YORK NOTES

ENGLISH LANGUAGE AND LITERATURE

REVISION AND EXAM PRACTICE

Suitable for AQA, Edexcel, Eduqas and OCR

MARY GREEN

PEARSON

YORK PRESS

HEL

YORK PRESS
322 Old Brompton Road, London SW5 9JH

PEARSON EDUCATION LIMITED
Edinburgh Gate, Harlow,
Essex CM20 2JE, United Kingdom
Associated companies, branches and representatives throughout the world

First published 2017

10 9 8 7 6 5 4 3 2 1

ISBN 978–1–2921–6979–8

Typeset by Carnegie Book Production
Printed in Slovakia

Text credits: 'Walking Away' from *The Gate and Other Poems* by Cecil Day Lewis reprinted by permission of Peters Fraser & Dunlop (www.petersfraserdunlop.com) on behalf of the Estate of Cecil Day Lewis. Excerpt from "Follower" from OPENED GROUND: SELECTED POEMS 1966-1996 by Seamus Heaney. Copyright © 1998 by Seamus Heaney. Reprinted by permission of Farrar, Straus and Giroux, LLC and Faber and Faber Ltd. Excerpt from "Bayonet Charge" from COLLECTED POEMS by Ted Hughes. Copyright © 2003 by The Estate of Ted Hughes. Reprinted by permission of Farrar, Straus and Giroux, LLC and Faber and Faber Ltd. 'Mother, any distance' from *Book of Matches* by Simon Armitage reprinted by permission of Faber and Faber Ltd. Letter to *The Times*, 3 July 1905 – Bernard Shaw reproduced by permission of The Society of Authors, on behalf of the Bernard Shaw Estate. Extract from *The Woman in Black* by Susan Hill, published by Vintage Books © Susan Hill 1983. Reproduced by permission of Sheil Land Associates Ltd. 'Absence' from *The Collected Poems* by Elizabeth Jennings, published by Carcanet Press, reprinted by permission of David Higham Associates Limited. 'Cold Knap Lake' from *Collected Poems* by Gillian Clarke (Carcanet, 1997) reprinted by permission of Carcanet Press Limited. Tatamkhulu Afrika: 'Nothing's Changed' from *Maqabane*, Mayibuye Books, 1994, p.33. Copyright © 1994 Tatamkhulu Afrika. Reprinted by permission of the author's estate. 'Before You Were Mine' from *Collected Poems* by Carol Ann Duffy. Published by Picador, 2015. Copyright © Carol Ann Duffy. Reproduced by permission of the author c/o Rogers, Coleridge & White Ltd., 20 Powis Mews, London W11 1JN. 'War Photographer' from *New Selected Poems* by Carol Ann Duffy. Published by Picador, 2009. Copyright © Carol Ann Duffy. Reproduced by permission of the author c/o Rogers, Coleridge & White Ltd., 20 Powis Mews, London W11 1JN. 'Valentine' from *New Selected Poems* by Carol Ann Duffy Published by Picador, 2009. Copyright © Carol Ann Duffy. Reproduced by permission of the author c/o Rogers, Coleridge & White Ltd., 20 Powis Mews, London W11 1JN.

Photo credits: Nanisimova/Shutterstock for page 13 middle / Evgeny Karandaev/Shutterstock for page 16 bottom / Andresr/© iStock for page 19 bottom / jjmillan/Shutterstock for page 20 middle / Genadi Dochev/Shutterstock for page 21 bottom / Steve Oehlenschlager/Shutterstock for page 23 bottom / fotorince/Shutterstock for page 24 bottom / Kalcutta/Shutterstock for page 28 bottom / Fabien Monteil/Shutterstock for page 29 bottom / topseller/Shutterstock for page 31 bottom / irabel8/Shutterstock for page 32 bottom / Mike Joppe/Shutterstock for page 37 top / jukurae/Shutterstock for page 39 bottom / conrado/Shutterstock for page 40 top / antoniodiaz/Shutterstock for page 41 bottom / jaymast/Shutterstock for page 42 bottom / mgfoto/© iStock for page 43 bottom / lbarrosphoto/© iStock for page 46 middle / M. Ali khan/Shutterstock for page 51 bottom / Samuel Borges Photography/Shutterstock for page 53 bottom / Inga Locmele/Shutterstock for page 57 bottom / Carlos Amarillo/Shutterstock for page 63 top / Tomwang112/© iStock for page 65 bottom / Syda Productions/© iStock for page 66 middle / Rawpixel.com/Shutterstock for page 67 bottom / Elnur/Shutterstock for page 68 middle / irin-k/Shutterstock for page 72 bottom / asiseeit/© iStock for page 76 bottom / michaeljung/Shutterstock for page 78 top / Pressmaster/Shutterstock for page 83 middle / legenda/Shutterstock for page 90 bottom / JasaShmasa/Shutterstock for page 91 bottom / Amy Johansson/Shutterstock for page 92 middle / fotyma/© iStock for page 92 bottom / elnavegante/Shutterstock for page 93 middle / Everett Historical/Shutterstock for page 94 bottom / Vitalii Hulai/Shutterstock for page 95 top / Ivan Ponomarev/Shutterstock for page 96 middle / duncan1890/© iStock for page 97 top / duncan1890/© iStock for page 98 top / Ross Strachan/Shutterstock for page 99 bottom / AF Archive/Alamy for page 102 middle / igolby/Shutterstock for page 103 bottom / Geraint Lewis/Alamy for page 104 middle / Ben Bryant/Shutterstock for page 106 top / Photo-Jope/Shutterstock for page 106 bottom / Everett Historical/Shutterstock for page 114 bottom / Alla Shcherbak/Shutterstock for page 117 middle / pixelheadphotodigitalskillet/Shutterstock for page 119 middle / Dennis W Donohue/Shutterstock for page 120 bottom / nd3000/Shutterstock for page 123 bottom / kukuruxa/Shutterstock for page 126 middle / wavebreakmedia/Shutterstock for page 127 bottom / FloridaStock/Shutterstock for page 129 middle

CONTENTS

PART ONE: THE BASICS

PART TWO: GCSE ENGLISH LANGUAGE

PART TWO: GCSE ENGLISH LANGUAGE

PART THREE: GCSE ENGLISH LITERATURE

THE ASSESSMENT OBJECTIVES

Whichever GCSE English Language and English Literature course you are following, your work will be examined through the Assessment Objectives below.

ENGLISH LANGUAGE

AO1 to AO4 relate to the Reading sections of the exam, and AO5 and AO6 to the Writing sections:

AO1	• Identify and interpret explicit and implicit information and ideas. • Select and synthesise evidence from different texts.
AO2	Explain, comment on and analyse how writers use language and structure to achieve effects and influence readers, using relevant subject terminology to support their views.
AO3	Compare writers' ideas and perspectives, as well as how these are conveyed, across two or more texts.
AO4	Evaluate texts critically and support this with appropriate textual references.
AO5	• Communicate clearly, effectively and imaginatively, selecting and adapting tone, style and register for different forms, purposes and audiences. • Organise information and ideas, using structural and grammatical features to support coherence and cohesion of texts.
AO6	Use a range of vocabulary and sentence structures for clarity, purpose and effect, with accurate spelling and punctuation. (20% of total marks.)

ENGLISH LITERATURE

AO1	Read, understand and respond to texts. Students should be able to: • maintain a critical style and develop an informed personal response • use textual references, including quotations, to support and illustrate interpretations.
AO2	Analyse the language, form and structure used by a writer to create meanings and effects, using relevant subject terminology where appropriate.
AO3	Show understanding of the relationships between texts and the contexts in which they were written.
AO4	Use a range of vocabulary and sentence structures, for clarity, purpose and effect, with accurate spelling and punctuation.

Look out for the AO labels throughout this book to help keep you on track!

CHAPTER 1: The basics: Spelling, punctuation and grammar

GRAMMATICAL TERMS A06 A04

HOW'S YOUR SPaG?

We all make mistakes with our spelling, punctuation and grammar, so this section is designed to help you avoid the most obvious ones. But what is your SPaG like to begin with?

❶ Here is one student's not very successful story opening. Can you identify the errors?

> We was all siting on the harbor wall washing the boats sale bye suddenly a cry went up man overbord someone called, there was a terrific crack I saw a huge wooden mast fall from a yot it crashes into the see near wear a man in a yellow lifejacket floundered around what I call, in disbelieve, thats my dad!

WORD CLASSES

In English there are eight main word classes. A word can belong to more than one word class, depending on how it is used. For example:

● *She spread out the **plan** on the table.* (noun)
● *I **plan** to leave tomorrow.* (verb)

The table below lists the word classes and some sub-classes, with examples.

Nouns		Pronouns	Verbs		Adjectives
common	**proper**		**auxiliary**	**main**	
hat	London	I	have	see	big
		who			

Adverbs	Determiners	Prepositions	Conjunctions	
			coordinating	**subordinating**
quickly	the	of	or	because

❷ Copy the table, then add the words below to the correct column. Some words belong in more than one column.

> while   together   table   go   himself   his   although   happy   you my/your   to   will   a/an   but   on   responsible   may   sharply   and   if in   Saturday   make   tall   Italy   me   soon   April   actor   run   book

DETERMINERS

When completing the table, you may have found it difficult to identify the **determiners**. Remember that a determiner shows a noun as **known** or **unknown**. For example, in the phrase 'this cat', the determiner 'this' refers to a specific, known cat.

Examples of determiners:

- Articles: 'the', 'a', 'an'
- Demonstratives: 'this', 'those'
- Possessives: 'my', 'your', 'his', 'her'
- Quantifiers: 'some', 'many'
- Certain question words: 'who', 'what'

MODIFIERS

When you modify something, you alter or adapt it. A **modifier** is not essential to a sentence, but it adds detail. It can make the meaning of a sentence more precise. For example, in the phrase 'the cream-cheese sandwich', 'sandwich' is modified by 'cream-cheese' to mean a particular type of sandwich. 'Cheese' is modified by 'cream' to mean a particular type of cheese.

TOP TIP

Remember, modifiers will make your writing more interesting.

❸ Modify the words 'teacher' and 'tea' to give more precise detail.

NOUN PHRASES

A **phrase** is a group of words that modifies a particular word, called the 'head'. A **noun phrase** is a phrase that has a noun as its head. For example:

- *Grey parrots can mimic.* 'Grey' modifies 'parrots', so 'grey' belongs to the noun phrase.
- *Most African grey parrots can mimic.* All the words in bold help to modify 'parrots', so they all belong to the noun phrase.

❹ Write down the noun phrases in these sentences. There may be more than one noun phrase in a sentence.
  - *Uncle Ray's rabbit in the hutch is snoring.*
  - *The small boy was a lost and bewildered newcomer.*

PREPOSITIONAL PHRASES

When **prepositional phrases** modify nouns they are adjectival, telling you which one, what type, how much or how many. For example: *The trees **by the river** sway gently.*

When prepositional phrases modify verbs they are **adverbial**. They tell you when, where, why or how. For example: *The river is flooding **because of the downpour**.*

❺ Write down the prepositional phrases in these sentences. Note whether they are adjectival or adverbial phrases.
  - *She's annoyed because of the holiday cancellation.*
  - *It seems the robin on the windowsill visits daily.*

PROGRESS LOG [tick the correct box]   Needs more work ☐   Getting there ☐   Under control ☐

SENTENCE CONSTRUCTION AND CLAUSES

Depending on their construction, sentences are described as simple, compound or complex. All sentences contain a subject and a verb. The subject is who or what the sentence is about. The verb tells you what the subject is doing, how it is feeling or its state.

SIMPLE SENTENCES

A **clause** is a group of words built around a verb as its head. A **simple sentence** has one **main clause** and it may contain an object as well as a subject and verb:

> *Leon   bought a guitar.*

subject + verb + object

   S   V   O

To find the object you can ask 'What?' So: 'Leon bought what?'

Sometimes a simple sentence may include an **indirect object**. To find this you could ask: 'Who or what received the direct object?'

> *Leon bought a guitar for Sally.*

   S   V   O   **indirect object**

You can add phrases to a simple sentence and vary their position.

> *Leon sang a ballad in the recording studio.*

             adverbial phrase

> *In the recording studio, Leon sang a ballad.*

GET IT RIGHT!

A simple sentence does not need to have a direct object. It can just be a noun and a verb: 'Will sang.' 'He sang.' 'The boy sang.'

TOP TIP

You can use minor sentences to create a sense of urgency or emphasis, such as 'On my way!' The verb in minor sentences is usually implied rather than stated: 'I **am** on my way.'

COMPOUND SENTENCES

A **compound sentence** is made up of two independent clauses joined with a **coordinating conjunction**. Each of the independent clauses should make sense on its own. For example:

- *Rory turned his room upside down, **but** he couldn't find his mobile phone.*
- *Rory complained to his mother, **and** he shouted at his brother.*

❶ What type of sentences are these?
- *The snake slithered.*   • *All in good time.*
- *Claire enjoys school, but she is always late for lessons.*

COMPLEX SENTENCES

A **complex sentence** usually has a main clause and a **subordinate clause**, which is dependent on the main clause to make sense. It can be connected by a **subordinating conjunction**:

> *Niyusha loved Coco **because** he was a dog like no other.*

The subordinating conjunction shows the kind of link between the main clause and the subordinate one. 'Because' is a conjunction of **reason**.

A complex sentence can also be formed using a present or past **participle**:

> *Having agreed with the plan, Hannah had second thoughts.*

You could also say: *'Hannah, having agreed with the plan, had second thoughts.'* 'Having agreed with the plan' is a **non-finite clause** that does not make sense on its own. To form a full sentence, the participle and **non-finite verb** 'having' must be linked to a **finite verb**. In the example, 'had' is the finite verb.

*'Lena **played** the drums'* is a **finite clause** because it has a finite verb ('played'). Finite clauses have a verb in the past or present tense and make sense on their own.

TOP TIP

Non-finite clauses are useful because they can be placed in different parts of a sentence, adding variety to your writing.

- A **noun clause** is a subordinate clause that acts like a noun. It begins with words such as 'what', 'when', 'where', 'whether', 'whatever'. For example: ***Whatever route you choose** is fine with me.*
- A **relative clause** (sometimes known as an **adjectival clause**) is used to modify a noun or pronoun. It begins with a **relative pronoun** ('which', 'that', 'who', 'whose', 'whom') or sometimes a subordinating conjunction ('when' or 'where'). For example: *My neighbour, **who loves soccer**, never misses a match.*

ADVERBIAL CLAUSES

An **adverbial clause** functions as an **adverb**. It modifies the meaning of an **adjective**, verb or adverb. It asks a question: 'Why?', 'When?', 'Where?', 'How?', 'How much?', 'What condition?'

The adverbial clause is connected to the main clause by a subordinating conjunction, which comes at the beginning of the adverbial clause:

adverbial clause

Commercial and illegal logging must be controlled, if rainforests are to survive.

main clause   subordinating conjunction ('if')

❷   Find the adverbial clauses in these sentences:
- *Poor squatters cut down trees because they need money.*
- *In order to cultivate the coca plant, drug cartels use rainforest land.*
- *While tribespeople use rainforest resources, they take care of the forest.*

APPLYING YOUR SKILLS

❸   Combine these simple sentences to make complex ones. Use conjunctions and relative pronouns where you can.
- *Jake always ate well. He was a great chef. He cooked at home.*
- *Sian had a strong singing voice. She didn't practise enough. She had too much to do.*
- *Kai loved sky-diving. He had training. He finished work. He practised his skills.*

Remember:
- Vary the style of your sentences, i.e. dropping or replacing words, but you must keep the meaning!

PROGRESS LOG [tick the correct box]   Needs more work ☐   Getting there ☐   Under control ☐

SENTENCE TYPES AND TENSES

You can use four types of sentences to communicate your intentions:

- **Declarative:** Most sentences are declarative. They make a statement about someone/something: *'The mask was encrusted with fake diamonds.'*
- **Interrogative:** A question: *'Did you get the midday train?'*
- **Exclamatory:** Exclamatory sentences have an exclamation mark, which indicates strong feelings: *'The diamonds weren't real!'*
- **Imperative:** A command in which the subject (second person 'you', singular or plural) is left out: *'Try your best.'* (**'You** try your best.')

SUBJECT–VERB AGREEMENT

A singular subject in a sentence needs a singular verb. A plural subject needs a plural one. It is easy to make a mistake by wrongly identifying the subject:

- *A **herd** of elephants **is** thundering across the plain.* 'Herd' is the subject (not elephants) and there is only one herd.
- ***Herds** of elephants **are** thundering across the plain.* 'Herds' is the subject and there is more than one herd.

When used on their own in a sentence, 'either' and 'neither' are always the subject, so the verb must be singular:

- *Either of the two young footballers **is** ready to join the team.*
- *Neither of the singers **is** ready to perform yet.*

If you use 'either/or' and 'neither/nor', the subject nearest to the verb is the one that decides:

- *Neither the Farley twins nor **Jason has** won the prize.* (singular)
- *Either Jason or the **Farley twins have** won the prize.* (plural)

❶ Write a sentence in the present tense, using each of the following words as the subject: 'geese', 'book of rules', 'Kate or Jack', 'either of the acrobats', 'neither of the clowns'.

> **GET IT RIGHT!** ⭐
>
> A common mistake when using the verb 'to be' is to confuse 'was' and 'were':
>
> *You **was** late again!* ✗
>
> *You **were** late again!* ✔

TENSES

When you write about things that are **going** to happen, you need to use a present tense verb:

- *He **is** going on Tuesday.*

Many verbs follow similar spelling patterns when they change tenses or shift from singular to plural. For example:

- **Simple present tense:** 'I help', 'you help', 'he/she/it help**s**'
- **Simple past tense:** 'I help**ed**', 'you help**ed**', 'he/she/it help**ed**'

However, there are also many irregular verbs, such as the verb 'to be':

- **Simple present singular:** 'I am', 'you are', 'he/she/it is'
- **Simple present plural:** 'we are', 'you are', 'they are'
- **Simple past singular:** 'I was', 'you were', 'he/she/it was'
- **Simple past plural:** 'we were', 'you were', 'they were'

> **TOP TIP** ⭐
>
> Writers sometimes use the present tense to create particular effects, such as a strong sense of immediacy. For example, a story about a shipwreck might be more powerful written in the present tense than in the past tense.

The table below shows some irregular verbs in the third person singular.

Verb	Present third person singular	Past third person	Past participle
to blow	blows	blew	blown
to do	does	did	done
to draw	draws	drew	drawn
to eat	eats	ate	eaten
to fly	flies	flew	flown

THE ACTIVE AND THE PASSIVE

Verbs can be **active** or **passive**. In the active voice, the subject performs the action on the object:

Scruff   *ate*   *my homework.*

subject   **verb**   **object**

In the passive voice, the sentence is switched around. The active voice is more direct than the passive, but you might decide to use the passive if you want to focus on the item that is being acted on:

My homework was eaten by Scruff.

subject   **verb**   **agent**

TOP TIP

Try to avoid using dialect or colloquialism unless you are using it for characterisation though voice or speech. Even then it should only be used very sparingly.

❷ Change the following sentences to the passive. Decide whether or not you need to use 'by'.

- *The rapper performed a series of hits.*
- *She declared her intentions.*
- *Danny and Marlon anticipated the result.*

APPLYING YOUR SKILLS

❸ Rewrite this paragraph, correcting the subject–verb agreements and the tenses.

I were the first to get home on Wednesday, so I makes myself a cup of cappuccino with our new coffee maker. It do you good to relax sometimes. It weren't for long though, because five minutes later there were a loud banging on the door. When I opens it I sees my little brother stood there, sinking under the weight of his schoolbag, with tears streaming down his face.

Remember:

- A singular subject in a sentence needs a singular verb; a plural subject needs a plural verb.
- Do not confuse past and present tense.

PUNCTUATION

Punctuation is extremely important as it helps to give meaning to writing. If used incorrectly, it may confuse your reader.

COMMAS

A comma separates the **main clause** in a sentence from the **subordinate clause**:

> *Bingley was by no means independent, but Darcy was clever.*

> **independent (main) clause**   **subordinate clause**

A comma can also be used to separate items in a list or a series of descriptions:

> *He was an odd mixture of light-heartedness and gloom, untidiness and fussiness, risk-taking and fear, so that even though she had lived with him for years, she felt she hardly knew him.*

A comma should not be used to join two independent clauses (this is an error called a **comma splice**), because both clauses can stand on their own:

> *Lottie turned the ignition to get the car going, the car remained silent.*

Instead you should do one of the following:

- Replace the comma with a full stop and a capital letter: *Lottie turned the ignition to get the car going. The car remained silent.*
- Add a conjunction: *Lottie turned the ignition to get the car going,* **but** *the car remained silent.*
- Add a **semicolon**: *Lottie turned the ignition to get the car moving; the car remained silent.*

GET IT RIGHT!

It is important to get basic punctuation right, as it can change the meaning of a sentence. What do these sentences mean with and without a comma?

- *Let's start baking, George!*
- *Let's start baking George!*

COLONS

A **colon** is used to indicate a pause. It has several functions.

It is used before lists:

> *Beth waited discontentedly while Max dithered. Finally, Max drew up a list: tents, tent pegs, sleeping bags, water carrier, torch, ear plugs.*

You can also use colons in play scripts to separate the name of the character from the words they speak:

> *Arjun: Hurry up, we'll be late.*

> *Oli: Don't panic. I'm almost ready.*

You can use colons to create impact in your writing. Look at this sentence:

> *Horror is one thing you can be certain to find in a Gothic tale.*

Withholding a word until the end of the sentence gives it emphasis, so a more dramatic way of saying this would be:

> *There's one thing you can be certain to find in a Gothic tale: horror.*

The clause before the colon is a main clause and can stand on its own.

SEMICOLONS

A semicolon links two ideas, events or pieces of information:

Her difficulty in life was too little money; her comfort was good friendship.

Semicolons can also be used to separate items in a long list:

Giles always writes a lengthy list of travel items before he packs his holiday bag: toothbrush and toothpaste; floss; razor and shaving foam; shampoo; shower gel; soap; deodorant; corn plasters; insect repellent; bandages; blister pack; throat sweets and so on and so on!

DASHES

Dashes can be used to separate parts of a sentence, but they are mainly used for emphasis or additional explanation:

Help from strangers is not unusual – we see it daily.

BRACKETS

Round brackets ( ) are used to include extra information or an afterthought without altering the meaning of the sentence:

Beth waited discontentedly while Max dithered. Finally, Max drew up a list: tents, tent pegs (spare ones), sleeping bags, water carrier, torch, ear plugs (two pairs).

TOP TIP

Square brackets [ ] are often used to clarify or inform within a quoted text. For example: *Smith notes that 'she [Jane Austen] often depicted women whose lives depended on marriage for economic security'.*

ELLIPSES

Ellipses (a series of three dots) show where words have been deliberately left out. They can be used to create an effect, such as suspense:

At last the horse began to trot, but only to go round in circles so that Matt was at his wits' end, until the sound of galloping made him turn …

❶ Add at least fifty words to the following paragraph starter. Include a semicolon, a dash, brackets and ellipses.

Once he knew the contents of the letter, he left early – before dawn – choosing the fastest route. As he drove away …

TOP TIP

Ellipses and square brackets can also be used to show that words from a quoted text are missing: *As Smith comments, 'Charlotte Lucas in Pride and Prejudice is obliged to marry the ridiculous […] Mr Collins'.*

DIRECT SPEECH

Direct speech refers to words that are actually spoken. They should be contained within speech marks. Direct speech also includes other punctuation features, which are shown on page 14.

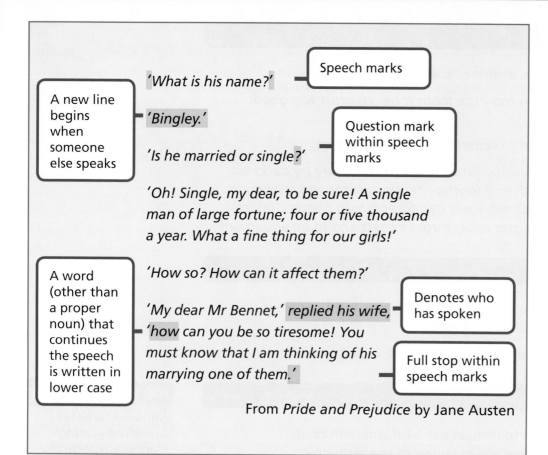

Speech marks	'What is his name?'
A new line begins when someone else speaks	'Bingley.'
Question mark within speech marks	'Is he married or single?'
	'Oh! Single, my dear, to be sure! A single man of large fortune; four or five thousand a year. What a fine thing for our girls!'
	'How so? How can it affect them?'
A word (other than a proper noun) that continues the speech is written in lower case	'My dear Mr Bennet,' replied his wife, 'how can you be so tiresome! You must know that I am thinking of his marrying one of them.'
Denotes who has spoken	
Full stop within speech marks	

From *Pride and Prejudice* by Jane Austen

TOP TIP
You may find that older texts, such as nineteenth-century novels by Austen and Dickens, sometimes use different punctuation rules from modern texts. For example, in this passage Austen uses an exclamation mark instead of a question mark in the line, 'how can you be so tiresome!'

REPORTED SPEECH

Reported speech is an **account** of what has been said. It does not show the actual words spoken, and no speech marks are used, but it should keep the meaning and the spirit of the words. Look at this example of reported speech based on the extract above. Note how tense and point of view change, as well as other features:

Mrs Bennet replied **to her husband with some exasperation** *that* **he was** *tiresome since he must know that* **she intended Mr Bingley** *to marry one of* **their daughters***.

TOP TIP
Reported speech may need to include words that convey the feelings expressed in actual speech. Other information, such as nouns and proper nouns, may also be needed.

APPLYING YOUR SKILLS

❷ Read this example of direct speech from *Pride and Prejudice*. Change it into reported speech, using suitable punctuation, tense and point of view. You could begin: *Mr Bennet told his family that …*

'About a month ago I received this letter; and about a fortnight ago I answered it, for I thought it a case of some delicacy, and requiring early attention. It is from my cousin, Mr Collins, who, when I am dead, may turn you all out of this house as soon as he pleases.'

Remember:

- The tense and point of view will change.
- Read your finished paragraph to check that it is clear who or what is being referred to – for example, have you used suitable nouns?

PROGRESS LOG [tick the correct box] Needs more work ■ Getting there ■ Under control ■

PARAGRAPH ORGANISATION

Paragraphs give shape and structure to a piece of writing. They allow the reader to follow shifts in thinking.

SETTING OUT PARAGRAPHS

To indicate that you are beginning a new paragraph in your writing, you should indent the line:

> *Jimmy and his skateboard flew under the dilapidated railway bridge, along a series of concrete slabs made smooth by constant use. Skateboarding was Jimmy's main occupation.*
> *Usually, Tarik was with him, but today Jimmy was alone.*

A new paragraph should be used to indicate a change of idea, topic, place or time.

- Idea: ***However,*** *the theme of love is also important in …*
- Topic: ***In contrast,*** *Text A is focused on …*
- Place: ***Another*** *notorious place was the Clink …*
- Time: ***Meanwhile,*** *a great deal had changed.*

You should also use a new paragraph when a different person starts speaking (which is a rule of **direct speech**):

> *May looked disconcerted. 'But what have you done …'*
> *'With the key?' interrupted Jenny.*

CONNECTIVES

When you begin a new paragraph you can signal the change using **connectives**, which link paragraphs and show the relationship between them. The connectives in the examples above are shown in bold. The table below shows some common connectives and how to use them.

TOP TIP

The **topic sentence** does not have to be the first sentence in a paragraph. You can create a preliminary sentence first.

TOP TIP

A paragraph can be any length. It can even be a single sentence if you want to create impact by setting a statement or question apart from the rest of the text.

TOP TIP

It is easy to fall into the habit of over-using certain connectives, such as 'then'. Try to use a variety of connectives in your writing.

Addition of ideas	Order or sequence	Examples	Cause and effect
In addition	Firstly	For example	Consequently
As well as	Secondly	For instance	As a result
Besides	Next	Such as	Since
Also	Later	As can be seen	Because

Compare & contrast	Qualify	Purpose	Sum up
Similarly	However	To this end	Finally
In the same way	Still	For this purpose	To sum up
In contrast	Yet	For this reason	In conclusion
On the other hand	Having said that	In order to	

APPLYING YOUR SKILLS

❶ Find the start of new paragraphs in this report:

Exceptionally heavy rain over a prolonged period this morning caused flash floods and brought disruption to several areas in the West Midlands. Flood warnings were issued yesterday. Roads have been inundated and transport is at a standstill. Those most affected are to the south of Birmingham. In addition, rail and property has been affected. There are unconfirmed reports that lines have been closed in the South East. There are no reports of injury or major damage to property, but five hundred homes are without power. Three schools are closed. Finally, heavy rain is expected to continue today and tomorrow moving eastwards. The environment agency has issued further flood warnings.

Remember:

● Read the text through with expression to check you have started the new paragraph in the right place.

PROGRESS LOG [tick the correct box]   Needs more work ☐   Getting there ☐   Under control ☐

SPELLING

(A06) (A04)

You do not always spell English words as they sound, but there are some useful spelling rules that can help you remember how to spell certain words.

PLURALS

When you add 's' to nouns that end in 'y', change 'y' to 'ie' when there is a consonant before the 'y':

> *lorry → lorries   cherry → cherries   memory → memories*

If there is a vowel before the 'y', just add 's':

> *donkey → donkeys   journey → journeys   tray → trays*

Add 'es' to nouns that end in '-ch', '-s', '-sh', '-x', '-z':

> *peach → peaches   glass → glasses   wish → wishes   fox → foxes*
> *buzz → buzzes*

(Exception: *stomach → stomachs*)

Nouns ending in 'f' or 'fe' often change to 'v' when 'es' is added:

> *wolf → wolves   knife → knives*

For most nouns that end in 'ff' or have two vowels before 'f', just add 's': 'cuffs', 'chiefs'.

PREFIXES AND SUFFIXES

Prefixes that end in a vowel do not change when added to a word. However, remember that double letters can occur.

ante → antenatal   *un → unnecessary*

semi → semicircle   *mis → misspell*

pre → premeditate   *ir → irregular*

When you add a **suffix** beginning with a vowel to a word that ends in a silent 'e', you usually drop the 'e'. However, if the word ends in 'ce' or 'ge' you keep the 'e'.

adventure → adventurous   *notice → noticeable*

excite → excitable   *manage → manageable*

When you add 'all', 'full' or 'till' to a word, drop the second 'l':

all → also, always, almost   *full → hopeful, fulfill*   *till → until*

❶ Look at the following words. Which ones are spelt incorrectly? Are there any exceptions? Which are literary terms?

> quays   heros   countrys   sniffs   vallies   librarys   loaves
> parodies   rooves   quizzes   motifs   ironies   dreadfull
> misunderstood   paradoxes   irigation   reversible   outrageous
> ambiguities   advantagous   misspoken

TOP TIP

Suffixes and prefixes build words, change meaning and can help to extend your vocabulary. They also change word classes. For example, adding 'ance' to the adjective 'resist' turns it into the noun 'resistance'.

HOMOPHONES

Words that sound the same but that mean different things are called **homophones**. There are many homophones and it is easy to make mistakes. Look at these homophones:

- **its** = shows belonging; **it's** = shortened form of 'it is'
- **their** = belonging to them; **there** = that place; **they're** = shortened form of 'they are'
- **whose** = belonging to someone; **who's** = shortened form of 'who is'

❷ Look at the following homophones. Copy down any that you confuse in your writing. Look up their meanings to help you remember the different spellings.

> to, two, too   fair, fare   hare, hair   right, rite, write, wright
> weather, whether   aloud, allowed   accept, except   missed, mist
> stationary, stationery   principal, principle

TOP TIP

Create your own spelling notebook A–Z. Record any words you are unsure of, particularly homophones.

IMPROVING YOUR SPELLING

Try recording a word with a similar pattern as a prompt:

Correct word	Reminder
*mem*ento	*mem*ber
toma*toes*	*toes*

Or, you can split complex words into sound sections that help visualise the spelling. Say each word out loud and listen to its rhythm to help you remember:

a-cco-mmo-date   di-le-mma   a-ppear-ance   def-in-ite-ly

Mnemonics are phrases used as memory aids. For example, you can create a nonsense phrase to remind you how to spell a word or name:

Word	Phrase reminder
ochre	**O**nly **c**arrots **h**ave **r**adar **e**yes.
Arctic	**A**ll **r**abbits **c**an **t**alk **i**n **c**ode.

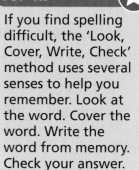

APPLYING YOUR SKILLS

❸   Identify the spelling errors in this paragraph. How many are homophones? Which **homophones** are spelled correctly?

Loseing no time, he grabbed two peices of the tough, fibreous rope and tide them together with a complex not I had never scene before. He pulled the join untill it was tight enough not to brake. With one quick move he through it towards the stout branch above us. It missed. He threw it hire. It missed again.

Remember:

● You should recognise an error quickly; if you are unsure, leave it as it is.
● Record the correct spellings of any errors you did not identify.

PROGRESS CHECK FOR CHAPTER 1

GOOD PROGRESS

I can:

● Use different types of sentences to create effects ☐
● Use different types of sentences that are mostly grammatically correct ☐
● Use a range of punctuation successfully most of the time ☐
● Spell most words correctly including complex words and use an increasingly wide range of vocabulary ☐

EXCELLENT PROGRESS

I can:

● Use the full range of sentence types to create a variety of effects ☐
● Use a range of sentences including complex structures and to a high level of grammatical accuracy ☐
● Use different kinds of punctuation to create effects, and rarely make errors ☐
● Spell accurately to a high level and use an ambitious range of vocabulary ☐

CHAPTER 2: Reading creative or fiction texts

WHAT'S IT ALL ABOUT?

In this section of the English Language exam, you will be asked to read either an extract (or extracts) from modern novels (twentieth or twenty-first century) or novels from the nineteenth century.

TIMING AND APPROACH

Read the source text carefully. You may find it helpful to read it once, then read the questions, then read the source text again, annotating it to help you answer the questions.

The exam paper will direct you to focus on a particular section of the source text for each question, so another possible approach is to reread and annotate the text for each question in turn as you answer it. However, do not spend too long reading the text before you start writing – no more than fifteen minutes.

EARNING THE MARKS

The number of marks for each question will be written on the paper. It is important to remember that, however good your answer, this is the maximum number of marks you can earn for that question.

The skills you will need, depending on the question, include the following:

- Identify **relevant information** from the source text – usually **facts**, **phrases** or **reasons**.
- **Explain** and **analyse** how the writer uses **language** for a particular **purpose**.
- **Analyse** how the whole of the source text is **structured**.
- **Evaluate** how well the writer has created a particular **impression** of some aspect of the source text, such as **character**, **setting** or **atmosphere**.

You will also be expected to give a personal response to the text – saying what you feel about it, and why, supporting your ideas with evidence.

AQA Paper 1, Section A
Edexcel Paper 1, Section A
Eduqas Component 1, Section A
OCR Component 2, Section A

GET IT RIGHT!

Depending on the exam board/ organisation, you may be asked to compare two source texts in this section. When you write about the second text, try not to repeat what you have written about the first. Refer back to the first, instead. For example: 'Similarly, the writer in …'.

TOP TIP

There are no marks for spelling, punctuation or grammar in this section, but if you express yourself clearly and accurately it will be easier for the examiner to understand your answers and credit you for them.

FINDING EXPLICIT INFORMATION

WHAT IS EXPLICIT INFORMATION AND HOW DO YOU IDENTIFY IT?

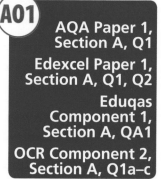

A01

AQA Paper 1, Section A, Q1

Edexcel Paper 1, Section A, Q1, Q2

Eduqas Component 1, Section A, QA1

OCR Component 2, Section A, Q1a–c

The simplest kind of information in a text is **explicit** information. This means information that is stated as fact. For example:

The bus stop was 200 metres away. Emily sprinted desperately towards it.

The most obvious fact here is 'The bus stop was 200 metres away.' This is stated explicitly. You might guess that Emily wants to catch the bus, but that is not stated explicitly.

The exam question will direct you to a section of the text, like this:

*Read again the first part of the text, lines 1–10. List **four** things from this part of the text about Emily's daily routine.*

Make sure you focus on the correct section. Underline or circle four facts in the extract, then list them.

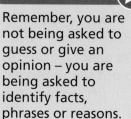

GET IT RIGHT!

Remember, you are not being asked to guess or give an opinion – you are being asked to identify facts, phrases or reasons.

❶ Read this story opening. What explicit information can you find in it?

It was a hot afternoon, and the railway carriage was correspondingly sultry[1], and the next stop was at Templecombe, nearly an hour ahead. The occupants of the carriage were a small girl, and a smaller girl, and a small boy. An aunt belonging to the children occupied one corner seat, and the further corner seat on the opposite side was occupied by a bachelor who was a stranger to their party, but the small girls and the  *small boy emphatically[2] occupied the compartment. Both the aunt and the children were conversational in a limited, persistent way, reminding one of the attentions of a housefly that refused to be discouraged. Most of the aunt's remarks seemed to begin with 'Don't.' and nearly all of the children's remarks began with 'Why?' The bachelor said nothing out loud.*

From 'The Storyteller' by Saki (H. H. Munro)

sultry[1] – hot and humid
emphatically[2] – very definitely

❷ Why would it be incorrect to write *'The children and their aunt are going to Templecombe'*?

EXAM FOCUS

Below are six points that a student might make about the extract. Look at the comments about each point:

1 'It was a hot afternoon.'

> **1. Correct – you can make short quotes from the text if the meaning is clear**

> **2. Correct – a simple sum**

2 There are five people in the compartment.

3 There is a fly in the compartment.

> **3. Incorrect – the conversation is compared with a fly**

> **4. Correct – 'persistent'**

4 The children and their aunt speak to each other often.

5 The children ask many questions.

> **5. Correct – 'Why?'**

> **6. May turn out to be true – we cannot be sure yet**

6 The bachelor is irritated by the children.

APPLYING YOUR SKILLS

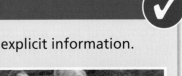

❸ Read this further extract from 'The Storyteller' and list four pieces of explicit information.

The child moved reluctantly to the window. 'Why are those sheep being driven out of that field?' he asked.

'I expect they are being driven to another field where there is more grass,' said the aunt weakly.

'But there is lots of grass in that field,' protested the boy; 'there's nothing else but grass there. Aunt, there's lots of grass in that field.'

'Perhaps the grass in the other field is better,' suggested the aunt fatuously.[1]

'Why is it better?' came the swift, inevitable question.

'Oh, look at those cows!' exclaimed the aunt. Nearly every field along the line had contained cows or bullocks, but she spoke as though she were drawing attention to a rarity.

'Why is the grass in the other field better?' persisted Cyril.

The frown on the bachelor's face was deepening to a scowl. He was a hard, unsympathetic man, the aunt decided in her mind.

fatuously[1] – stupidly, pointlessly

Remember:

- Only list points that are definitely correct.
- Do not mistake a character's opinion for a fact.

FINDING IMPLICIT INFORMATION

WHAT IS IMPLICIT INFORMATION AND HOW DO YOU IDENTIFY IT?

(A01)

AQA Paper 1, Section A, Q1

Edexcel Paper 1, Section A, Q2

Eduqas Component 1, Section A, QA1

OCR Component 2, Section A, Q1a–c

Writers may imply information, suggesting or hinting at it with description or word choices rather than stating it explicitly. Identifying implicit information is a key skill in English Language and Literature. Consider these lines:

- *Sam's face was turning purple. His knuckles were clenched and white.*
- *Sam was furious.*

Most readers would find the first version more interesting and enjoy inferring (deducing) the implied information that is stated explicitly in the second version. They would identify the signs that Sam is furious.

Read this continuation of 'The Storyteller' and think about this question: 'What does the writer imply about the characters?'

> *The smaller girl created a diversion by beginning to recite 'On the Road to Mandalay'.[1] She only knew the first line, but she put her limited knowledge to the fullest possible use. She repeated the line over and over again in a dreamy but resolute and very audible voice; it seemed to the bachelor as though someone had had a bet with her that she could not repeat the line aloud two thousand times without stopping. Whoever it was who had made the wager was likely to lose his bet.*
>
> *'Come over here and listen to a story,' said the aunt, when the bachelor had looked twice at her and once at the communication cord.[2]*
>
> From 'The Storyteller' by Saki (H. H. Munro)
>
> *'On the Road to Mandalay'*[1] – a poem by Rudyard Kipling
> *communication cord*[2] – a way for passengers to let a train driver know if there is an emergency

How would you approach this question?

- The question says 'characters' (plural), so try to find information about all three characters.
- Look only for implied information.

The table below shows some implied information and evidence.

Character	Implied information	Evidence
Girl	She is determined to keep repeating the line.	'resolute'
Bachelor	He is exasperated by the children, especially the girl.	It seems as if she will keep repeating the line 'two thousand times'. This hints at his exasperation by exaggerating his fears.
Aunt	She feels she ought to stop the children irritating the bachelor.	She decides to tell them a story after the bachelor 'looked twice at her and once at the communication cord'. This hints that he might pull the emergency cord rather than have to listen to the girl.

❶ What other implied information can you find about the girl – for example, in the writer's choice of the phrase 'created a diversion'?

❷ What could be implied about the bachelor by the particular way in which the writer hints at the man's worries about the girl?

EXAM FOCUS

Here are three further points that a student thinks are implied in the extract. Look at the comments about each point:

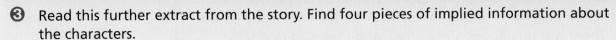

2. Correct – he appears to consider pulling the emergency communication cord to get someone to stop her!

1 The girl wants to irritate the bachelor.

2 The bachelor is irritated by the girl.

3 The aunt feels embarrassed by the children.

1. Not necessarily – she may just not care if she does

3. Correct – she responds to the bachelor's glances

APPLYING YOUR SKILLS ✔

❸ Read this further extract from the story. Find four pieces of implied information about the characters.

The children moved listlessly towards the aunt's end of the carriage. Evidently her reputation as a storyteller did not rank high in their estimation.

In a low, confidential voice, interrupted at frequent intervals by loud, petulant questions from her listeners, she began an un-enterprising and deplorably uninteresting story about a little girl who was good, and made friends with everyone on account of her goodness, and was finally saved from a mad bull by a number of rescuers who admired her moral character.

'Wouldn't they have saved her if she hadn't been good?' demanded the bigger of the small girls. It was exactly the question that the bachelor had wanted to ask.

Remember:
● Look for information about **all** the characters.
● Look for clues in description and word choices.
● A writer's word choices may imply information.

QUOTING OR PARAPHRASING EFFECTIVELY

HOW CAN YOU QUOTE OR PARAPHRASE A TEXT EFFECTIVELY TO SUPPORT YOUR POINTS?

A01

AQA Paper 1, Section A, Q1, Q2, Q4

Edexcel Paper 1, Section A, Q2, Q3, Q4

Eduqas Component 1, Section A, QA2, QA3, QA4

OCR Component 2, Section A, Q1b–c, Q2, Q3, Q4

In all your English exams, you should give evidence and support your comments on a text by quoting or paraphrasing.

- **Quoting** means giving the exact words used, in quotation marks. You should quote if the exact word choice is important.
- **Paraphrasing** means putting information into your own words. It is useful to show you **understand** the text and to make your response more **concise**.

If you are referring to implied information, give a short quotation (it can even be one word) to support your point. In other parts of the exam, you will need to explain the significance of your quotation or paraphrase.

CHOOSING A QUOTATION

Read the extract below, then answer the question that follows.

> She was a tall woman of imperious mien,[1] handsome, with definite black eyebrows. Her smooth black hair was parted exactly. For a few moments she stood steadily watching the miners as they passed along the railway: then she turned towards the brook course. Her face was calm and set, her mouth was closed with disillusionment. After a moment she called:
> 'John!' There was no answer. She waited, and then said distinctly:
> 'Where are you?'
> 'Here!' replied a child's sulky voice from among the bushes. The woman looked piercingly through the dusk.
> 'Are you at that brook?' she asked sternly.
> For answer the child showed himself before the raspberry-canes that rose like whips. He was a small, sturdy boy of five. He stood quite still, defiantly.
>
> From 'The Odour of Chrysanthemums' by D. H. Lawrence
>
> *imperious mien*[1] – a commanding appearance

❶ What words or phrases describing the woman's appearance suggest:

- A strong, decisive character?
- That she has some reason to be unhappy?

TOP TIP ⭐

Select your evidence carefully. If there are several possible quotations you could use to make a point, choose the best one or two.

PRESENTING QUOTATIONS

Suppose you want to quote an **adverb** to show that the woman in the extract is a firm parent. You might say:

- *She is a strict parent: 'she asked sternly'. The adverb shows ...*
- *She is strict with her boy ('she asked sternly') and expects him to ...*
- *She speaks to her son 'sternly' when she suspects that he ...*

Any of these is acceptable. However, the third method is often the most effective – **embedding** the quotation. Use this at least some of the time, as it will make your writing more fluent. Always remember to use quotation marks around words or phrases that are taken directly from the text.

❷ Write two sentences commenting on the character of the mother in the extract above, embedding the following quotations:

- *'distinctly'*
- *'piercingly'*

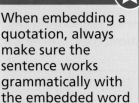

GET IT RIGHT!

When embedding a quotation, always make sure the sentence works grammatically with the embedded word or phrase.

PARAPHRASING

Use paraphrasing when it is a detail or character action in the text that is important rather than the author's word choice.

EXAM FOCUS

Read this paragraph in which a student has quoted from a text and paraphrased where necessary. Some of its features have been highlighted:

The woman's 'hair ... parted exactly' suggests that she is decisive and takes care with her appearance. She demands to know where her son is, speaking 'distinctly' so that he has no excuse for not answering her. She looks 'piercingly' into the gloom, suggesting that she is determined to find her son, and that he cannot hide from her.

Paraphrase

Explains the significance of the adverb choice

Embedded quotation with **ellipsis** (...) to preserve the sentence's grammar

Embedded quotation; paraphrase of 'through the dusk' helps to explain

APPLYING YOUR SKILLS

❸ Write two sentences showing what you learn about the boy in this extract.

Remember:

- In the first sentence, paraphrase the **explicit** information about the boy.
- In the second, use an embedded quotation to analyse his responses to his mother.

PROGRESS LOG [tick the correct box]   Needs more work ▮   Getting there ▮   Under control ▮

ANALYSING LANGUAGE FEATURES AND EFFECTS

HOW DOES THE CHOICE OF PARTICULAR WORDS AND PHRASES CREATE EFFECTS?

A02

AQA Paper 1, Section A, Q2

Edexcel Paper 1, Section A, Q3

Eduqas Component 1, Section A, QA2, QA3, QA4

OCR Component 2, Section A, Q2, Q3

Writers use language in different ways for different purposes. For example, they may want to create a striking image, suggest a hidden meaning or build tension.

Read the extract below. How does the writer use **words and phrases** to show that Yvette is in danger?

> *She* [Yvette] *heard somebody shouting, and looked round. Down the path through the larch trees the gipsy was bounding. The gardener, away beyond, was also running. Simultaneously she became aware of a great roar, which, before she could move, accumulated to a vast deafening snarl. The gipsy was gesticulating. She looked round, behind her.*
>
> From *The Virgin and the Gipsy* by D. H. Lawrence

How would you answer the question?

- First, decide what the **focus of the question** is – 'that Yvette is in danger'.
- **Choose examples** of **words and phrases** that help to show danger.
- Select the **most appropriate ones** and **use correct grammatical terms**.
- **Describe the effects**.

The table below describes two examples from the text.

TOP TIP ⭐

Only use literary terms if you are sure of them. You will still get credit for selecting words and describing their effects.

Signs of danger	Words/phrases	Terms (where useful)	Effect
The gipsy is running towards Yvette.	*was bounding*	Verb (past continuous)	Powerful verb emphasises gipsy's sense of urgency. Use of continuous verb suggests that the gipsy is in the background, some distance from Yvette.
Yvette's attention is drawn in two directions at once.	*Simultaneously*	Conjunctive **adverb**	Points out Yvette's sudden awareness of danger. Heightens tension further.

EXAM FOCUS

Read the start of this successful response to the question. Some of its qualities have been highlighted:

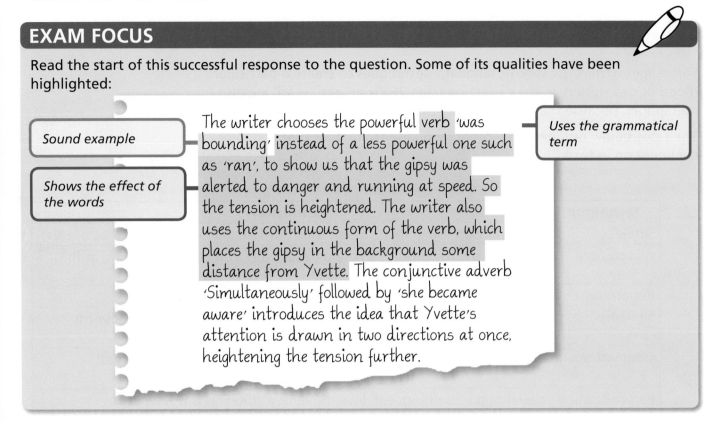

Sound example

Shows the effect of the words

The writer chooses the powerful verb 'was bounding' instead of a less powerful one such as 'ran', to show us that the gipsy was alerted to danger and running at speed. So the tension is heightened. The writer also uses the continuous form of the verb, which places the gipsy in the background some distance from Yvette. The conjunctive adverb 'Simultaneously' followed by 'she became aware' introduces the idea that Yvette's attention is drawn in two directions at once, heightening the tension further.

Uses the grammatical term

What mistakes **might** a student have made in answering this question?

● They might have commented on the sentence structure – not asked for here.

● They might have focused on the landscape instead of the danger.

● They might have mentioned the effects but not shown how they were created (the evidence).

● They might have identified the types of phrases or words incorrectly.

Reread the extract at the top of page 26, then answer these two questions:

❶ What **verbs**, **nouns** and **adjectives** best show that Yvette is in danger?

❷ Describe their **effects**.

NOW YOU TRY IT

Read this further extract from earlier in the text, then answer the question below.

> *And she felt too lazy, too lazy, too lazy. She strayed in the garden by the river, half dreamy, expecting something. While the gleam of spring sun lasted, she would be out of doors. Indoors Granny, sitting back like some awful old prelate,[1] in her bulk of black silk and her white lace cap, was warming her feet by the fire …*

prelate[1] – a high-ranking clergyman, such as a bishop

❸ How does the writer use words and phrases to describe Yvette's feelings of idleness?

Remember:

● Stick to the focus of the question.

● Mention words and phrases.

● Describe their effects.

CHOOSING TECHNIQUES TO CREATE EFFECTS

Sometimes writers use specific language techniques to create a particular mood or description. In the extract on page 26, 'roar' and 'snarl' are also **metaphors**, because they describe the rushing water as an animal.

The table below outlines some other language techniques that you might comment on in texts.

Technique	Definition
Simile	a comparison using 'like', 'as' or 'than': 'a face like a tomato'
Alliteration	repeated use of consonant sounds, especially at the start of words, as in 'dirty, dark and damp'
Repetition	words or phrases used more than once, for emphasis
Sibilance	strongly stressed consonants making a 'hissing' sound, e.g. 'whisper of silvery snow'
Onomatopoeia	words that sound like the thing they describe, such as 'Crash! Thud!'
Personification	describing something, e.g. love, time, or a flood, as if it is a person

Read this further extract from *The Virgin and the Gipsy*. Which of the **techniques** in the table above does the writer use to describe Yvette's desperate circumstances?

> *Yvette was blind to everything but the stairs. Blind, unconscious of everything save the steps rising beyond the water, she clambered up like a wet, shuddering cat, in a state of unconsciousness. It was not till she was on the landing, dripping and shuddering till she could not stand erect, clinging to the banisters, while the house shook and the water raved below, that she was aware of the sodden gipsy.*

How would you approach this question?

- Decide what its **focus** is – 'Yvette's desperate circumstances'.
- Find **examples** of Yvette's desperate circumstances and sum them up in your own words.
- Select the **most appropriate ones** and identify the **techniques** used.
- Describe the **effects**.

TOP TIP ⭐

Look for techniques that appeal to a range of senses, not only sight.

EXAM FOCUS

Read the start of this successful response to the question. Some of its qualities have been highlighted:

| Technique identified |

Repetition is one of the key ways the writer conveys how desperate Yvette is to find a place of safety away from the flood.

| Highlights writer's usage |

| Appropriate quotations, well embedded |

For example, repeating the words 'blind' and 'to/of everything' highlights how Yvette is unaware, 'unconscious', of her general surroundings and is only focused on the 'stairs' (also repeated as 'steps') that are above the water. Another form of repetition, alliteration, particularly 'b' in 'but' and 'beyond', helps to reinforce the word 'blind' and further emphasises Yvette's desperate need to survive.

| Effect described |

Reread the extract on page 28 and answer these questions:

4 Find **two other techniques** in the extract.

5 Describe their **effects**.

APPLYING YOUR SKILLS

Read this extract from later in the text, then use what you have learned about the effect of language choices (words, phrases and techniques) to answer the question below.

> *The bridge was gone. But the flood had abated, and the house, that leaned forwards as if it were making a stiff bow to the stream, stood now in mud and wreckage, with a great heap of fallen masonry and debris at the south-west corner. Awful were the gaping mouths of rooms!*

6 How does the writer use language to describe what has happened to the house?

Remember:

- Stick to the focus of the question.
- Mention words and phrases.
- Describe their effects.

ANALYSING THE EFFECTS OF DIFFERENT TYPES OF SENTENCES

HOW DO DIFFERENT SENTENCE TYPES CREATE EFFECTS?

A02

AQA Paper 1, Section A, Q2

Edexcel Paper 1, Section A, Q3

Eduqas Component 1, Section A, QA2, QA3, QA4

OCR Component 2, Section A, Q2, Q3

Writers vary the structure, length and style of their sentences to change the pace, introduce new information, add details or create emotional impact. You should be able to identify appropriate examples and explain their effect.

Read this short extract. How does the writer use **different sentence forms** to describe the ship's predicament?

> *The ship ground to a halt. Although the sailors on the ice pushed and shoved, yelled and shouted, and puffed and swore, the huge wooden beast wouldn't move. The pack ice seemed to have closed and the ship would be forever wedded to it.*
>
> *'Nothing for it,' said the Captain gloomily, leaping down. 'Abandon ship!'*

How would you approach this sort of question?

- Decide what the **focus of the question** is – 'the ship's predicament' (the problem it faces).
- Find **examples** of the problem being described.
- Select the **most appropriate evidence** and identify the **sentence forms**.
- Describe the **effects**.

Look back at pages 10–11 to remind yourself of the different sentence forms writers use to add variety and create effects in their work. The table below describes two examples of sentence forms from the text.

TOP TIP ★

If your question mentions sentence forms, it is likely to be part of a question worth 8 marks (probably 2–3 marks for this part), so although there are four stages here, you would need to do this very quickly in your head, or in brief notes.

Problem	Example	Sentence form	Effect
The ship meets trouble.	*The ship ground to a halt.*	Simple sentence	Suggests the abrupt, sudden nature of the moment.
The sailors try everything but cannot move it.	*Although the sailors on the ice pushed and shoved, yelled and shouted, and puffed and swore, the huge wooden beast wouldn't move.*	Complex sentence	The long subordinated sentence suggests all the men's efforts.

EXAM FOCUS

Read this successful response to the question. Some of its qualities have been highlighted:

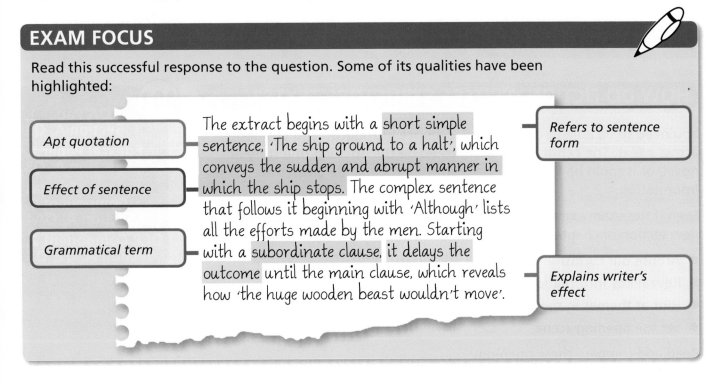

Apt quotation

Effect of sentence

Grammatical term

The extract begins with a short simple sentence, 'The ship ground to a halt', which conveys the sudden and abrupt manner in which the ship stops. The complex sentence that follows it beginning with 'Although' lists all the efforts made by the men. Starting with a subordinate clause, it delays the outcome until the main clause, which reveals how 'the huge wooden beast wouldn't move'.

Refers to sentence form

Explains writer's effect

What mistakes **might** a student have made in answering this question?

- They might have commented on the Captain's feelings – not asked for here.
- They might have mentioned the different forms but not mentioned the effects.
- They might have mentioned the effects but not specified the types of sentences used.
- They might have commented on vocabulary and not mentioned sentences at all.

Reread the extract on page 30, then answer these two questions:

❶ What two other sentence forms or styles are used in the extract?

❷ How do they contribute to the effect?

APPLYING YOUR SKILLS

Read this further extract from the same text, then answer the question below.

> *It was just before nightfall that it happened. Although the men had posted guards on all sides of the camp, somehow they must have missed its approach. Grabbing rifles and throwing off blankets, the men leapt into action. A flare went up. There it was! A huge, lumbering white monster appeared out of the gloom. It was a polar bear.*

❸ How does the writer use sentence forms to describe the drama of the polar bear's attack?

Remember:

- Stick to the focus of the question.
- Mention the sentence forms.
- Describe their effects.

ANALYSING THE STRUCTURE OF A TEXT

HOW DO FICTION WRITERS STRUCTURE TEXTS?

A02

AQA Paper 1, Section A, Q3

Edexcel Paper 1, Section A, Q3

Eduqas Component 1, Section A, QA4

OCR Component 2, Section A, Q2, Q3

You need to be able to explain how ideas are introduced and developed across a text. The extract in an exam could be the opening of a story or novel, or it could be from later on. You will probably be given this information.

Even if the exam extract is from later on in a story, it may be the start of a new section or chapter. In any opening, the writer may do several things:

- Arouse our **curiosity** – making us ask questions
- Reveal **key information** about characters and their situation
- Hint at **themes** in the story
- Set the **opening scene**

Read and compare these openings:

> **A** *None of them knew the colour of the sky. Their eyes glanced level, and were fastened upon the waves that swept toward them. These waves were of the hue of slate, save for the tops, which were of foaming white, and all of the men knew the colours of the sea.*
>
> From 'The Open Boat' by Stephen Crane
>
> **B** *There was no possibility of taking a walk that day. We had been wandering, indeed, in the leafless shrubbery an hour in the morning; but since dinner (Mrs Reed, when there was no company, dined early) the cold winter wind had brought with it clouds so sombre, and a rain so penetrating, that further out-door exercise was now out of the question.*
>
> From *Jane Eyre* by Charlotte Brontë
>
> **C** *It is a truth universally acknowledged, that a single man in possession of a good fortune, must be in want of a wife.*
>
> From *Pride and Prejudice* by Jane Austen

❶ What is revealed or suggested in each opening?

❷ What questions does each opening raise?

TOP TIP

Look for how a text engages the reader. For example, opening A gets our attention with a puzzling statement that becomes clearer when we realise the men are concentrating on the rough sea. We ask ourselves why this is so.

EXAM FOCUS

Read this extract from a response to a question based on opening **B**.
Some of its qualities have been highlighted:

> The opening makes us wonder why a walk is impossible, and then explains, providing a surprising amount of information. It moves from morning to afternoon through 'that day' in the narrator's memory when they had little to do, as shown by their 'wandering' on a cold winter's day. It reveals the time of day, the season and the weather. It also introduces 'Mrs Reed' as someone who decides what time lunch will be. The passage also raises questions: who Mrs Reed is, who the narrator is and why she is wandering about. Finally, the 'sombre' weather creates a gloomy mood.

Identifies the 'question and answer' format

Refers to evidence

Shows how the opening engages our interest

The student does not make the mistake of trying to analyse words or sentences in detail, concentrating instead on what the opening achieves and how ideas are developed and structured.

NOW YOU TRY IT

Read the continuation of opening **B**, then answer the question below.

> *I was glad of it: I never liked long walks, especially on chilly afternoons: dreadful to me was the coming home in the raw twilight, with nipped fingers and toes, and a heart saddened by the chidings of Bessie, the nurse, and humbled by the consciousness of my physical inferiority to Eliza, John, and Georgiana Reed.*
>
> *The said Eliza, John, and Georgiana were now clustered round their mama in the drawing-room: she lay reclined on a sofa by the fireside, and with her darlings about her (for the time neither quarrelling nor crying) looked perfectly happy. Me, she had dispensed[1] from joining the group.*

dispensed[1] – banned

❸ Write a comment explaining how this extract moves on from and develops the opening, both in the information it provides and in the further questions it raises. Consider how the writer:

- Reveals more of the narrator's character and probable age
- Goes on to hint at the narrator's position within the family
- Begins to make us sympathise with the narrator

Remember:

- Stick to the focus of the question – development of ideas.
- Show how the passage progresses.

STRUCTURING A FICTION TEXT

A passage may be structured in many ways. For example:

- In the **order in which an observer takes in the scene**
- From an **overall picture to fine detail**, or the opposite
- In the **order in which action occurs**, building up to a **climax**
- **Switching time frame**, using memories, action, plans and **foreshadowing**

Read this passage about a young woman moving home. Some of its features have been highlighted.

New paragraph shifts reader's attention to wagon's contents, first objects (furniture), then plants, then living things

Creates atmosphere, referring back to the previous paragraph

Opening sentence emphasises the young woman being left alone

Switches focus to the girl

Closer focus on what the girl does, arousing our curiosity

The sensible horses stood – perfectly still, and the waggoner's steps sank fainter and fainter in the distance.

The girl on the summit of the load sat motionless, surrounded by tables and chairs with their legs upwards, backed by an oak settle, and ornamented in front by pots of geraniums, myrtles, and cactuses, together with a caged canary – all probably from the windows of the house just vacated. There was also a cat in a willow basket, from the partly opened lid of which she gazed with half-closed eyes, and affectionately surveyed the small birds around.

The handsome girl waited for some time idly in her place, and the only sound heard in the stillness was the hopping of the canary up and down the perches of its prison. Then she looked attentively downwards. It was not at the bird, nor at the cat; it was at an oblong package tied in paper, and lying between them. She turned her head to learn if the waggoner were coming. He was not yet in sight; and her eyes crept back to the package, her thoughts seeming to run upon what was inside it. At length she drew the article into her lap, and untied the paper covering; a small swing looking-glass was disclosed, in which she proceeded to survey herself attentively. She parted her lips and smiled.

From *Far From the Madding Crowd* by Thomas Hardy

❹ Write down a short heading to summarise each paragraph.

❺ Comment on how the final paragraph of this passage is structured. For example, is anything hinted at? How is information revealed?

CONTRAST, CONFLICT AND RESOLUTION

Many stories involve contrast and conflict, usually leading to a **resolution** (the end of conflict), or a climax (the high point of excitement).

In the following extract, the character Cathy reports disagreeing with Linton. As you read, think about how the passage is structured.

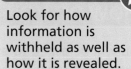

TOP TIP

Look for how information is withheld as well as how it is revealed.

> '*He said the pleasantest manner of spending a hot July day was lying from morning till evening on a bank of heath in the middle of the moors, with the bees humming dreamily about among the bloom, and the larks singing high up overhead, and the blue sky and bright sun shining steadily and cloudlessly. That was his most perfect idea of heaven's happiness: mine was rocking in a rustling green tree, with a west wind blowing, and bright white clouds flitting rapidly above; and not only larks, but throstles[1], and blackbirds, and linnets, and cuckoos pouring out music on every side, and the moors seen at a distance, broken into cool dusky dells; but close by great swells of long grass undulating in waves to the breeze; and woods and sounding water, and the whole world awake and wild with joy. He wanted all to lie in an ecstasy of peace; I wanted all to sparkle and dance in a glorious jubilee. I said his heaven would be only half alive; and he said mine would be drunk: I said I should fall asleep in his; and he said he could not breathe in mine, and began to grow very snappish. At last, we agreed to try both, as soon as the right weather came.*'
>
> From *Wuthering Heights* by Emily Brontë

throstles[1] – thrushes

TOP TIP

Choose verbs and verb phrases to help you analyse structure, such as 'focuses', 'narrows down', 'balances' and 'brings together'.

EXAM FOCUS

Read this opening to an analysis of contrast and conflict in the passage. Some of its features have been highlighted:

Cathy makes Linton's perfect day sound pleasant but unexciting, and then describes her own, which by contrast is full of movement, colour, sound and life. From 'He wanted ...' the conflict intensifies.

| Summarises the contrast |
| Describes the change |
| Identifies turning point |

APPLYING YOUR SKILLS

⑥ Continue the analysis of the passage, making at least two more points.

Remember:

● Consider how the pace is increased.

● Show how the passage develops and reaches a resolution

FORMING AN INTERPRETATION: EVALUATING A TEXT

HOW DO YOU INTERPRET AND EVALUATE A TEXT?

A04

AQA Paper 1,
Section A, Q4

Edexcel Paper 1,
Section A, Q4

Eduqas
Component 1
Section A, QA5

OCR Component 2,
Section A, Q4

You will be asked to **evaluate** part of a text **critically** and **support** this with **textual references**. You will have to give a personal response to an aspect of the text, such as **characterisation**, **setting** and atmosphere, or **themes**. To do so, you will need to consider language effects and comment on how successful you think they are.

Read the extract below. How far does the writer succeed in revealing the narrator's character?

> *It was a great comfort to turn from that chap to my influential friend, the battered, twisted, ruined, tin-pot steamboat. I clambered on board. She rang under my feet like an empty Huntley & Palmer biscuit-tin kicked along a gutter; she was nothing so solid in make, and rather less pretty in shape, but I had expended enough hard work on her to make me love her. No influential friend would have served me better. She had given me a chance to come out a bit – to find out what I could do. No, I don't like work. I had rather laze about and think of all the fine things that can be done. I don't like work – no man does – but I like what is in the work – the chance to find yourself.*
>
> From *Heart of Darkness* by Joseph Conrad

How would you answer this question?

- Think about **your own response** to the character and the reasons for it.
- Focus on the **details** described, the narrator's **language**, and what both **say** about him.
- Choose **examples** of details and language that you find **effective**.
- Comment on how these express the narrator's **character**.

EXAM FOCUS

Read this extract from a successful response. Some of its features have been highlighted:

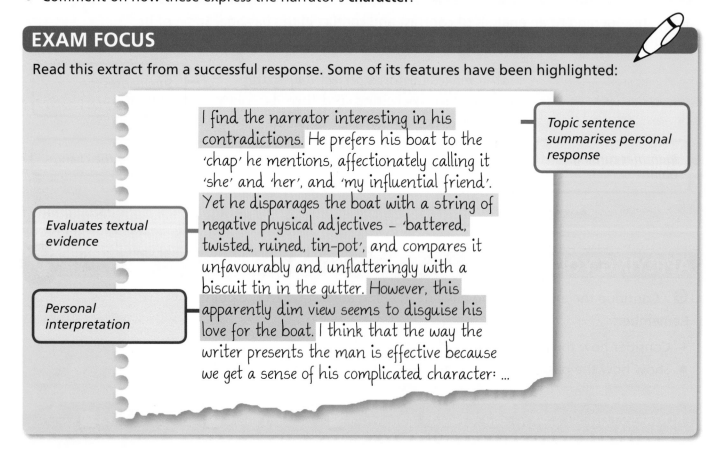

I find the narrator interesting in his contradictions. He prefers his boat to the 'chap' he mentions, affectionately calling it 'she' and 'her', and 'my influential friend'. Yet he disparages the boat with a string of negative physical adjectives – 'battered, twisted, ruined, tin-pot', and compares it unfavourably and unflatteringly with a biscuit tin in the gutter. However, this apparently dim view seems to disguise his love for the boat. I think that the way the writer presents the man is effective because we get a sense of his complicated character: ...

Topic sentence summarises personal response

Evaluates textual evidence

Personal interpretation

❶ Reread the extract, then add a point interpreting and evaluating what the narrator says about his attitude towards work.

NOW YOU TRY IT

Read this further passage from *Heart of Darkness*, then answer the question below.

Going up that river was like travelling back to the earliest beginnings of the world, when vegetation rioted on the earth and the big trees were kings. An empty stream, a great silence, an impenetrable forest. The air was warm, thick, heavy, sluggish. There was no joy in the brilliance of sunshine. The long stretches of the waterway ran on, deserted, into the gloom of overshadowed distances. On silvery sand-banks hippos and alligators sunned themselves side by side. The broadening waters flowed through a mob of wooded islands; you lost your way on that river as you would in a desert, and butted all day long against shoals[1], trying to find the channel, till you thought yourself bewitched.

shoals[1] – shallows

❷ A reader has commented that the way this passage is written makes the jungle voyage convincingly real. How far do you agree?

Remember:

- Give your own impressions.
- Evaluate how the writer has created them.
- Support your views with textual evidence.

THE LANGUAGE OF EVALUATION

It can be particularly useful to have some **adjectives** (or phrases meaning similar things) at your fingertips to explain whether a text is effective or not. For example, consider using words such as:

- 'intense', 'memorable', or 'powerful' (leaves a lasting impression)
- 'vivid' or 'colourful' (strong, bright or rich imagery)
- 'engaging', 'compelling' or 'enticing' (drawing you in)
- 'dramatic' (full of tension and action)

Always make sure the comments you select fit with what you have been asked to focus on.

TOP TIP

If you are studying for the OCR exam, you can also gain marks for comparing writers' ideas and perspectives over two or more texts (AO3). For more guidance, see Chapter 4, where AO3 is covered in relation to non-fiction texts.

SUPPORT IDEAS USING EVIDENCE FROM THE TEXT

You will have noticed that in the task on page 37 you were asked to 'support your opinions with references to the text (or texts)'. This means providing evidence. You could use several types of evidence, depending on what aspect of the text you are asked to comment on:

- What characters do and say
- How the writer uses descriptive language
- What details are included
- Ideas that the text raises or explores

❸ Find an example of each type of evidence about the character Errol in the passage below. Then decide which you would need to support with a quotation and which you could simply refer to.

> *Errol looked at his watch again and drummed his fingers on the desk. 'Come on, come on!' he said aloud, his haunted face creasing tightly. He felt trapped, vulnerable, like a mouse with no hole to run to. Even the stuffed owl in the shadowy corner of the ill-lit basement room seemed to be glaring at him as if he were prey.*

PEE AND PEA

You may have been taught the PEE or PEA techniques:

- PEE – Point, Evidence, Explanation
- PEA – Point, Evidence, Analysis

PEA is more useful, as **analysis** is a higher-level skill than **explanation**. However, for this question you also need **evaluation**, showing your assessment of the writer's skills.

If you use PEA, try not to list the PEA and Evaluation in the same order every time. You do not need to evaluate in every point you make.

Read this paragraph.

Point   Evidence

> *Errol is portrayed as anxious,* **in that** *he looks repeatedly at his watch and drums on the table.* **These actions are an** *effective way to show that he is tensely waiting for something to happen.*

Analysis and evaluation

Now look at this new version of the paragraph.

> *Errol's repeated glances at his watch and his drumming on the table are effective ways to show that he is tensely waiting for something, revealing his anxious nature.*

❹ Identify the PEA and Evaluation in the second version.

❺ Rewrite the following sentences to vary the PEA and Evaluation order. Start: 'A persuasive sense of menace is created by …'

> *The character feels in danger, as shown by the adjectives 'trapped, vulnerable', and the strong verb 'glaring', implying threat. The word choices create a persuasive sense of menace.*

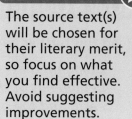

TOP TIP

The source text(s) will be chosen for their literary merit, so focus on what you find effective. Avoid suggesting improvements.

GET IT RIGHT!

To achieve a high mark you must **evaluate** the text if the task requires it. This means assessing how far it has achieved its purpose – normally to bring to life the characters or events being described.

EXAM FOCUS

Read this response to Question 2 on page 37, about the first person narrative in the extract from *Heart of Darkness*.

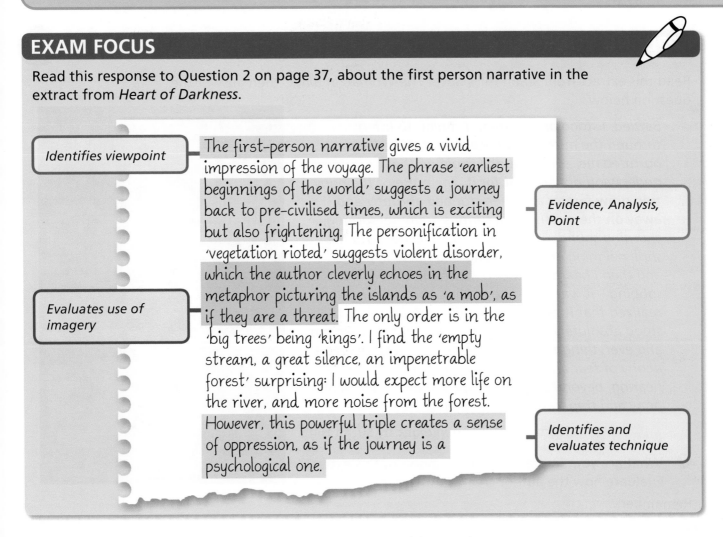

Identifies viewpoint

The first-person narrative gives a vivid impression of the voyage. The phrase 'earliest beginnings of the world' suggests a journey back to pre-civilised times, which is exciting but also frightening. The personification in 'vegetation rioted' suggests violent disorder, which the author cleverly echoes in the metaphor picturing the islands as 'a mob', as if they are a threat. The only order is in the 'big trees' being 'kings'. I find the 'empty stream, a great silence, an impenetrable forest' surprising: I would expect more life on the river, and more noise from the forest. However, this powerful triple creates a sense of oppression, as if the journey is a psychological one.

Evidence, Analysis, Point

Evaluates use of imagery

Identifies and evaluates technique

What mistakes **might** a student have made in answering this question?

- They might have summarised the story of the passage.
- They might have just given a personal response ('*It's like when we went to Center Parcs ...*').
- They might have missed the connections between parts of the text.
- They might have failed to provide textual evidence.

Read this further extract from *Heart of Darkness*:

> *Trees, trees, millions of trees, massive, immense, running up high; and at their foot, hugging the bank against the stream, crept the little begrimed steamboat, like a sluggish beetle crawling on the floor of a lofty portico.[1] It made you feel very small, very lost, and yet it was not altogether depressing, that feeling. After all, if you were small, the grimy beetle crawled on – which was just what you wanted it to do.*
>
> *portico[1] – roof supported by columns in classical architecture*

6 How far do you agree that the author effectively portrays the narrator's experience?

APPLYING YOUR SKILLS

Read this extract from Susan Hill's novel *The Woman in Black*, then answer the question below.

> *Baffled, I stood and waited, straining to listen through the mist. What I heard next chilled and horrified me, even though I could neither understand nor account for it. The noise of the pony trap grew fainter and then stopped abruptly and away on the marsh was a curious draining, sucking, churning sound, which went on, together with the shrill neighing and whinnying of a horse in panic, and then I heard another cry, a shout, a terrified sobbing – it was hard to decipher – but with horror I realized that it came from a child, a young child. I stood absolutely helpless in the mist that clouded me and everything from my sight, almost weeping in an agony of fear and frustration, and I knew that I was hearing, beyond any doubt, appalling last noises of a pony and trap, carrying a child in it.*

From *The Woman in Black* by Susan Hill

❼ What are your impressions of the **mood** of this extract? Evaluate how the author creates this mood.

Remember:

- Give your impressions.
- Analyse how they are formed.
- Evaluate the text.
- Include evidence in the form of paraphrase or quotations.

PROGRESS CHECK FOR CHAPTER 2

GOOD PROGRESS

I can:

- Identify explicit and implicit information ☐
- Clearly explain most effects of the writer's language choices ☐
- Select a range of suitable quotations to support my ideas ☐

EXCELLENT PROGRESS

I can:

- Analyse thoughtfully the effects of the writer's language choices ☐
- Select the most appropriate quotations to support my ideas ☐
- Interpret and evaluate a text ☐

CHAPTER 3: Writing imaginative, descriptive and narrative texts

WHAT'S IT ALL ABOUT?

Depending on the course you are following for your English Language exam, you will have to:

- Respond to a given stimulus, such as a title or a photograph
- Write either a story, part of a story or an imaginative description

On some courses you will be given a choice, but on others you will not.

SKILLS REQUIRED

Whatever the task set, you will need these core skills to demonstrate your creative and descriptive ideas:

- Adopt an appropriate writing style (for example, using vivid description).
- Choose interesting ideas that are raised by the question.
- Organise your writing for clarity and interest, using paragraphs with **connectives** and **discourse markers** to link them where necessary.
- Create striking effects in your writing – for example, creating a sense of place and character by using **imagery** such as **similes** and **metaphors**.
- Use accurate grammar, spelling and punctuation.

TOP TIP

In the months leading up to the exam, focus on developing key skills that you can use on the day. For example, to extend your vocabulary read as much fiction as you can and note any new words that appeal to you.

AUDIENCE AND VOICE

You may be asked to write for a specific audience, such as young people or adults, but it is useful to have an audience in mind anyway. You should write in **Standard English** unless a character or narrator is speaking, when some informal language may be acceptable. Think about the voice of the story. How will it sound? Will you use **dialect** and **colloquialisms**?

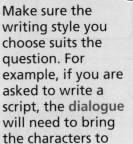

TOP TIP

Make sure the writing style you choose suits the question. For example, if you are asked to write a script, the **dialogue** will need to bring the characters to life.

EFFECTIVE DESCRIPTIVE WRITING

WHAT MAKES A DESCRIPTION LEAVE A STRONG IMPRESSION ON THE READER?

A05 A06

AQA
Paper 1,
Section B

Edexcel Paper 1,
Section B

Eduqas
Component 1,
Section B

OCR Component 2,
Section B

There is a difference between description in a purely descriptive piece of writing and description in a story when you are writing in the exam:

● When writing a story, you need to move the plot along and cannot spend too much time on description.

● In a purely descriptive piece, you have more time to consider the detail and **imagery** you want to use.

SHOW DON'T TELL

When you 'tell' a reader something, you are simply informing them. 'Showing' is a technique that helps a reader to visualise what you are describing, making your writing more vivid and exciting.

Read these two descriptions of a setting:

> Repetition used to highlight the rain

> Contrast shows how the rain affects everyone alike

Telling: *There was so much rain between Friday and Sunday.*

Showing: *Rain, rain and more rain. It trickled from caps and hoods, soaked the rich and poor alike, assaulted meagre streets and expansive boulevards. Umbrellas collapsed from exhaustion. Cars juddered to a halt. Still it rained.*

> Powerful verbs heighten the effect of the rain

TOP TIP ⭐

Some 'telling' is necessary in a narrative, because information may be needed to move the story along. Note how in the 'telling' example, we learn that it rains 'from Friday to Sunday', but this information is not given in the 'showing' example.

❶ What specific things are **shown** in the second description? (If you were drawing a picture, what would be in it?)

❷ Find an example of **personification** in the second description.

DESCRIBING A PERSON

You can use the same method of 'telling' or 'showing' when describing a person. For example:

Telling: *Nina was completely drenched.*

Showing: *Rivulets of water streamed from Nina's hair and ran down her forehead on to her nose. Water dripped from her coat into her already waterlogged shoes, which squelched with every miserable step she took.*

❸ What specific things does the writer **show** us in this description? Find:

- Powerful verbs
- Vivid **adjectives**
- Repetition
- Other vocabulary choices you think add to the description

If you continued the description about Nina using 'telling', it might read like this:

TOP TIP

Most images appeal to the sense of sight, but you can also appeal to the other senses (sound, touch, taste). Note how Nina's 'waterlogged' shoes 'squelched'. The image appeals to the senses of sound and touch.

Useful sentence giving information

Too close to where? Needs to show where Nina is and what the bus looked like

Nina reached the bus stop. As the bus came round the corner, it came too close and she got wet again.

Needs more vivid description showing how she 'got wet'

GET IT RIGHT!

Avoid **tautology**. For example, if you use a powerful verb you do not need an adverb with a similar meaning to describe it: 'He **strolled slowly** along the street. To 'stroll' is to walk slowly so you do not need the adverb here.

❹ Rewrite the 'telling' example above using the 'showing' technique to create a vivid picture. You can write more than one sentence. You could begin: 'As the [add adjectives] bus veered round the corner ...'

- Use specific, detailed verbs, rather than 'came', 'got wet'.
- Use literary techniques, such as a simile.

APPLYING YOUR SKILLS

❺ Write a description of 100 words about a small fishing boat in a storm. Use the picture to help you.

Remember:

- Appeal to the senses.
- 'Show' rather than 'tell', using powerful verbs, adjectives and **adverbs**, comparisons such as **similes** and personification.

CREATING ATMOSPHERE AND MOOD

HOW DO LANGUAGE FEATURES SUCH AS PUNCTUATION OR VARIED SENTENCES CREATE EFFECTS?

A05 **A06**

AQA
Paper 1,
Section B

Edexcel Paper 1,
Section B

Eduqas
Component 1,
Section B

OCR Component 2,
Section B

Punctuation, repetition and a variety of sentence lengths can help to create different **moods**, tension and pace.

Read the extract below:

> *And this Thing I saw? How can I describe it? A monstrous tripod, higher than many houses, striding over the young pine trees, and smashing them aside in its career; a walking engine of glittering metal, striding now across the heather, articulate ropes of steel dangling from it, and the clattering tumult of its passage mingling with the riot of the thunder.*
>
> From *War of the Worlds* by H. G. Wells

❶ Sum up the mood of this extract by choosing the best words from the following:

| surprise | alarm | horror | fear | dismay | excitement |

❷ The table below shows how punctuation and sentence length contribute to the mood of the extract. Find each example in the passage above.

TOP TIP ⭐

If you are asked to write a description, decide on the mood you want to create before you begin writing.

Feature	Function	Effect
Questions instead of statements	Speaks directly to the reader	Conveys the speaker's alarm
Semicolon, commas	Lists tripod's actions and features in quick succession	Conveys the speaker's horror and fear
Short sentences followed by a long one	Marks a shift in pace	Creates a growing sense of the tripod's power and menace

RHETORICAL QUESTIONS

A **rhetorical question** is a question that expects no answer, usually because the answer is obvious or there is no answer. A rhetorical question can be used for effect, to:

● Emphasise a point
● Encourage the reader to accept a particular point of view
● Contemplate the unanswerable

❸ What effect do each of these rhetorical questions have?

- *I'm sure you'd agree with me, wouldn't you?*
- *Who can say what will happen in this world?*
- *Can we get the show on the road, please?*

EXAM FOCUS

Read this successful description of a pleasant surprise. Some of its qualities have been highlighted:

> Short sentence followed by a long one changes pace

> Mimi gasped. The food was displayed on a crisp white tablecloth: cheeses, pickles, brown rolls, white rolls, pizza, samosas, pakoras, sausage rolls, patties, meringues, eclairs, angel cake, banana cake, chocolate cake and more. Wasn't it just perfect?

> Semicolon and commas used to list details

> Rhetorical question to emphasise a point

REPETITION

Another way of emphasising a point is by using repetition. Usually the same words and phrases are repeated, but punctuation or sentence length can also be repeated to emphasise mood. For example, asking more than one question (as in the extract from *War of the Worlds*) emphasises the speaker's shock.

Read the following passage:

> *Quick! Along Mitcham Street I sprint, round the corner and into Pickett's yard. Then up to the far end and into the shadows. I stop. Catch my breath. Steady myself. Lean against the wall. Listen.*

> Repeating short or minor sentences in succession creates pace and tension and reflects the character's feelings

> **TOP TIP**
>
> Using a series of short sentences to create tension can be effective, but do not overuse this technique otherwise it loses its impact. Use punctuation such as exclamation marks sparingly.

❹ What punctuation is used to create a sense of urgency?

APPLYING YOUR SKILLS

❺ Reread the passage above. Write another paragraph of about 100 words to continue the story. Describe how an unwelcome sound comes closer and closer to the narrator, then slowly fades as the danger passes.

Remember:

- Create tension as the sound comes closer.
- Release the tension as it fades.

PROGRESS LOG [tick the correct box]   Needs more work ☐   Getting there ☐   Under control ☐

GENERATING IDEAS AND STRUCTURING A DESCRIPTION

HOW CAN YOU USE THE STIMULUS GIVEN TO YOU IN THE EXAM EFFECTIVELY?

A05 **A06**

AQA
Paper 1,
Section B

Edexcel Paper 1,
Section B

Eduqas
Component 1,
Section B

OCR Component 2,
Section B

The exam paper will give you a prompt, or stimulus, to inspire your writing. This might be a photograph, a written scenario or a key sentence from a story. There are several ways of using this stimulus to develop your ideas.

WORD CHAINS

You could choose a key word or a feature of the picture to begin. For example, if you are presented with a photograph of the natural world, you might begin your planning by listing the features in the photo to create word chains. A word chain can help you expand your ideas, so it may spark an idea for a description.

First select one feature, such as 'wood'. Write down the next word that comes into your head (such as 'animal'), then continue to do this to create word associations. For example:

> *wood animal rabbit hare field pasture lush summer sun moon stars cosmos mystery*

❶ Create word chains of at least five words starting with each of the following:

| mask | | fish | | lightning | | train | | despair |

FIRST LINES

Another way to generate ideas is to focus on a key word from the stimulus and use it to create an opening sentence. For example, you could generate a sentence around the word 'mask':

> *The mask hung on a nail at the back of the junk shop.*

You can then add detail:

Phrase adds detail   Adjective adds detail

The mask with the hollow eyes hung from a rusty nail at the back of the junk shop.

❷ Create first sentences from any of the remaining words in Question 1 (not 'mask').

❸ Copy and complete the sentences below, adding detail with words, phrases and **imagery**. Try to capture such feelings as amazement, delight, sadness, shock or anger.

- *The … fairground lights, which … twinkled … in the dark.*
- *They walked … along the … beach for the last time.*
- *The … laptop, …, had been completely dismantled.*

STRUCTURE YOUR DESCRIPTION

In the exam, you will need to organise your ideas quickly. Keep them in your head or note them down if you have time. If you were describing the junk shop, you might structure your description in the following way:

- **Paragraph 1:** Begin with a general description of the shop and its atmosphere. Is it mysterious? Enticing? Disturbing?
- **Paragraph 2:** Describe the specific details of the mask and why you were drawn to it.
- **Paragraph 3:** Move on to a different object or introduce a person, and so on.

Zoom in on details, using techniques such as powerful verbs, **adjectives** and **similes**.

Use **prepositions** or **prepositional phrases** to describe the precise relationship of one thing or person to another: 'The key was **inside** a tatty envelope, which had been pushed **behind** the mirror **on** the wall.'

> **TOP TIP**
>
> Remember, moving from a general description (the overall view) to a specific one (a focus on one thing) is a useful technique to use in your writing.

EXAM FOCUS

Read this successful description of a cat. Some of its features have been highlighted:

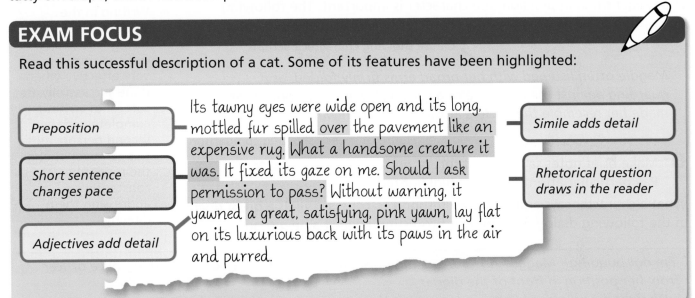

Preposition	Its tawny eyes were wide open and its long, mottled fur spilled over the pavement like an expensive rug. What a handsome creature it was. It fixed its gaze on me. Should I ask permission to pass? Without warning, it yawned a great, satisfying, pink yawn, lay flat on its luxurious back with its paws in the air and purred.	Simile adds detail
Short sentence changes pace		Rhetorical question draws in the reader
Adjectives add detail		

APPLYING YOUR SKILLS

❹ Choose **one** of the following titles and create a plan for a description:
   - 'The Race'
   - 'The Lake'
   - 'Being Carefree'

Remember:

- Generate some ideas, based on the titles, using the skills you have learned.
- Then draw two boxes, one for each paragraph, and make notes in each box.
- In the first box write notes for a general description.
- In the second and third write notes for a specific description. Add further boxes if you wish.
- Make notes on using other techniques you have learned in this unit (such as powerful verbs and images.)

PROGRESS LOG [tick the correct box]   Needs more work ▢   Getting there ▢   Under control ▢

CREATING CONVINCING CHARACTERS AND VOICES

HOW CAN YOU MAKE YOUR CHARACTERS CONVINCING AND VIVID?

A05 **A06**

AQA
Paper 1,
Section B

Edexcel Paper 1,
Section B

Eduqas
Component 1,
Section B

OCR Component 2,
Section B

To create a convincing character you should:

- Decide what your character wants. What is their goal (for example, to achieve justice)?
- Consider if they are what they seem (perhaps they have a secret)
- Consider if something is troubling them (are they being threatened?)
- Decide what their strengths and weaknesses are (brave but rash?)

FIRST IMPRESSIONS

The reader's first impression of a character is important. The following description gives an insight into a character as well as her appearance:

Clause showing character's actions

Maggie often listened with her broad arms firmly folded, as if guarding against the influence of a speaker's views – a stance that made her resemble the buffers at the end of a railway line.

Figure of speech showing comparison

❶ Make brief notes saying what sort of person Maggie seems to be. Pay particular attention to the highlighted text.

What a character says and how they respond to others reveals a great deal: In the following **dialogue**, Maggie is protesting against a new road.

> *'I'm not budging!' Maggie insisted, looking up squarely into the eyes of the young police officer from her position in front of the digger.*
>
> *He sighed, and glanced anxiously towards the approaching sergeant. 'Look, Miss, I'm sorry, but you'll have to shift eventually. All the others have given up. You're the last man standing, as it were.'*
>
> *'For your information,' Maggie said evenly, 'I'm a woman. And I'm sitting down. What's more, I'm staying sitting down.'*

❷ What does this extract tell us about Maggie as a person? Think about:
- Her goals (what does she want?)
- Things that might be that troubling or difficult for her

❸ Write five sentences about a teenage son or daughter refusing to do what a parent wants.
- In the first sentence, convey the teenager's personality through their physical movements and appearance (for example, hand gestures).
- The remaining sentences should be dialogue, in which the character reveals more of their personality.

  You could start: *'He stood in the kitchen ...'*

TOP TIP ⭐

Writing in the second person (using 'you') can be difficult, but it is very effective when done successfully. Be careful of writing completely in the second person, as this can overwhelm the reader by constantly addressing them directly.

POINT OF VIEW AND VOICE

A narrative can be told from different points of view.

Point of view (POV)	Voice	Effect on reader
First person, 'I'	Intimate	Draws in the reader, who experiences only one POV
Second person, 'you' single or plural	Commanding, urgent	Reader feels as though they are almost a character in the story
Third person, 'he'/'she'/'it'	More distant	Reader is able to experience more than one POV

Most narratives are told in the third or first person. Point of view is important because there are things you could not say in all viewpoints:

- **Third person:** *Joe sat with his head in his strong, capable hands. He was exhausted, yet still looked remarkably handsome.*
- **First person:** *I sat with my head in my strong, capable hands. I was exhausted, yet still looked remarkably handsome.*

❹ What different impressions do you get of the character?

TOP TIP

What one character says about another also reveals something about the first character's personality. Keep this in mind when writing narratives.

EXAM FOCUS

Read this successful opening, written in the second person:

> *Second person, chatty, demands attention*

> *Creates mystery: what times, where, why?*

You know what it's like when all you want to do is curl up into a tight invisible bundle, and sleep for ever, but you daren't give in, you daren't let up for a second? Well, this is one of those times. To give in, now, I'm telling you, would be disastrous – it would take me right back to the beginning.

> *Rhetorical question pulls in the reader*

APPLYING YOUR SKILLS

❺ Write a 100-word character sketch of a market trader who sells fruit and vegetables. Decide what viewpoint to use and add a feature that suggests your character has a secret.

Remember:

- Create a vivid first impression.
- Give your character a goal.

GENERATING IDEAS AND STRUCTURING A NARRATIVE

HOW CAN YOU PLAN A STORY?

In the exam, you may be asked to write a narrative or story. Planning what you are going to write before you start is a key skill.

Look at this question:

Write a story that involves a dangerous situation.

To start planning an answer to this question, you could create a spider diagram with the word 'danger' in the centre. You could then address the following questions:

● Who is in danger?

● What is the danger?

● Where is it happening?

Or you could begin by sketching a quick mental image of your main character, including name, gender, one or two character traits, circumstances (who or what is putting them in danger), appearance. For example:

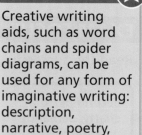

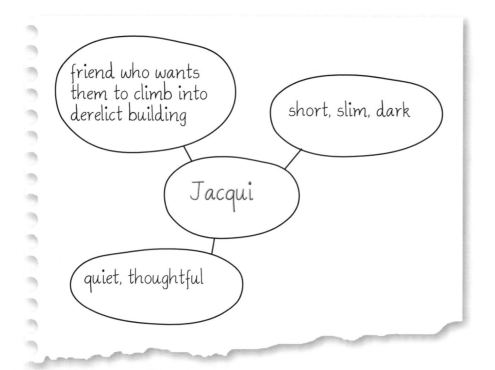

> **TOP TIP**
>
> Creative writing aids, such as word chains and spider diagrams, can be used for any form of imaginative writing: description, narrative, poetry, play scripts and other forms.

❶ Copy the 'character' diagram above and complete it as if you were planning an answer to the question.

❷ Keep the key word 'danger' in mind and think about **who** is in danger – the main character or someone else. Note down some thoughts to start developing your ideas.

CREATE A PLOT

When planning your plot, you need to think about:

- The start of your story (your main character's circumstances)
- Where your story will go (what does the character do, how does this affect the events?)
- How it will end (well or badly?)

Most stories follow a linear structure:

introduction → complication → crisis → resolution

Many narratives have more than one crisis or stage (see Freytag's pyramid on page 99), but you will have limited time in an exam so limit yourself to one key event where everything reaches a **climax**.

The opening should arouse the reader's curiosity, so they want to read on. The conclusion needs to have impact, too. You could end with a twist or a **cliffhanger**:

> *He was caught now, completely and utterly. The prospect that he might stare Death in the face had never once occurred to him.*
> *'Are we ready?' said a voice.*

OTHER NARRATIVE DECISIONS

When planning a narrative, you will also need to consider:

- What **point of view** will you write from – first person ('I') or third person ('he'/'she'/'it') or the unusual second person 'you' (see page 49)
- If you choose the **first person**, will this be the main character or someone else?
- What **tense** will you write in?
- How many other **characters** will you have? (Not too many.) What is their **relationship** to the main character?

❸ Write down answers to these points for the story you are planning.

TOP TIP ⭐

Try to include some direct speech, to 'show' rather than 'tell' what the characters are doing and thinking. Make sure it fits naturally with your story.

DIFFERENT NARRATIVE APPROACHES

Some narratives begin at a point in the plot when some or even all of the action has already taken place. This is referred to as *in media res* (Latin for 'in the middle of things'). For example:

> *I peered through a small gap in the fence. I couldn't believe it! There was nothing but rubble with grass growing between the debris. I'd only been away three weeks. Where was the school?*

The events that lead to this moment are revealed throughout the story in various ways, such as description, **dialogue** or **flashback**.

FLASHBACKS

A flashback is an event that has happened at an earlier time and is recalled in the main story as it is being told. It is used to give:

● Essential information that has a bearing on the plot
● Insights into a character's nature and actions

When using flashbacks, make sure you signal them clearly and make it obvious when you return to the main story, otherwise the reader will be confused.

GET IT RIGHT!

Remember, flashbacks can make the story richer, but they take the reader away from the main action, so only use them if they are essential to the story.

EXAM FOCUS

Read this well-constructed use of flashback. Some of its features have been highlighted:

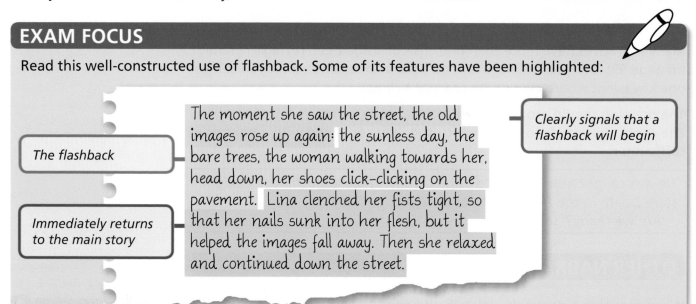

The flashback

Immediately returns to the main story

> The moment she saw the street, the old images rose up again: the sunless day, the bare trees, the woman walking towards her, head down, her shoes click-clicking on the pavement. Lina clenched her fists tight, so that her nails sunk into her flesh, but it helped the images fall away. Then she relaxed and continued down the street.

Clearly signals that a flashback will begin

APPLYING YOUR SKILLS

❹ Add a fifty-word flashback to the extract below. The narrative relates to the theme of danger.

David hauled the faded, velvet armchair through the rickety gate and swung the gate shut with his right boot. It shuddered on its hinges. He grinned.

Remember:

● Signal when the flashback begins and when you return to the main story.

PROGRESS CHECK FOR CHAPTER 3

GOOD PROGRESS

I can:

● Create mood in descriptions, using language effectively ☐
● Create some convincing characters and narrative voices ☐
● Generate sound ideas, and structure descriptions and narratives clearly ☐

EXCELLENT PROGRESS

I can:

● Create a rich atmosphere in descriptions, using detailed and effective language ☐
● Create a range of convincing characters and narrative voices ☐
● Generate original and engaging ideas, and structure descriptions and narratives in imaginative ways to engage the reader ☐

CHAPTER 4: Reading non-fiction texts

WHAT'S IT ALL ABOUT?

In the English Language exam, you will be asked to read short non-fiction texts or extracts, either modern (twentieth or twenty-first century) or from the nineteenth century. The texts will express viewpoints – sometimes similar, sometimes different – and be on related topics. They could be in a range of forms, such as magazine articles, news stories, letters or journals.

> **AQA Paper 2, Section A**
> **Edexcel Paper 2, Section A**
> **Eduqas Component 2, Section A**
> **OCR Component 1, Section A**

TIMING AND APPROACH

You may find it helpful to read the source text once, then read the questions, then read the text again, annotating it to help you answer the questions. Another possible planning approach is to reread and annotate the source text for each question in turn as you answer it. However, if you follow this approach, make sure you keep a close eye on the clock!

EARNING THE MARKS

The number of marks for each question will be written on the paper. Remember that you can gain **only** the marks that are given for that question. You must answer all questions on the exam paper to gain the maximum marks.

The exam paper will tell you what to focus on for each question. The skills you will need, depending on the question and the exam board/organisation, are likely to involve some or all of the following:

- Identify specific information (such as facts or quotations).
- Select information from both texts and integrate them in your answer.
- Analyse how language and structure are used for effect.
- Write about similarities and differences between the texts.
- Write a comparison of how writers in each extract convey attitudes and ideas.
- Say what you think or feel about the texts and why, using evidence to support your views.

> **TOP TIP**
>
> If you are asked to use correct 'subject terminology' or 'techniques' when writing about the effects writers create, you are expected to use terms such as: 'image', 'verb' and 'irony'.

> **TOP TIP**
>
> There are no marks for spelling, punctuation or grammar in this section, but if you express yourself clearly and accurately it will be easier for the examiner to understand your answers and credit you for them.

TEXTS

Turn over to find texts similar to those you might encounter in your exam. They are both non-fiction viewpoint pieces:
one a modern piece from a broadsheet newspaper;
the other a letter to *The Times* from 1864.
Both discuss the effects on children
of reading stories.

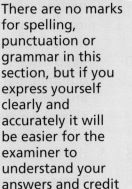

TEXT A: TWENTY-FIRST CENTURY NON-FICTION

From 'Why do we read scary books?'

Lou Morgan, *The Guardian*, 29 October 2015 (theguardian.com)

Some of my favourite books when I was 13 or so were horror stories. Point Horror, Stephen King, Bram Stoker, James Herbert … all the names you'd expect to see on the list. I used to sneak into second-hand bookshops and buy anthologies of vampire stories, smuggling them home in my bag or my coat because my mother didn't

5 approve. 'They'll scare you,' she always said. And she was right – they did. But that was the point.

Fear is one of our primal emotions: it's one that is hardwired into us, just as it is in all animals. On a very basic level it has kept us alive as a species; encouraging us to stay away from long drops and big fires, helping us dodge sabre-tooth tigers and other

10 Things With Big Sharp Teeth And Claws that might quite enjoy adding us to their dinner. Last time I looked though, there weren't too many sabre-tooth tigers to worry about on my local high street.

We're a peculiar lot, when you think about it: we work so hard to make our world, our environment safer … and then we actively seek out things that will make us afraid.

15 Horror movies, urban legends, ghost stories. We hunt down the darkness and we revel in it. Why? Because, this way, we can control it.

When I asked my corner of Twitter what scared them (in a very quick and – admittedly – deeply unscientific survey), I got answers ranging from "human cruelty" to "being insignificant". Imprisonment – both in a place and in our own bodies. Abandonment.

20 Helplessness. Pain, loss and grief. These are the big things that frighten us, the things we think could destroy us. These are the things that keep us up at night. *These* are the new sabre-tooth tigers.

The difference is that if you're faced with a sabre-tooth tiger, a spear is going to make you feel a lot better about your odds of survival. How do we battle the fear of losing

25 the people we love, and being powerless to stop it? How do we face that down?

Simple. We seek out stories; stories which give us a place to put our fears. Books in particular let us pour our fear into them before we have so much of it sloshing around in our heads that we drown in it. Stories that frighten us or unsettle us – not just horror stories, but ones that make us uncomfortable or that strike a chord somewhere

30 deep inside – give us the means to explore the things that scare us … but only as far as our imaginations and our experiences allow. They keep us safe while letting us imagine we're in peril. Stories, after all, are never *about* what they're about: there is always a pocket somewhere within them for us to drop in our own emotions, our own fears. A box right at the heart of it all waiting to be filled, somewhere we can lift up

35 the lid and look at the darkness … and close it again when we've had enough.

There is always space for us at the middle of a story – any story. We make it ours just by reading it. A book is a perfectly personalised map through the nightmare forest, because we already know where the monsters are. We put them there ourselves.

Horror stories reflect their times: just as the repressed Victorians loved their vampires,

40 we seem to gravitate towards technology, zombies, dystopia and psychological terrors. When I wrote my own horror novel, *Sleepless*, I wanted to add the intense pressures and stresses of exams into that mix – and (particularly as someone with a long, slightly embattled history of manic depression) the fear of not being able to trust your own mind.

TEXT B: NINETEENTH-CENTURY NON-FICTION

Reverend Lord Sidney Goldolphin Osborne, letter to *The Times*, 1864

The author claims that doctors are often called to the bedsides of restless, fearful and sleepless children who, rather than having a physical illness, are really suffering from reading the wrong books: '... reading which, keeping the mind on the strain, has wrought it up to an excitement from which it cannot calm down by any power of its own'. He continues:

It is quite true that there are many most excellent books for the amusement of young children. I have seen some I hold to be most pernicious,[1] which are yet considered quite harmless ... I once took up and read in the nursery of a friend a book which in you or me might only raise a smile, but which I am satisfied might give the children
5   for whom it was written night after night of pure terror. It was written something after this fashion: It was the history of two truant kittens, which in a fit of naughty disobedience had absconded[2] from home. Their adventures were many; they were cleverly told in child language; they were such as must interest a child deeply in the fate of the brother and sister catlings; there were beautifully executed pictures of
10 such things as awful owls with eyes of fire hovering over them at night, murderous-looking dogs coming down on them by day, bulls breathing from their nostrils as if they were chimneys on fire, bandit cats, giants awfully armed, seizing them to carry them to dark caves, etc.

Of course, the moral was, kittens and children who are disobedient will be subject to
15 such terrible tribulations. It struck me that such a book was enough to scare sleep from any young child allowed to pore over its pages; many such tales would make it subject to the dreams and screams which, terrifying the parents, invoke the [doctor]; they then all say it is stomach [ache], and proceed to inflict all kinds of intestinal torture to no purpose, for the child, confined to its bed, is given more and more of
20 such intoxicating literature. Weakened by the senna[3] and traditional grey powder, it gets worse and worse; the [doctor] is puzzled, the mother alarmed; more advice is called in; the child is sent to the sea, there gets well under the more novel and natural fascination of shells and seaweed. Fortunately the books are left behind; it is forbidden to read at all, but not because what it read was bad reading for it.

25 When shall we learn that, just as prudence should dictate the food a child should eat, so should it regulate the food afforded to its brain? There is no greater folly than this system of rubbing off the natural angles of childishness by a course of reading appealing to childish simplicity, but wrapping up amusement in clever mimicry of the most exciting of all literature, the novel. Childish sentiment runs to dumb animals and
30 their young; tales may be written on these to afford the utmost amount of childlike, gleeful interest – may be made joyous as well as instructive. I never fear sleeplessness from over laughing. Children are born to laugh a good deal; it is time enough to excite their tears by sentiment when that season has come when sorrow must mix more or less with their joy.

Glossary:
pernicious[1] – damaging
absconded[2] – run away
senna[3] – a herbal laxative

IDENTIFYING FACTUAL INFORMATION

HOW SHOULD YOU DEAL WITH THE QUESTION?

A01

AQA Paper 2,
Section A, Q1

Edexcel Paper 2,
Section A, Q1, Q4

Eduqas
Component 2,
Section A, QA1,
QA3

OCR Component 1,
Section A, Q1a–b

In the exam, some questions may ask you to find factual or **explicit** information. This is information that is directly stated in the text. You will need to find this information fairly quickly and write it down.

- Identify key words in the question. Common key words will ask you to find information, facts or quotations. For example: 'pick', 'name', 'find', 'identify', 'select quotations', 'how many?', 'how much?', 'what?'
- Search for the information in the text. Sometimes you may be given lines within which to search (for example, 'from lines 1–7').

EXAM FOCUS

Look at this exam-style question relating to Text A. The key words are in bold.

Identify one phrase from lines 1–5 that tells you what kind of books the writer bought.

A student might have given one of the following answers:

The phrase that tells us what kind of books the writer bought is:

- *'horror stories'* (Incorrect: not stated as the ones she 'bought', a key word)   ✗
- *'books by Stephen King'* (Incorrect: specific writers not asked for)   ✗
- *'scary books'* (Incorrect: student's own words not asked for)   ✗
- *'anthologies of vampire stories'* (Correct: satisfies all key words)   ✔

TRUE OR FALSE QUESTIONS

You may be asked to identify whether statements are true or false. You will need to use a slightly different technique to the one you would use for finding factual information. This is because:

- The statements will not be directly quoted from the text
- To decide whether a statement is true or false, you need to **interpret** the text – to work out the answer from the information.

For example, is the following statement (based on lines 1–6 of Text A) true or false?

Vampire stories have never frightened Lou Morgan.

A student might have said the statement is true.

- They might have assumed that because the writer chose to read vampire stories, she was not frightened by them.
- They might not have realised that these actual words are not in the text and that they were required to **interpret** the question.

The statement is false because vampire stories **did** frighten the writer (although she enjoyed being frightened).

TOP TIP ★

In the exam, the texts you are given may be referred to as 'texts', 'resources' or 'extracts'.

TOP TIP ★

Do not spend too long on questions that will only earn you 1 or 2 marks. Identify the key words in the question as quickly as possible.

APPLYING YOUR SKILLS

Answer the following questions about Text A. Spend no longer than five or six minutes on all four questions. Time yourself.

1 Name an author whose books were the writer's favourites (lines 1–6).

2 Select a quotation from lines 42–47 that tells us what the writer wanted to include in her own horror story.

3 Decide whether the following statements about lines 1–16 are true or false.

- *Morgan thinks that human beings are contradictory.*
- *Morgan's mother disapproved of her reading fiction.*

Now answer the following questions about Text B. Spend no longer than five or six minutes on all four questions. Time yourself.

4 What are the main animal characters in the children's book the writer discusses?

5 Find a phrase in the second paragraph that describes what Osborne says is the moral of the children's book.

6 Decide whether the following statements about lines 9–34 are true or false.

- *Osborne thought that the illustrations in the children's book were badly drawn.*
- *Osborne believes that children's reading should both teach useful things and make children feel happy.*

Remember:

- Read the questions carefully.
- Look for information relating to them in the section of the text indicated in the question.
- Identify the part of the section the statement seems to relate to by locating key words.

SELECTING AND SYNTHESISING INFORMATION FROM TWO TEXTS

HOW CAN YOU COMPARE TWO TEXTS?

You will be asked to comment on both non-fiction source texts that have been provided. The writers may express similar or contrasting points of view – or both.

To successfully compare two texts, you need to consider the writers' views in both of them and select suitable examples to back up your points. The views expressed may be **explicit** or **implicit**.

> **A01**
>
> AQA Paper 2, Section A, Q2
>
> Edexcel Paper 2, Section A, Q7a
>
> Eduqas Component 2, Section A, QA5
>
> OCR Component 1, Section A, Q2

EXPLICIT OPINIONS

A writer may state their views directly. For example, in Text B the writer says: 'It is quite true that there are many most excellent books for the amusement of young children.' It is clear from this sentence that the writer thinks there are good books available that can entertain children.

IMPLICIT OPINIONS

An opinion that is implied or hinted at is an implicit opinion. To identify this, you have to 'read between the lines' or work out what it means. For example, in Text A on page 54 the writer says: 'Stories, after all, are never *about what they're about.*'

This statement seems confusing, but it is being used to make the reader think carefully about what stories really mean. The writer is implying that she thinks stories are not simply about what happens. They have deeper meanings. In the case of horror stories, she thinks these deeper meanings are about how we deal with fear.

> **TOP TIP** ⭐
>
> Remember, if the question asks you to **find** opinions, you must identify them **in the text**, not give your own opinions about the points the writer is making and whether or not you agree with them.

WRITING YOUR RESPONSE TO BOTH TEXTS

Look at the exam-style question below. The key words are in bold.

> *What do the **writers think** are the **effects** of reading **horror stories**?*

The table below gives examples from both texts, along with an analysis of the writer's opinion (whether explicit or implicit).

Quotation/evidence	Writer's opinion	Explicit/implicit
Text A *We hunt out the darkness and we revel in it*	We seek what frightens us [in horror stories] because it excites us.	Implicit
Text B *I am satisfied [the book] might give children ... night after night of pure terror*	Horror stories make children terrified.	Explicit

STRUCTURING YOUR RESPONSE

You can structure your written response in several ways. For example, you could write about one writer's viewpoint in one paragraph, then write about the other writer's views in the next paragraph. This method is clear and organised, but less interesting to read than other structures.

Alternatively, you can integrate (**synthesise**) the two views. You could discuss both writers' views within paragraphs. This is more difficult to do. Practise this skill so you can write confidently and fluently.

When comparing two texts, make sure you use **connectives**, particularly those that compare and contrast ('on the one hand … on the other hand', 'similarly', 'in contrast') and those that qualify ('however', 'having said that').

EXAM FOCUS

Read how one student has synthesised two views on the effect that horrors stories have:

> Both Morgan and Osborne are interested in the effect that horror stories have on us, particularly on young people or children. Morgan believes that we seek out horror stories deliberately because they frighten us. They encourage us to explore 'the darkness' and 'the things that scare us', which she sees as a good thing. On the other hand, Osborne thinks that reading horror stories creates 'pure terror' in young children, and that this in turn, rather than being positive, causes physical and psychological damage.

> *Effective opening that gives an overview of the similarities between the writers' points of view*

> *Contrasting connective helps to order thoughts*

> *A reminder of Morgan's view while Osborne's is being discussed*

APPLYING YOUR SKILLS

Look again at this question:

*What do the **writers think** are the **effects** of reading **horror stories**?*

❶ Write a paragraph in response. Use the paragraph in the Exam Focus section as a guide if you need to.

Remember:

• Select suitable quotations that reveal the writers' opinions.
• Make sure you understand the implicit opinions expressed.

UNDERSTANDING PERSUASIVE LANGUAGE

HOW SHOULD YOU ANALYSE PERSUASIVE LANGUAGE IN A TEXT?

A01 **A02**

AQA
Paper 2,
Section A, Q3

Edexcel Paper 2,
Section A, Q2,Q3,
Q5, Q6

Eduqas
Component 2,
Section A, QA2,
QA4

OCR Component 1,
Section A, Q3

You will be asked to comment on the way writers try to persuade us to accept their point of view. A typical question referring to Text B might be:

Osborne is trying to persuade us to share his point of view. How does Osborne use language to convey this?

How would you answer this question?

- Consider the **register** and **tone** of the text, and how they persuade.
- Underline **phrases** and **sentences** that you find persuasive.
- Make notes analysing the **effect** of these phrases and sentences.
- Select phrases and describe their effects.

The table below outlines some of these effects.

Phrase	Effect
'most pernicious ... quite harmless'	The writer contrasts the strong, formal adjective 'pernicious' with the simple 'quite harmless', suggesting how wrong the latter view is.
'night after night of pure terror'	The writer repeats 'night' and uses the adjective-noun combination 'pure terror' to stress the children's intense and sustained suffering.
'adventures', 'cleverly told in child language' 'interest a child deeply', 'beautifully executed pictures'	The writer uses positive phrases to emphasise the stories' appeal to children, before describing their harmful effects. The contrast emphasises his point.
'awful owls with eyes of fire'	One of several vivid visual details used by the writer, helping readers to imagine the effect on children.
'terrible tribulations'	The writer's use of 'tribulations' – a powerful formal word for ordeals or hardships – makes the judgement on children seem very harsh, especially when emphasised by **alliteration**.

❶ Following the examples in the table, analyse the persuasive effect of the following phrases. Try to say which technique is being used in each case.

- *'dreams and screams'*
- *'all kinds of intestinal torture'*
- *'intoxicating literature'*

TOP TIP

Not all source texts will be explicitly persuasive, but they will have a particular perspective on an event or topic.

ANALYSING DEVICES AND SENTENCE STRUCTURES

In addition to commenting on the effect of words and phrases, you should also comment on persuasive language devices such as:

- **Rhetorical questions** (e.g. *'Have we all gone mad?'*)
- **Triads** (lists of three)
- **Alliteration** (as in *'terrible tribulations'*)
- **Imagery (metaphors, similes, personification)**

In addition, comment on sentence structures. For example, sentences may have an overall rhetorical effect, such as Osborne's long sentence beginning, *'Their adventures were many ...'*. This lists ways in which the book would appeal to children, with the list items gradually lengthening to build to a climax of frightening pictures.

TOP TIP

A good way to understand the effect of a word choice is to ask yourself how the effect would be different if a different word with a similar meaning had been used.

EXAM FOCUS

Read this successful analysis of the effects of Text B. Some of its qualities have been highlighted:

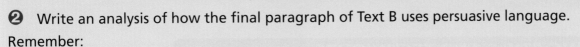

The shortness of the phrase 'scare sleep from a child', together with its alliteration, suggests how easily children can be affected. Similarly, the linking of 'dreams and screams' in a rhyme is apt in a text about children but also emphasises how wrong it is to scare them, because we normally think of 'dreams' as being innocent and positive. Osborne gains our sympathy for his argument by focusing us on one child, and saying they are 'weakened by the senna'. The short phrases listing stages in the child's decline, from 'it gets worse and worse' to the child being 'sent to the sea' to recover, show how easily a child can be affected.

> Terminology used correctly and helpfully

> Fully analyses effect

> Comments on technique

> Analyses effect of sentence structure

APPLYING YOUR SKILLS

❷ Write an analysis of how the final paragraph of Text B uses persuasive language.

Remember:

- Select persuasive words and phrases and analyse their effect.
- Use the correct terms for language devices if you know them, and analyse their effect.
- Comment on the effects of sentence structures.

PROGRESS LOG [tick the correct box]   Needs more work ☐   Getting there ☐   Under control ☐

COMPARING WRITERS' VIEWPOINTS AND TECHNIQUES

HOW CAN YOU COMPARE ATTITUDES AND TECHNIQUES IN TWO TEXTS?

You will be asked to compare the two texts provided in the exam. You may be given a statement in quotation marks to which you must respond, or this might take the form of a more general question.

A question based on the texts in this chapter might be:

> *Compare how the two writers convey their different attitudes to stories.*

In your answer, you should:

- Compare their different **attitudes**
- Compare the **methods** they use to convey their attitudes
- Support your ideas with **quotations** from both texts

How would you answer this question?

- Decide what the writers' **different attitudes** are.
- Select **quotations as evidence** for these attitudes.
- **Annotate** your texts and, if you have time, make two quick lists to **plan** your comments on their **methods**.
- Write your answer, in paragraphs, moving from **attitudes** to **methods**, such as **style and structure**.

AQA Paper 2, Section A, Q4

Edexcel Paper 2, Section A, Q7b

Eduqas Component 2, Section A, QA6

OCR Component 1, Section A, Q4

GET IT RIGHT! ⭐

The phrase 'how the two writers convey' refers to methods used by each writer, including language, form and structure. Try to write about **all** of these.

COMPARING ATTITUDES

To compare attitudes, you need to briefly summarise the main points each writer makes, as shown in the table below. You may find it helpful to summarise one writer, for example starting with Text A, then add the attitudes of the second that are either similar or very different.

Text A	Text B
Horror stories help us to confront our fears in a manageable way.	*Children cannot cope with frightening stories: these stories create unmanageable fears.*
We can relate personally to stories and make them our own.	*This is not a personal thing – all children are frightened by scary stories and may get ill because of them.*

IDENTIFYING STYLE AND TECHNIQUES

Read some of the techniques used in Text A paragraphs 1–3:

- Morgan uses an **anecdote** about her teenage book-buying habits.
- She **lists** authors and, later, things we 'seek out' to 'make us afraid'.
- She **quotes** her mother ('They'll scare you'), then **surprises** us by agreeing with her.

- She **uses humour** – using capitals for 'Things With Big Sharp Teeth And Claws', that are made to sound amusingly civilised in the understatement 'adding us to their dinner'.

- She **entertains** us with the surprising image of sabre-tooth tigers on 'my local high street'.

- She **asks the question** 'Why?', then answers it.

❶ Read the rest of Text A.

- Make a list of language techniques used in the remainder of the text.

- Decide which are the most important and what short quotations you could use as evidence for them.

- Compare Lou Morgan's techniques with those used by Osborne in Text B. Make notes on their similarities and differences.

EXAM FOCUS

Read this successful extract comparing techniques in the texts:

> Both authors use anecdote. Morgan describes her own teenage book-buying, which she then justifies ('that was the point'), while Osborne describes a children's book he once picked up. Morgan, however, uses more humour. In 'dodge sabre-tooth tigers', the informal verb has a comic effect, and her description of animals 'that might quite enjoy adding us to their dinner' also uses wittily ironic understatement to joke about our fears.
>
> While Osborne uses some humour, as in 'catlings', on the whole he is more serious. His strong, negative adjective 'pernicious' conveys the serious effects on children, and he evokes our sympathy in 'night after night of pure terror', in which repetition emphasises the effect, and 'terrible tribulations', which strongly conveys the children's suffering, emphasised by alliteration.

Topic sentence states a basic similarity

Embedded quotation with analysis of effect and purpose of style

Linking phrase identifies a similarity and prepares for a contrast

Fluently expresses effect

WRITING ABOUT STRUCTURE

Compare the writers' use of structure as a technique. To do this, try to get an overview of how each text develops. Think of a short heading that would sum up the attitudes or arguments in each paragraph. There are some examples over the page.

TOP TIP ⭐

Although both texts will express a viewpoint, they may have different purposes and target audiences, which will influence their style.

For Text A, these might begin with:

- *Morgan's teenage love of horror stories*
- *The importance of fear*
- *Our attraction to horror*
- *Modern fears*

EXAM FOCUS

Here is how a student might have written about the structure of Morgan's text:

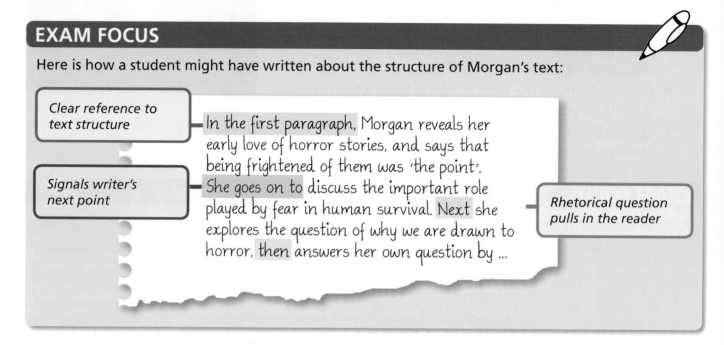

Clear reference to text structure

In the first paragraph, Morgan reveals her early love of horror stories, and says that being frightened of them was 'the point'. She goes on to discuss the important role played by fear in human survival. Next she explores the question of why we are drawn to horror, then answers her own question by ...

Signals writer's next point

Rhetorical question pulls in the reader

❷ Reread Text B. Find similar short headings to sum up the three paragraphs.

APPLYING YOUR SKILLS

❸ Write a response to the question at the start of this unit, which asks you to compare how the two writers convey their different attitudes to stories in the two texts.

Remember:

- Use the bullet points in the question to help you cover all its aspects.
- Write about differences in attitude, then in style and structure.
- Select quotations as evidence and analyse their effects.

PROGRESS CHECK FOR CHAPTER 4

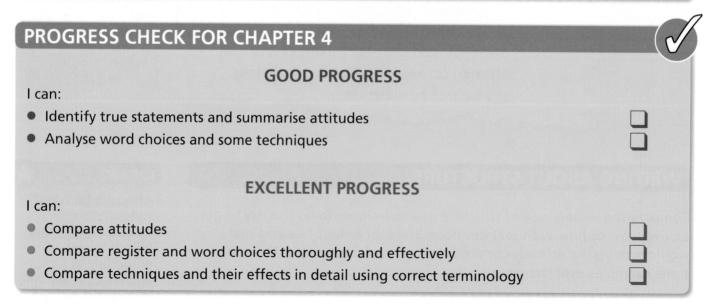

GOOD PROGRESS

I can:

- Identify true statements and summarise attitudes ☐
- Analyse word choices and some techniques ☐

EXCELLENT PROGRESS

I can:

- Compare attitudes ☐
- Compare register and word choices thoroughly and effectively ☐
- Compare techniques and their effects in detail using correct terminology ☐

CHAPTER 5: Writing to present a viewpoint

WHAT'S IT ALL ABOUT?

When you are asked to write non-fiction, transactional writing (such as an article or a report) in your English Language exam, you need to:

- Give information
- Argue and express your viewpoint
- Persuade

> AQA Paper 2, Section B
>
> Edexcel Paper 2, Section B
>
> Eduqas Component 2, Section B
>
> OCR Component 1, Section B

TIMING AND APPROACH

You should aim to spend about five minutes planning. It is also important to allow five minutes at the end to check and improve your work.

EARNING THE MARKS

The table below shows what you will be marked on and what you must do to achieve a high score.

What you will be marked on	What this means
Content and organisation	Content: ● Your ideas ● How well you have fitted your writing to the given purpose and audience Organisation: ● The fluency of your writing and mastery of language techniques ● Structure and paragraphing
Technical accuracy	Sentence structure ● Vocabulary ● Spelling, punctuation and grammar ● Appropriate **register** (degree of formality) and use of **Standard English** (without slang, **dialect** or non-standard grammar)

> **TOP TIP**
>
> Remember to set out your answer appropriately, depending on what you are asked to do. For example, if you are asked to write a formal letter, begin and end the letter correctly and write in the correct formal tone.

WHAT IS WRITING TO EXPRESS A VIEWPOINT?

WHAT ARE 'EXPRESSING' AND 'PERSUADING'?

AQA Paper 2, Section B

Edexcel Paper 2, Section B, Q8 or Q9

Eduqas Component 2, Section B, QB1, QB2

OCR Component 1, Section B, Q5 or Q6

When writing to **express** a viewpoint, you are aiming to **persuade** readers to agree with you. However, your expectations will depend on the **purpose** of the writing. For example:

● In a magazine article about reality TV, you may just want readers to sympathise with your views and be entertained by them.

● In a job application or a letter to voters, you will want to do everything you can to persuade your readers and make them act in a particular way, because you will benefit if they do so.

These differences show the importance of three factors:

● **Purpose:** what the writing is intended to do (for example, persuade readers to vote for you)

● **Audience:** who it is aimed at (for example, the age group, level of education, interests, etc.)

● **Form:** where the writing will appear (for example, in a letter, an article, the text for a speech)

In the exam, you may be given a provocative statement, such as:

School uniform is an attempt to prevent teenagers from expressing themselves. Few adults are obliged to wear a uniform, so teenagers should not have to either.

This will be followed by a task that identifies purpose, audience and form, such as:

Form   Audience

Write a letter to your school governors in which you explain your views on this statement.

Purpose

❶ Identify the purpose, audience and form in the following exam-style tasks:

● *'Zoos are just animal prisons, out-dated institutions with no place in the modern world.' Write an article for the weekend magazine of a **broadsheet** newspaper explaining your views on this subject.*

● *'Television is the worst thing that ever happened to modern society.' Write the text of a speech intended to influence a group advising the government on its media policies.*

REGISTER AND TONE

Register refers to the type of language used in a text, especially how formal it is. Compare these two comments:

● *Me and my workmates reckon it's time you realised you've got to look after us if we're going to pull out the stops and crack your deadlines. Sorry, but if you won't bite the bullet and get a new drinks machine, we're off.*

GET IT RIGHT! ★

In the exam, your response to this task should always be in a fairly formal register, even if you are asked to write for a student audience.

- *My colleagues and I agree that you should appreciate the need to provide us with adequate facilities in order to maximise our efficiency. Regrettably, if you do not invest in a new beverage machine, we will be obliged to withdraw our labour.*

❷   Neither of these statements is perfect – for example, the second one is too long-winded.

     - Which is more formal? Which vocabulary and grammar features create this effect?
     - Which is more impressively persuasive?

Tone refers to a writer's apparent attitude towards the subject – for example, humorous, angry, critical or passionate. The tone should not change dramatically within a piece of writing, but some variety can be effective. For example, you might use humour, then become more serious.

EXAM FOCUS

Read this part of a successful response to the first task in Question 1. Some features of purpose, audience and form have been highlighted:

> One of my fondest childhood memories is of being photographed with Bobo the chimpanzee in London Zoo. Despite relatives asking 'Which one is you?', the experience probably led to me now sponsoring a family of chimps in the wild. But zoos also contribute to conservation in more immediate ways, such as their extensive breeding programmes for endangered species.

Humour leads to serious point

Formal register and calmly informed tone suggest knowledge

Affectionate personal tone, but still uses formal Standard English

APPLYING YOUR SKILLS

❸   Identify the purpose, audience and form in the following task. Then write the first three sentences of a response.

'It is all too easy to sign an online petition for a good cause and feel you are "doing your bit" for social change, when in fact you are just easing your conscience.'

Write an entry for a blog focusing on social media in which you explain your views on this statement.

Remember:

- Write appropriately for your purpose, audience and form.
- Choose the right tone and register.

KEY FEATURES OF NON-FICTION TEXTS EXPRESSING A VIEWPOINT

WHAT LANGUAGE TECHNIQUES ARE EFFECTIVE IN EXPRESSING A VIEWPOINT?

(A05)

AQA Paper 2, Section B

Edexcel Paper 2, Section B, Q8 or Q9

Eduqas Component 2, Section B, QB1, QB2

OCR Component 1, Section B, Q5 or Q6

RHETORICAL DEVICES

Rhetorical devices are language techniques used for effect, especially to persuade. The table below outlines some useful rhetorical devices.

Device	Explanation	Example
Tricolon (triple, triad)	Using three words or phrases in a row, often with the most powerful coming last	*... a policy that is uninformed, ineffective, and irresponsible*
Rhetorical question	Question making a point rather than seeking an answer	*Do they think we're complete idiots?*
Alliteration	Repeated use of consonant sounds, especially at the start of words; often used with the tricolon	*The rainforest is difficult, dangerous and often deadly.*
Parallelism	Achieving contrast by repeating a grammatical form	*Zoos claim to provide a lasting refuge for endangered species; all they really offer is a fleeting distraction for bored spectators.*

❶ Look at the exam-style task below.

'Fashion is just manufacturers exploiting the insecurity of shoppers, especially the young.'

Write an article for a youth-market magazine expressing your views on this subject.

Write a paragraph from the article in which you agree or disagree with the statement. Try to use all four devices from the table. Add other sentences in between if you wish.

PROVIDING EVIDENCE

To help persuade readers to accept your viewpoint, you should provide evidence. You could combine this with information that shows how you are qualified to speak on the subject. Evidence can take several forms:

- **Anecdote** – a very short story. For example: *'The last time I visited a zoo, a female gorilla very deliberately turned her back on me. I felt ashamed ...'.* (Anecdotes are often a good way to begin.)

- Referring to a study, or to other more informal 'research'. For example: *'A study published in 2015 found that ...'* or *'Many students I have spoken to say that ...'.*

- Statistics (can be used as evidence or for effect in reference to a study) – *'A shocking 59 per cent ...'.*

- References to the texts in Section A of the exam paper.

> **TOP TIP**
>
> Use rhetorical devices sparingly. If you use them too frequently, especially one particular device, readers will feel you are trying to manipulate them.

❷   Write a short anecdote that you could use when responding to the exam-style task in Question 1.

EXAM FOCUS

Read this part of a successful response to Question 1:

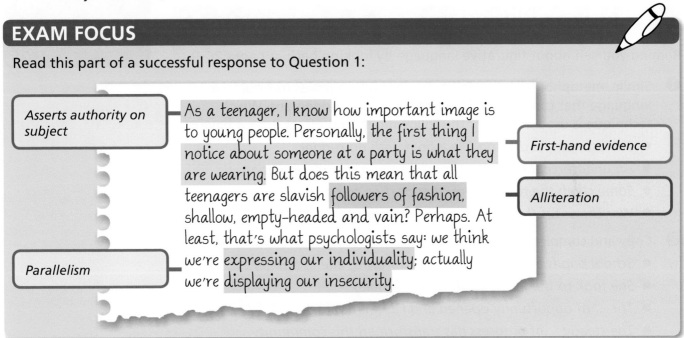

Asserts authority on subject

Parallelism

As a teenager, I know how important image is to young people. Personally, the first thing I notice about someone at a party is what they are wearing. But does this mean that all teenagers are slavish followers of fashion, shallow, empty-headed and vain? Perhaps. At least, that's what psychologists say: we think we're expressing our individuality; actually we're displaying our insecurity.

First-hand evidence

Alliteration

DIRECT APPEALS AND CALLS TO ACTION

Some persuasive texts have very clear objectives. They might be:

- Encouraging people to report bullying
- Making people buy beauty products
- Asking people to donate to a charity

Texts like this may make direct appeals to the reader or urge them to take a particular action. For example:

- *Don't let animals like Flossy suffer needlessly: donate £5 now to ...*

APPLYING YOUR SKILLS

❸   Write the opening paragraph in response to the exam-style task in Question 1. Use the three language techniques covered in this unit to explain your viewpoint.

Remember:

- Try to provide evidence in some form.
- Speak directly to the reader if it seems appropriate.

USING LANGUAGE TO ARGUE OR PERSUADE

HOW CAN LANGUAGE TECHNIQUES STRENGTHEN AN ARGUMENT?

A05

AQA Paper 2, Section B

Edexcel Paper 2, Section B, Q8 or Q9

Eduqas Component 2, Section B, QB1, QB2

OCR Component 1, Section B, Q5 or Q6

Some persuasive writing presents a reasoned argument, often using rhetorical devices. Other texts support their argument with an appeal to the reader's imagination and emotions, using **figurative** and **emotive** language.

FIGURATIVE LANGUAGE

Remind yourself about figurative language by looking back at pages 26–9.

❶ **Simile**, **metaphor** and **personification** are all examples of figurative language that can be used to express a critical judgement. Which technique is used in each of the following? What effect does it have?

- *The economy is drifting like a boat with no rudder.*
- *An unenforceable law is as much use as a chocolate teapot.*
- *Some climb the rope ladder of education to success.*
- *War chews up the poor and spits them out.*

❷ Copy and complete the following sentences using figurative language.

- *School pupils all in their identical uniforms, like ... (simile)*
- *She took to the job as easily as a ... (simile)*
- *The ... of opportunity opened and I ... (metaphor)*
- *The steady ... of progress has transformed this community (personification)*

EMOTIVE LANGUAGE

Emotive language aims to create a particular emotional response in readers. For example:

- *Mine closures ripped the heart out of our community.*
  (strong physical metaphor)
- *Workmen used a chainsaw to hack off ...*
  (visual detail and **onomatopoeia**)
- *Thanks to your help, vulnerable baby elephants like Bertha can look forward to happy lives.*
  (adjectives and humanisation of 'Bertha' appeal to our sympathies)

❸ Rewrite these sentences using emotive language for persuasive effect:

- *This unnecessary new road will go through some nice countryside.*
  (Imply that this will cause serious environmental damage.)
- *Many poorly qualified school-leavers find themselves unemployed.*
  (Imply that their talents will be wasted.)

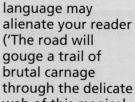
TOP TIP

Too much emotive language may alienate your reader ('The road will gouge a trail of brutal carnage through the delicate web of this magical ecosystem.'). Use it carefully.

EXAM FOCUS

Read this extract from a student's essay on unemployment. Some examples of figurative and emotive language have been highlighted:

Emotively negative metaphor

Emotive language

For some, just escaping the trap of unemployment is a struggle. Others find themselves chained by financial commitments to brain-numbingly repetitive work, longing for some sense of personal fulfilment. Identifying your strengths and passions and finding out how they can help you to contribute to society is like finding a key that unlocks a door to a secret garden.

Metaphor implying being trapped

Positively emotive simile, implying opportunity

What mistakes **might** a student have made in using figurative and emotive language in this response? Look at this alternative response:

Mixes two inaccurate metaphors

Cliché, and boredom is not literally fatal

For some, just finding that bus ticket out of the dungeon of unemployment is a struggle. Others find themselves glued by financial commitments to work that literally bores them to death, longing for some sense of personal fulfilment. Identifying your strengths and passions and finding out how they can help you to contribute to society is like winning the lottery.

Does not really suggest being trapped

Exaggerated and a cliché

APPLYING YOUR SKILLS

❹ Write at least one persuasive paragraph that uses some figurative and emotive language to argue a case for or against one of the following:

● Lowering the voting age to 16
● Re-legalising fox-hunting
● Introducing a tax on sugary foods

Remember:

● Use a mixture of types of figurative language – simile, metaphor and personification.
● Choose suitable emotive words and phrases, but use them sparingly.

PROGRESS LOG [tick the correct box]   Needs more work ■   Getting there ■   Under control ■

USING DIFFERENT TYPES OF SENTENCES

HOW CAN SENTENCE TYPES ADD IMPACT TO YOUR WRITING?

In all your writing you should use a variety of sentence types and lengths. You should choose the sentence type carefully to achieve the effect you want. The three main types of sentence are **simple**, **compound** and **complex**.

SIMPLE SENTENCES

Simple sentences contain only a subject and a verb. Sometimes they also contain an object. For example:

Subject   Verb

A few students walk. Most catch the bus.

Verb   Object

Simple sentences are usually short. You can use them effectively at the start of a paragraph to make a point that you then go on to develop. Simple sentences can also be used for dramatic effect. For example:

> *They need our help. No one else cares.*

A **minor sentence**, which is grammatically incomplete, can also achieve dramatic effect:

> *They are throwing away their lives. **For nothing.***

TOP TIP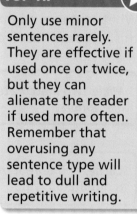

Only use minor sentences rarely. They are effective if used once or twice, but they can alienate the reader if used more often. Remember that overusing any sentence type will lead to dull and repetitive writing.

COMPOUND SENTENCES

Compound sentences join two simple sentences using a **coordinating conjunction**, such as 'and', 'but', 'or' , 'nor', 'so' or 'yet'. For example:

- *They know what they want **and** will do anything to get it.*
- *We work hard, **yet** we remain unrecognised.*
- *Relationships are a compromise, **so** we have to make sacrifices.*

COMPLEX (SUBORDINATED) SENTENCES

Complex sentences include a **main clause** that makes sense on its own, and at least one **subordinate clause** that only makes sense in relation to the main clause.

❶   Identify the main clause and the subordinate clause in each of the following sentences:

- *Owain, although he lives in Wales, plays for England.*
- *Having been brought up in the UK, they are completely bilingual.*
- *Switzerland, which is advanced in many ways, gave women the vote only in 1990.*

EXAM FOCUS

Read this extract from a student's response showing a variety of sentence types to express a viewpoint:

> Simple sentence introduces topic of paragraph

> Conjunction in compound sentence

Another problem with social media is that it is actually anti-social. Yes – I mean it. All too often I see my fellow teenagers glued to their phones while they completely ignore the person sitting next to them. Despite being addicted to Facebook, Snapchat and Instagram, which are the current favourites of my own peer group, they can barely find time to speak to each other in person. Electronic friends are somehow more appealing or safer than live ones.

> Shorter simple sentence for dramatic effect

> Complex sentence with two subordinate clauses

What mistakes **might** a student have made here?

- They might have started with a long, complex sentence, and lost the reader's interest.
- They might have used two or three very short sentences, losing impact.
- They might have overloaded the complex sentence with more subordinate clauses, making it confusing.
- They might have ended the paragraph with a long, complex sentence instead of a shorter one that makes an effective concluding point.

TOP TIP

Addressing or questioning the reader directly can be effective: 'Take a close look. Is he really what he seems?'

APPLYING YOUR SKILLS

❷ Rewrite the passage below using a variety of sentence lengths and types for effect.

Social media apps are the new social glue. We used to be limited to face-to-face communication. Now we can talk to each other in many ways. We can invite all our friends to a party on Facebook in seconds. Facebook is very easy to use. Even my granddad uses it. Some people talk about the threat of social media. They point to cyber-bullying. They also say it is used by terrorists. Any form of communication can be used for good or bad. The internet is a way to join our intelligences. We become one huge interconnected human mind. This could be the way forward for humanity.

Remember:

- Use all three types of sentence: simple, compound and complex.
- Start or end with a short, simple sentence for effect.
- Use a minor sentence if it will create impact.
- Avoid overloading complex sentence with lots of subordinate clauses.

PROGRESS LOG [tick the correct box]   Needs more work ▪   Getting there ▪   Under control ▪

USING PUNCTUATION TO PERSUADE

HOW CAN PUNCTUATION HELP YOU GET YOUR MEANING ACROSS?

You can make your persuasive sentences even more effective – and earn marks for technical accuracy – by using a range of punctuation. Using punctuation correctly and creatively is important for clarifying your ideas.

A05 A06

AQA
Paper 2,
Section B

Edexcel Paper 2,
Section B, Q8 or
Q9

Eduqas
Component 2,
Section B, QB1,
QB2

OCR Component 1,
Section B, Q5 or
Q6

FULL STOPS

A sentence usually ends with a full stop. Remember that all sentences (except **minor sentences** for effect) must have a subject and a verb:

Subject

Cars pollute. They are noisy. They squash hedgehogs.

Verb

COMMAS TO CLARIFY

Commas divide clauses in order to make the meaning instantly clear. They allow you to write sentences that will not confuse your reader:

> *WhatsApp, which enables 'group chat', works on wi-fi, avoiding the need for a mobile signal.*

You also need commas in lists, which can give your writing a sense of plenty and variety:

> *You can get anything you want online: from socks, sweatshirts, baseball caps and cheerleader jackets, to iPhones, selfie-sticks and frozen pizzas.*

Look at how the commas in these sentences make them more persuasive:

● *People should learn more languages: it is useful to speak Punjabi, Welsh is spoken in Snowdonia, and Belgium uses French and Flemish.*

● *Dedication is the key: after eating, Sammy, Elva and Gil always practise.*

❶ Punctuate these sentences:

   ● *Although many apps are free downloading them uses up your data*

   ● *It is free simple to use and readily available and what's more it works*

TOP TIP

Avoid commas that do nothing to change or clarify meaning. For example, this sentence does not need any commas: 'My friend Pam the plumber could fix that tap for you in ten minutes if you paid her.'

DASHES AND PARENTHESES

Clauses can also be divided with **dashes** or **round brackets** (like these):

● *Marmite – you either love it or loathe it – apparently divides the world.*

● *You can even buy vegetarian black sausage – though why you'd want to beats me.*

Use a dash to add drama, humour or to suggest that information is interesting but not essential. This effect is slightly stronger with parentheses:

Actors like Jennifer Lawrence and Kit Harington (tipped for a BAFTA) show that it is possible to combine drama and psychological insight.

SEMICOLONS AND COLONS

The **semicolon** (;) and **colon** (:) are useful in viewpoint writing (see pages 12–13):

- *Friendship can be temporary; parenting lasts a lifetime.*
- *There is only one reason to take a bus: the price.*

QUESTION AND EXCLAMATION MARKS

Use a question mark with every question, even a **rhetorical** one. Use exclamation marks sparingly for a surprising, amusing or ironic point:

And why do we wear uniform? To make us feel we belong!

> **GET IT RIGHT!**
>
> Never use more than one exclamation mark at a time!

EXAM FOCUS

Read this response to see how a student has used punctuation:

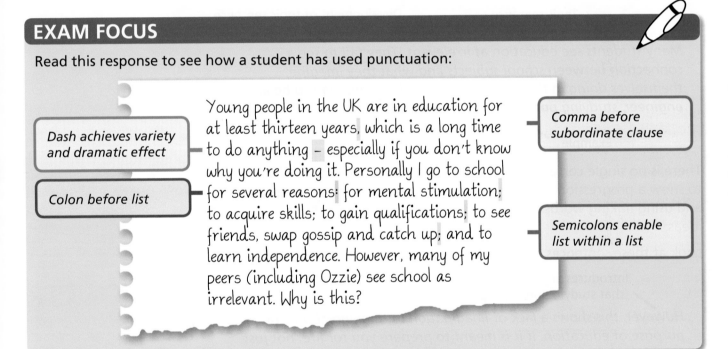

Dash achieves variety and dramatic effect

Colon before list

Young people in the UK are in education for at least thirteen years, which is a long time to do anything – especially if you don't know why you're doing it. Personally I go to school for several reasons: for mental stimulation; to acquire skills; to gain qualifications; to see friends, swap gossip and catch up; and to learn independence. However, many of my peers (including Ozzie) see school as irrelevant. Why is this?

Comma before subordinate clause

Semicolons enable list within a list

❷ How is punctuation used in the final two sentences above?

APPLYING YOUR SKILLS

❸ Write a paragraph on cyber-bullying and how to deal with it. Use the punctuation techniques outlined in this unit.

Remember:

- Use commas to clarify.
- Use dashes and round brackets to divide clauses effectively.
- Use colons and semicolons to divide ideas.

PROGRESS LOG [tick the correct box]   Needs more work ▮   Getting there ▮   Under control ▮

USING STRUCTURES CREATIVELY

HOW CAN STRUCTURE CONVEY YOUR MESSAGE?

In your exam, you will receive marks for developing your ideas in each paragraph and throughout your whole response.

A05

AQA Paper 2, Section B

Edexcel Paper 2, Section B, Q8 or Q9

Eduqas Component 2, Section B, QB1, QB2

OCR Component 1, Section B, Q5 or Q6

STRUCTURE WITHIN PARAGRAPHS

Effective paragraphs usually:

- Focus on one central idea each
- Begin with a **topic sentence**
- Show a progression of ideas
- Use **connectives** to link ideas

For example:

Topic sentence   Development of topic sentence

Many students see education as irrelevant. They fail to see a connection between school subjects and what they imagine themselves doing in the future. For example, if you plan to be an engineer, studying poetry may seem pointless ...

Linking phrase

Example

There is no single correct way to structure a paragraph, but you should try to show a progression of ideas, enhanced by your choice of sentence types, and using linking words and phrases to show the relationship between ideas.

Look at these sentences, which develop the paragraph above:

Introduces argument opposing previous idea (that studying poetry is pointless)

However, this shows a lack of imagination in thinking about the purpose of education. If it is meant to prepare you for life, not just for a job, then perhaps poetry could be worthwhile after all.

Explains why it shows a 'lack of imagination'

CONNECTIVES

Connectives (such as 'although' and 'moreover') are words and phrases that link ideas and prepare readers for each new development. Connectives help to shape the whole paragraph. In the example above, 'However' prepares the reader for a contradiction of the view that poetry is pointless for engineers.

❶ Write a topic sentence for a paragraph suggesting that schools should focus more on verbal than written communication skills. Then continue the paragraph, using at least two connectives and building to a concluding point.

EXAM FOCUS

Read this paragraph and the notes on how it is structured:

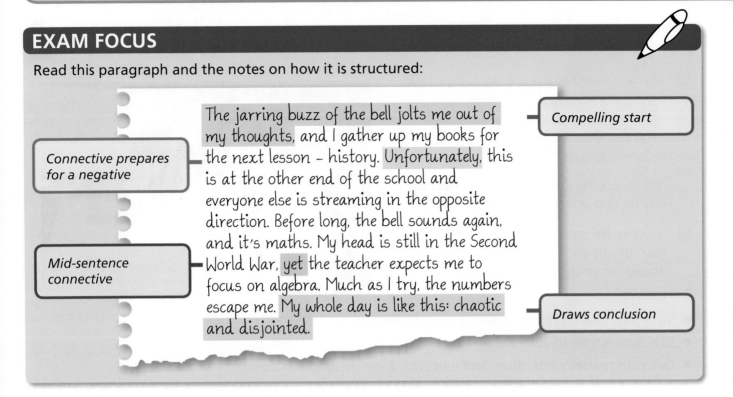

Compelling start

Connective prepares for a negative

The jarring buzz of the bell jolts me out of my thoughts, and I gather up my books for the next lesson – history. Unfortunately, this is at the other end of the school and everyone else is streaming in the opposite direction. Before long, the bell sounds again, and it's maths. My head is still in the Second World War, yet the teacher expects me to focus on algebra. Much as I try, the numbers escape me. My whole day is like this: chaotic and disjointed.

Mid-sentence connective

Draws conclusion

OVERALL STRUCTURE

Your writing should always have a clear overall structure. You should plan this out before you start writing, but be prepared to adapt your plan if you have better ideas as you write.

Here is a possible structure for a task asking you to write about the value of education.

(1) Start by introducing the subject. You could get the reader's attention with:

- An **anecdote** (as in the Exam Focus box)
- A quotation: *'Education is not preparation for life; education is life itself.'* (John Dewey)
- A statistic: *'Over 70 per cent of school leavers ...'*
- A controversial claim: *'Secondary schools exist to keep teenagers out of their parents' way and off the streets until they are old enough to do something useful.'*

(2) Then explain its significance, perhaps raising questions to be addressed.

Two or three paragraphs **explaining the problem** and **arguing for a solution** – for example, proposing that schools should have whole-morning lessons.

(3) Now add a paragraph considering at least one **alternative viewpoint** – such as that teenagers get bored easily.

(4) End with a **conclusion** dismissing opposing arguments, perhaps weighing them up ('On balance ...'), drawing ideas together and leaving readers with a memorable message.

APPLYING YOUR SKILLS

❷ Write a plan for a response to this task:

'Studying history in school is a waste of time. Pupils should be learning skills that focus on the here and now in modern Britain.'

Write a letter to your school governors explaining your views on this claim.

❸ Now write an engaging opening paragraph and a concluding paragraph based on your plan.

Remember:

● Your plan should reflect a development of ideas.

● Use connectives in your paragraph.

● Get your reader's attention, and end with a compelling statement.

PROGRESS CHECK FOR CHAPTER 5

GOOD PROGRESS

I can:

● Write in an appropriate register for purpose, audience and form ☐

● Use a range of language techniques and punctuation ☐

● Plan a structured response ☐

EXCELLENT PROGRESS

I can:

● Write in a consistent and appropriate tone for a purpose ☐

● Use figurative and emotive language persuasively ☐

● Use sentence types and punctuation in varied and creative ways ☐

CHAPTER 6: GCSE English Language practice papers

PAPER 1: READING AND WRITING IMAGINATIVE/ CREATIVE TEXTS

Although the following practice papers may not be exactly like the ones you will face in an exam, they will test you on the key skills you need and help you revise. Marks have been allocated to each question for guidance. These vary across the exam boards/organisations.

This paper relates to:

- AQA Paper 1: Explorations in creative reading and writing
- Edexcel Paper 1: Fiction and imaginative writing
- Eduqas Component 1: Twentieth-century literature reading and creative prose writing
- OCR Component 2: Exploring effects and impact

Time allowed: We recommend that you spend 1 hour 45 minutes on this paper (some boards allow 2 hours).

TEXT A

This extract is from the opening of a short story by H. G. Wells. A medical scientist is showing a visitor his laboratory in London.

'The Stolen Bacillus'

'This again,' said the Bacteriologist, slipping a glass slide under the microscope, 'is well, – a preparation of the Bacillus of cholera – the cholera germ.'

The pale-faced man peered down the microscope. He was evidently not accustomed to that kind of thing, and held a limp white hand over his disengaged eye. 'I see very
5   little,' he said.

'Touch this screw,' said the Bacteriologist; 'perhaps the microscope is out of focus for you. Eyes vary so much. Just the fraction of a turn this way or that.'

'Ah! now I see,' said the visitor. 'Not so very much to see after all. Little streaks and shreds of pink. And yet those little particles, those mere atomies, might multiply and
10   devastate a city! Wonderful!'

He stood up, and releasing the glass slip from the microscope, held it in his hand towards the window. 'Scarcely visible,' he said, scrutinising the preparation. He hesitated. 'Are these – alive? Are they dangerous now?'

'Those have been stained and killed,' said the Bacteriologist. 'I wish, for my own part,
15   we could kill and stain every one of them in the universe.'

'I suppose,' the pale man said, with a slight smile, 'that you scarcely care to have such things about you in the living – in the active state?'

'On the contrary, we are obliged to,' said the Bacteriologist. 'Here, for instance –' He walked across the room and took up one of several sealed tubes. 'Here is the living

---

20   thing. This is a cultivation of the actual living disease bacteria.' He hesitated. 'Bottled cholera, so to speak.'

A slight gleam of satisfaction appeared momentarily in the face of the pale man. 'It's a deadly thing to have in your possession,' he said, devouring the little tube with his eyes. The Bacteriologist watched the morbid pleasure in his visitor's expression. This

25   man, who had visited him that afternoon with a note of introduction from an old friend, interested him from the very contrast of their dispositions. The lank black hair and deep grey eyes, the haggard expression and nervous manner, the fitful yet keen interest of his visitor were a novel change from the phlegmatic[1] deliberations of the ordinary scientific worker with whom the Bacteriologist chiefly associated. It was

30   perhaps natural, with a hearer evidently so impressionable to the lethal nature of his topic, to take the most effective aspect of the matter.

He held the tube in his hand thoughtfully. 'Yes, here is the pestilence imprisoned. Only break such a little tube as this into a supply of drinking-water, say to these minute particles of life that one must needs stain and examine with the highest

35   powers of the microscope even to see, and that one can neither smell nor taste – say to them, "Go forth, increase and multiply, and replenish the cisterns,"[2] and death – mysterious, untraceable death, death swift and terrible, death full of pain and indignity – would be released upon this city, and go hither and thither seeking his victims. Here he would take the husband from the wife, here the child from its

40   mother, here the statesman from his duty, and here the toiler from his trouble. He would follow the water-mains, creeping along streets, picking out and punishing a house here and a house there where they did not boil their drinking-water, creeping into the wells of the mineral water makers, getting washed into salad, and lying dormant in ices. He would wait ready to be drunk in the horse-troughs, and by

45   unwary children in the public fountains. He would soak into the soil, to reappear in springs and wells at a thousand unexpected places. Once start him at the water supply, and before we could ring him in, and catch him again, he would have decimated the metropolis.'[3]

Glossary:
[1] *phlegmatic* – unemotional, calm, down to earth
[2] *cisterns* – water storage tanks
[3] *decimated the metropolis* – killed everyone in London

SECTION A: READING

Answer **all** questions in this section.

You are advised to spend about 45 minutes on this section.

❶ Read again the first four paragraphs of the text.

List **four** things from this part of the text about the visitor.

[4 marks]

❷ Look in detail at this extract from lines 16–32 of the text:

'I suppose,' the pale man said, with a slight smile, 'that you scarcely care to have such things about you in the living – in the active state?'

'On the contrary, we are obliged to,' said the Bacteriologist. 'Here, for instance –' He walked across the room and took up one of several sealed tubes. 'Here is the living thing. This is a cultivation of the actual living disease bacteria.' He hesitated. 'Bottled cholera, so to speak.'

A slight gleam of satisfaction appeared momentarily in the face of the pale man. 'It's a deadly thing to have in your possession,' he said, devouring the little tube with his eyes. The Bacteriologist watched the morbid pleasure in his visitor's expression. This man, who had visited him that afternoon with a note of introduction from an old friend, interested him from the very contrast of their dispositions. The lank black hair and deep grey eyes, the haggard expression and nervous manner, the fitful yet keen interest of his visitor were a novel change from the phlegmatic[1] deliberations of the ordinary scientific worker with whom the Bacteriologist chiefly associated. It was perhaps natural, with a hearer evidently so impressionable to the lethal nature of his topic, to take the most effective aspect of the matter.

How does the writer use language here to describe the visitor?

You could comment on the writer's choice of:

● Words and phrases
● Language features and techniques
● Sentence forms

[8 marks]

❸ You now need to think about the **whole** of the **text**.

This text is the opening of a story.

How has the writer structured the text to interest you as a reader?

You could write about:

- What the writer focuses your attention on at the beginning
- How and why the writer changes this focus as the text develops
- Any other structural features that interest you

[8 marks]

❹ Now look at the last part of the text from line 33 to the end.

A student, having read this section of the text said: 'The writer is very effective in bringing to life the threat of the bacillus and the bacteriologist's attitude towards it.'

To what extent do you agree?

In your response, you could:

- Write about your own impressions of the bacillus and the bacteriologist
- Evaluate how the writer has created these impressions
- Support your opinions with references to the text

[20 marks]

SECTION B: WRITING

You are advised to spend about 45 minutes on this section.

Write in full sentences.

You are reminded of the need to plan your answer.

You should leave enough time to check your work at the end.

⑤ You are going to enter a creative writing competition.

Either: Write a description suggested by this picture:

Or: Write a story about a scientific experiment that goes wrong.

(24 marks for content and organisation
16 marks for technical accuracy)

[40 marks]

PAPER 2: READING AND WRITING NON-FICTION TEXTS

This paper relates to:

- AQA Paper 2: Writers' viewpoints and perspectives
- Edexcel Paper 2: Non-fiction and transactional writing
- WJEC Eduqas Component 2: Nineteenth and twenty-first century non-fiction reading and transactional/ persuasive writing
- OCR Component 1: Communicating information and ideas

Time allowed: We recommend that you spend 1 hour 45 minutes on this paper (some boards allow 2 hours).

TEXT A

Fashion Goes Pop

Alice Fisher, *The Guardian*, **20 March 2011 (theguardian.com)**

Spring is a fertile time. Not just for the lambs and the budding trees, but for fashion and trends. The first months of each year bring the latest round of catwalk shows from New York, London, Milan and Paris, and the concurrent awards season sent the best dressed in film and music trotting up the red carpets to the Grammys,
5 the Brits, the Baftas and the Oscars. Spring is an orgy of style.

In the old days, if you wanted to look at the beautifully ridiculous, the conceptual or the just plain silly, the fashion shows were your best bet. Awards ceremonies, by contrast, used to be elegant oceans of pretty, colourful gowns by Valentino, Marchesa and Versace. They were so sedate that, in 2001, when Björk wore a swan
10 dress by fashion designer Marjan Pejoski and laid six eggs on the red carpet at the Oscars, she was lampooned for years. In 2011, a decade later, nobody would blink if Björk had taken off and flown to her seat. This spring, at the Grammys, Katy Perry sported angel wings, 10-year-old actress and pop star Willow Smith turned up in 8in platform trainers, US singer Nicki Minaj added leopard-print highlights to her
15 pompadour[1] hair to match her leopard-print dress and Lady Gaga arrived in an egg, carried like a Roman emperor.

The designers' most outrageous creations were papped[2] on celebrities at red-carpet events rather than at the fashion shows. In fact, the most talked-about turn on the catwalk this season wasn't by Kate Moss, Lara Stone or any other model – it was
20 Lady Gaga's debut at the Thierry Mugler womenswear show in Paris. Something odd is happening with celebrities and style. The stars are becoming more daring, more avant garde than the designers.

Nowadays, the biggest female names in music don't particularly set themselves apart from their predecessors through musical style – most of them create
25 surprisingly traditional pop – but the way they look is a whole new world ...

The new stars do seem to be more humorous and self-aware than their pop predecessors. When Jessie J won the Critics' Choice at this year's Brit Awards she wore a Vivienne Westwood minidress. 'I look like the evil queen from *Snow White*,' she told reporters. 'I just need to go and find my dwarfs now.' Similarly, when asked
30 about her big-cat Givenchy couture[3] at this year's Grammys, Minaj described her outfit as 'miraculous meets her cub meets ferocity meets fabulosity meets the

runway'. Katy Perry is more pragmatic. 'We're all unique. That's why we all win and we all can exist. People don't just want vanilla. They want 31 flavours. I couldn't do what Rihanna does. I couldn't do what Gaga does. They can't do what I do.'

35 What these stars do is create a break in the monotony of style that has smothered culture of late. Trends used to wash from catwalk to stage to club and pavement unhampered. They may not be of vast cultural significance, but these new celebrities' style is vivid and fun. We have come a long way from laughing at a star for laying eggs on a red carpet to applauding one for arriving in an egg. It's going
40 to be entertaining to see how much further we can go.

Glossary:
pompadour[1] – a hairstyle in which the hair is brushed upwards for height
papped[2] – photographed by paparazzi (independent photographers who take pictures of celebrities)
couture[3] – fashionable made-to-measure clothing

TEXT B

Letter from George Bernard Shaw to *The Times* 3 July 1905

Sir, The Opera management of Covent Garden regulates the dress of its male patrons. When is it going to do the same to the women?

On Saturday night I went to the Opera. I wore the costume imposed on me by the regulations of the house. I fully recognize the advantage of those regulations.
5 Evening dress is cheap, simple, durable, prevents rivalry and extravagance on the part of male leaders of fashion, annihilates class distinctions and gives men who are poor and doubtful of their social position (that is, the great majority of men) a sense of security and satisfaction that no clothes of their own choosing could confer ...

10 But I submit that what is sauce for the gander is sauce for the goose. Every argument that applies to the regulation of the man's dress applies equally to the regulation of the woman's. ...

At 9 o'clock (the Opera began at 8) a lady came in and sat down very conspicuously in my line of sight. She remained there until the beginning of the last act. I do not
15 complain of her coming late and going early; on the contrary, I wish she had come later and gone earlier. For this lady, who had very black hair, had stuck over her right ear the pitiable corpse of a large white bird, which looked exactly if someone had killed it by stamping on the beast, and then nailed it to the lady's temple, which was presumably of sufficient solidity to bear the operation.
20 I am not, I hope, a morbidly squeamish person; but the spectacle sickened me. I presume that if I had presented myself at the doors with a dead snake round my neck, a collection of black beetles pinned to my shirtfront, and a grouse in my hair, I should have been refused admission. Why, then, is a woman to be allowed to commit such a public outrage? Had the lady been refused admission, as she should
25 have been, she would have soundly rated the tradesman who imposed the disgusting headdress on her under the false pretence that 'the best people' wear such things, and withdrawn her custom from him; and thus the root of the evil

30 would be struck at; for your fashionable woman generally allows herself to be dressed according to the taste of a person who she would not let sit down in her presence. I once, in Drury Lane Theatre, sat behind a matinee hat decorated with the two wings of a seagull, artificially reddened at the joints so as to produce the illusion of being freshly plucked from a live bird. But even that lady stopped short of a whole seagull. Both ladies were evidently regarded by their neighbours as ridiculous and vulgar; but that is hardly enough when the offence is one which

35 produces a sensation of physical sickness in persons of normal human sensibility.

I suggest to the Covent Garden authorities that, if they feel bound to protect their subscribers against the dangers of my shocking them with a blue tie, they are at least equally bound to protect me against the danger of a woman shocking me with a dead bird.

Yours truly,
G. Bernard Shaw

SECTION A: READING

Answer **all** questions in this section.

You are advised to spend about 45 minutes on this section.

❶ Read again the first two paragraphs of **Text A**.

Choose **four** statements below which are TRUE. Choose a maximum of four statements.

[4 marks]

A Fashion shows take place in large cities.

B The Brits and the Baftas are fashion shows.

C The writer thinks that modern fashion shows are ridiculous.

D Marchesa is a fashion designer.

E Björk was once ridiculed for one of her outfits.

F The writer thinks that celebrities wear boring outfits at awards ceremonies.

G Katy Perry wore angel wings to an awards ceremony.

H Modern audiences are surprised when celebrities wear outrageous costumes.

② You need to refer to **Text A** and **Text B** for this question:

Use details from **both** texts. Write a summary of the differences in attitudes to fashion in the two articles.

[8 marks]

③ You now need to refer **only** to **Text B**, Shaw's letter.

How does Shaw use language to express his views on fashion persuasively?

[12 marks]

④ For this question, you need to refer to the **whole of Text A** together with **Text B**, the letter to *The Times*.

Compare how the two writers convey their different attitudes to fashion.

In your answer, you could:

- Compare their different attitudes
- Compare the methods they use to convey their attitudes
- Support your ideas with references to both texts

[16 marks]

SECTION B: WRITING

You are advised to spend about 45 minutes on this section.

Write in full sentences.

You are reminded of the need to plan your answer.

You should leave enough time to check your work at the end.

⑤ 'Clothes are not just functional – they are an essential way in which we express our individuality.'

Write an article for a broadsheet newspaper in which you explain your views on this statement.

(24 marks for content and organisation
16 marks for technical accuracy)

[40 marks]

CHAPTER 7: The basics: Core Literature skills and effects

HOW TO COMMENT ON TEXTS AND USE QUOTATIONS

When commenting on a text in your Literature exam, you should always support what you say with references or by using quotations effectively.

AO1 **AO2**

AQA
Paper 1,
Paper 2
Edexcel Paper 1,
Paper 2
Eduqas
Component 1,
Component 2
OCR Component 1,
Component 2

USING QUOTATIONS

Using quotations accurately can make your answer more sophisticated. Remember:

- Always use single quotation marks (' ') around the quotation.
- Only put quotation marks around words taken from the text.
- Embed the quotation into the sentence, so that it flows easily when read.
- Do not use a quotation and then repeat what it means in your own words.
- Do not overuse quotations. Use them to support the most important points.

EXAM FOCUS

Read this part of a student's response to a task on the character of Admiral Greystock in Anthony Trollope's novel *The Eustace Diamonds*. Some of its features have been highlighted:

> Identifies the character

> Refers to a specific word and makes an inference

Trollope presents Admiral Greystock, the father of Lizzie Eustace, as someone who, it was said by others, 'liked whist, wine – and wickedness in general.' The word 'wickedness' in particular suggests that he was a notorious character.

> Apt quotation

A higher-level response would explore the point further, focusing on particular words and their effect to identify further implications:

> Apt quotations well embedded in the text

> Focuses in on a particular word and draws inferences to make a wider point

In the opening page of 'The Eustace Diamonds' Trollope refers to Admiral Greystock, Lizzie Eustace's father. He is a man said to like 'whist, wine – and wickedness in general' even on 'his dying bed', which suggests that he was not only notorious for his 'wickedness' but also determined to be so to the end, despite what others might think.

> Locates the reference precisely

❶ Rewrite this comment on Meera Syal's novel *Anita and Me* as a single sentence, embedding the quotation.

Meena describes how the Tollington women show their mutual dislike of each other. They 'snarl and send death rays to each other'.

DEVELOP A CRITICAL STYLE

The style in which you write your interpretation of a text is important.
In AO1 you are asked to write in a critical style.

What does it say?	What does it mean?	Dos and Don'ts
AO1 'maintain a critical style'	Write in a clear, formal style using **Standard English**, not in a chatty, informal style.	**Don't write:** *What the writer is sort of going on about is …* **Do write:** *The writer is making the underlying point that …*

When writing in a critical style, you should use a range of verbs to show the effects created in the text:

● *The writer presents/suggests/conveys/implies/explores/describes/demonstrates/reveals …*

● *The reader/audience infers/understands/recognises/perceives/deduces …*

❷ Choose alternative verbs to replace the underlined verbs.
   ● *The author **says** that the main character …*
   ● *In this scene Shakespeare **shows** …*
   ● *As events unfold, the audience **can tell** …*
   ● *The sense of fear is **shown** by …*

PLAN YOUR RESPONSE

Remember to write your response in paragraphs and to use **connectives**. You should plan for about six or seven paragraphs. Always include:

● An introduction: outline the main point or argument you will make
● A conclusion: sum up your argument (you could begin: 'Finally …')

TOP TIP

You can also make references without quotations to support a point, e.g. *In the first chapter the writer presents us with each main character, which allows the reader to gain an overall impression of them.*

TOP TIP

Once you are sure you understand the question, plan your answer quickly. List key ideas. Note down important names, places and key events.

APPLYING YOUR SKILLS

❸ Reread a section from the text you are studying when a key character appears for the first time. Write 100 words commenting on that character.

Remember:

● Comment on what you learn about the character from their first appearance.
● Include short, important quotations.

PROGRESS LOG [tick the correct box] Needs more work ■ Getting there ■ Under control ■

WRITING ABOUT AN EXTRACT

In the exam, you will be asked to write about an extract from at least one of the texts you have. To address the question:

- **First:** read through the extract
- **Second:** make sure you know where the extract occurs and what happens before and immediately after it
- **Third:** consider the importance of the extract (what we learn and how things change as a result)

A01 A02

AQA
Paper 1,
Paper 2

Edexcel Paper 1,
Paper 2

Eduqas
Component 1,
Component 2

OCR Component 1,
Component 2

UNDERSTANDING THE QUESTION

Questions related to texts can be detailed, so after you have read the question, ask yourself: what exactly am I asked to do?

Always identify **key words** and keep them in mind as you write. For example, the question may ask you to write about:

- A character or event
- The reader's or audience's response
- The relationship between characters
- How **mood** (such as fear or tension) is created
- How an idea or **theme** (such as marriage) is presented
- The context of the play/novel

❶ Identify the key words in these two exam-style questions:

> *Read the extract. Then answer the following question.*
>
> *With close reference to the extract, show how a character is presented.*

> *Write about the way suspense is treated in the novel.*
> - *Refer to the extract and the novel as a whole*
> - *Show your understanding of characters and events in the novel*
> *Refer to the context of the novel.*

TOP TIP ⭐

If you are asked to 'make close reference', you need to refer to specific examples and explain their effects. Use accurate terms for literary techniques, such as image, simile, irony.

ZOOM IN ON POWERFUL WORDS AND PHRASES

TOP TIP

Remember that much of the language used in fiction, poetry or drama will have hidden meanings so you will often need to infer what is meant.

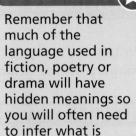

When you read the extract in the exam, make sure you zoom in on powerful words and phrases and the **effect** they create. For example, consider how Dickens presents Marley's ghost in this sentence from *A Christmas Carol*:

Powerful adjectives

The spirit raised a frightful cry, and shook its chain with such a dismal and appalling noise, that Scrooge held on tight to his chair.

Sound (as well as sight) is used to heighten the image of the ghost and Scrooge's discomfort

EXAM FOCUS

Read this successful response to the question of how Dickens presents Marley's ghost in the sentence above, which includes the effect on the reader:

Strong opening

Zooms in on key words and analyses their function

Shows the effect on the reader.

The writer exploits the sense of sound (as well as sight) to create the image of Marley's ghostly appearance. Powerful adjectives such as 'dismal' and 'appalling' describe the ghost's cry, so that Scrooge holds on 'tight to his chair' in fear. In this way, the reader sees how the ghost begins to cause a change in Scrooge's attitude, since he is not used to being afraid.

Shows sense of sound is used (followed by example)

APPLYING YOUR SKILLS

❷ Choose a page at random from a text you are studying and select an extract (about ten lines). Using the Exam Focus above as a model, write fifty words about the extract. Include comments on the effect it has on the reader

Remember:

- Identify where in the text the extract comes from.
- Identify and zoom in on key words and phrases, such as images or dialogue

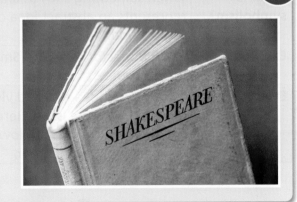

PROGRESS LOG [tick the correct box] Needs more work ☐ Getting there ☐ Under control ☐

COMMENTING ON KEY LITERARY TECHNIQUES

Writers use many techniques to create effects. The most common is **imagery**, which includes **similes** and **metaphors**.

A01 **A02**

AQA
Paper 1,
Paper 2

Edexcel Paper 1,
Paper 2

Eduqas
Component 1,
Component 2

OCR Component 1,
Component 2

LITERARY TECHNIQUE: IMAGE

What is an image?	In literature, an image is the mental picture that appeals to the senses and is conjured up by the words.
Example	*They told of…footsteps creaking upon staircases and fingers tapping at casements* [windows]… (Susan Hill, *The Woman in Black*)
Effect	These images, particularly 'footsteps creaking and 'fingers tapping' have associations with the supernatural and create a sense of foreboding.

LITERARY TECHNIQUE: METAPHOR

What is metaphor?	When a striking image is used to describe one thing as another to imply a resemblance.
Example	'The Spider, as Mr Jaggers had called him [Bentley Drummle], was used to lying in wait.' (Charles Dickens, *Great Expectations*)
Effect	The 'Spider' suggests someone who plots, waiting for the right moment to make a move or attack.

❶ In *Great Expectations*, Pip refers to another character, Joe, as a 'Hercules'. Write a sentence explaining the impression this metaphor creates. You may need to look up who Hercules was.

LITERARY TECHNIQUE: SYMBOLISM

What is symbolism?	When something such as an image, person or animal represents an abstract idea or quality that is widely understood.
Example	In *An Inspector Calls*, Eva Smith is a **symbol** of the poor and powerless.
Effect	It makes the idea real and vivid so that the audience is engaged with the issue. Here, the symbolism makes us question a society that allows the powerful to take no responsibility for the poor.

GET IT RIGHT! ⭐

Similes and metaphors both make comparisons between one thing and another. To tell the difference, remember that similes include the words 'like', 'as' or 'than' ('caught **like** a bird in a snare').

LITERARY TECHNIQUE: DRAMATIC IRONY

What is dramatic irony?	When the development of the plot allows the audience to know something that a character or characters do not.
Example	In *Blood Brothers*, Mickey and Edward meet and play together as children. They become blood brothers (cut their skin and mix their blood), which means they will always have to support each other.
Effect	The audience, which already knows the outcome, cannot but help feel sadness for the two small boys, because they are twins although they do not know it. Nor do they know that in the final act, Mickey will accidentally shoot Edward and will himself be shot by the police.

TOP TIP

Many of Shakespeare's plays contain dramatic irony. Note any examples of this technique in the play you are studying and make sure you understand why they are ironic.

Dramatic irony is a powerful technique. It often occurs in three stages:

- **Preparation:** The reader or audience or a particular character is made aware of something that the characters do not know.

- **Suspension:** The reader or audience becomes intrigued about what will happen; the character who has knowledge has to live with what he or she knows and decide whether to reveal it.

- **Resolution:** The truth is revealed, and the effect creates an outcome (which may or may not have been expected).

Dramatic irony can be used to tragic effect. In Shakespeare's *Romeo and Juliet*, Romeo thinks Juliet is dead and takes poison so he too will die. However, unlike Romeo, the audience – powerless to intervene – knows that Juliet is only in a deep sleep.

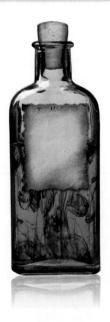

VOCABULARY CHOICES

Heightened language, such as powerful imagery, has a dramatic effect that grabs the reader's attention. Read this extract from *The Strange Case of Dr Jekyll and Mr Hyde*, in which vocabulary choices have specific effects:

TOP TIP

When studying a text, compile a list of examples of literary techniques the writer uses to describe character, setting and key events. Note their effects and commit them to memory so you can recall them in the exam.

Compound adjective and **abstract noun** evoke image of a creature out of control

And next moment, with ape-like fury he was trampling his victim underfoot and hailing down a storm of blows, under which the bones were audibly shattered.

Powerful verb conveys image of a violent onslaught

❷ Write a comment on the effect of the phrase 'the bones were audibly shattered'.

SENTENCE STRUCTURE

Writers also construct sentences to have particular effects on a reader. Look at this further example from *The Strange Case of Dr Jekyll and Mr Hyde*:

> *... yet, it was not so much these tokens of a swift physical decay that arrested the lawyer's notice, as a look in the eye and quality of manner that seemed to testify to some deep-seated terror of the mind.*
>
> Withholds most dramatic thought until the end to increase tension

The author might have written:

> *What arrested the lawyer's attention was the look in his eye and the quality of his manner that seemed to testify to some deep-seated terror of the mind, as well as the tokens of his swift physical decay.*
>
> Has less impact when placed in the middle (or beginning) of the sentence.

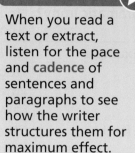

TOP TIP

When you read a text or extract, listen for the pace and cadence of sentences and paragraphs to see how the writer structures them for maximum effect.

DR. JEKYLL and MR. HYDE

THE TRANSFORMATION
"GREAT GOD! CAN IT BE!!"

APPLYING YOUR SKILLS

❸ Read this further extract from *The Strange Case of Dr Jekyll and Mr Hyde*, then answer the question below.

Sir, if that was my master, why had he a mask upon his face? If it was my master, why did he cry out like a rat and run from me? I have served him long enough. And then … the man paused and passed a hand over his face.

Think about techniques, sentences and vocabulary used for effect. Describe the effects of this extract in fifty words.

Remember:

● Sentence form has an effect.

● Similes are significant.

● Actions can reveal character.

PROGRESS CHECK FOR CHAPTER 7

GOOD PROGRESS

I can:

● Explain how writers use language to show action, ideas, character and mood ☐

● Use a selection of common literary terms to explain the effects of language ☐

● Refer to evidence, use appropriate quotations to support my points and make references to relevant parts of texts to show how a writer uses language ☐

EXCELLENT PROGRESS

I can:

● Analyse in detail and show how a writer uses language to explore characters and themes and create mood ☐

● Choose appropriate evidence, make inferences, include apt quotations and references and develop wider interpretations from a writer's use of language ☐

● Explain the function of settings and the effects of context ☐

CHAPTER 8: Shakespeare

CONTEXT IN SHAKESPEARE

The context of any work of art is the historical time and place in which it was written, who created it and under what conditions. There are many contextual details that can help your reading of a text.

A03

AQA Paper 1, Section A

Edexcel Paper 1, Section A

Eduqas Component 1, Section A

OCR Component 2, Section B

HISTORY AND POLITICS

- Shakespeare wrote during the reigns of Elizabeth I and James I of England (VI of Scotland).
- Power was held by the Crown and the Church.
- There was little democracy. The Divine Right of Kings meant that the monarch was answerable only to God, not to the people. It was a way of keeping power.
- Playwrights and poets were expected to write in praise of the monarch to reinforce the their power and encourage obedience from the people. For example, *Henry V* pays tribute to Elizabeth I and the Tudor line.
- James I was the patron of Shakespeare's acting company, the King's Men. *Macbeth* was written for James.

CULTURE AND SOCIETY

- The Italian Renaissance influenced Shakespeare. Renaissance means 'rebirth' and was a time of great artistic flowering. It came after the Middle Ages, which was seen as a period of cultural decline.
- Theatres developed from travelling companies. They attracted rich and poor alike, and were a source of education.
- Boys played female roles because women were not allowed to appear on stage. A boy probably played both Viola as a woman and Viola disguised as a man, Cesario, in *Twelfth Night*.

RELIGION, BELIEFS AND MORAL CODES

- Under Elizabeth I, the official Christian religion was the Protestant Church of England. However, the previous monarch, Mary I, had been Catholic and many people in England were also Catholics.
- The Great Chain of Being was God's hierarchy of life. God was at the top, then angels, kings and so on down to animals, plants and minerals.
- Audiences in Shakespeare's day believed in witchcraft, so they would take the supernatural powers in his plays seriously, such as the witches' curses and prophecies in *Macbeth*.
- Non-Christians were often regarded with suspicion. We can see this in plays such as *The Merchant of Venice*, but Shakespeare may in fact have been using the play to challenge the views of his contemporaries.
- Shakespeare's attitudes towards other races or groups can seem discriminatory but also inconsistent. For example, Othello, a North

TOP TIP ⭐

Use the internet to find out one interesting fact about life at the time the play you are studying is set. Can you link it to anything that happens in the play?

African, is respected as a powerful general but also subject to racial abuse and intolerance.

The exam question will focus on an issue or idea related to the Shakespeare play you are studying. In your response, you will need to link context closely to the question. For example, you might explore connections between the themes (for example, conflict) and:

- The position of women at the time
- Parents' attitudes to children in Shakespeare's day
- Patriotic ideas
- Elizabethan or Jacobean beliefs in the supernatural
- Renaissance ideals, such as **courtly love**
- Multiracial and colonial attitudes

EXAM FOCUS

Read how one student discusses the theme of love in *Romeo and Juliet.* Features relating to context have been highlighted:

> Before Romeo meets Juliet, he is infatuated with Rosaline, of whom he says the sun 'Ne'er saw her match since the world began'. His overblown response idealises Rosaline and suggests aspects of courtly love, considered at the time as a higher form of expression. Perhaps Shakespeare is criticising such love as unrealistic. After all, when Romeo meets Juliet, he sees her as flesh and blood and immediately forgets Rosaline.

Quotation supports context

Identifies the context

Suggests the effects Shakespeare was trying to achieve

APPLYING YOUR SKILLS

❶ Create a 'context' spider diagram for the Shakespeare play you are studying like the one on page 107.

- In the middle, write the name of the Shakespeare play you are studying.
- Around this, make notes about the context of the play (e.g. for *Macbeth* this might include Gunpowder Plot).
- Add events and details from the play that relate to the contexts (e.g. Macbeth murdering the rightful king).
- Finally, add your own explanation or ideas about how you think the contexts and play are linked (e.g. as a warning to possible conspirators).

Remember:

- Context can be specific events or wider social beliefs.
- Try to find quotations from the play to add to your diagram to support your points.

PROGRESS LOG [tick the correct box]   Needs more work ☐   Getting there ☐   Under control ☐

STRUCTURE AND PLOT IN SHAKESPEARE

Shakespeare's plays usually have five acts, with a variable number of scenes within each act. The scheme below is a way of showing the structure of a story – how a plot develops. The table gives examples from Henry V.

A02

AQA Paper 1, Section A

Edexcel Paper 1, Section A

Eduqas Component 1, Section A

OCR Component 2, Section B

Stage	What it means	Example from *Henry V*
Exposition	Setting presented. Main characters introduced. Plot begins with a problem or conflict.	Chorus explains the epic nature of the story to be told. Act I setting: England. Henry decides to fight French for English land in France, after insult from French king.
Rising action	Further characters may be introduced. Complications or obstacles arise related to the main conflict. Leads towards **climax**.	Act II Chorus explains preparations for war. Three plotters against Henry arrested. Plotters executed, but a drunk who insults Henry is freed, showing Henry's strength and discrimination. French king fortifies army, but is a weak leader.
Climax	Defining moment of play or novel, on which future of main characters and events turn. Moment of greatest tension.	Act III Chorus explains siege of Harfleur. Battle begins. Henry wins, but army exhausted. French demand surrender, but Henry proceeds to Calais. The French expect to win. Act IV Chorus describes the scene before the battle in English and French camps. Before Battle of Agincourt, Henry (disguised) visits soldiers in camp. Before battle gives St Crispin's Day speech (Act IV Scene 3).
Falling action	Tension falls, although there maybe moments of further tension/ uncertainty. Play moves towards ending.	Act IV The French are losing. Henry in charge. Battle moves to its close. English win. Henry forbids boasting (Act IV Scene V). Act V Chorus tells us that Henry returns to England. Years pass.
Dénouement	Play's outcome, good or bad. Problems unravelled. Something usually learned. Characters have been affected.	Act V Peace negotiations finally agreed. French Katherine agrees to marry Henry. two countries united. Epilogue Chorus tells us that Henry VI lost his father's successes in subsequent wars.

This structure is represented visually in 'Freytag's Pyramid', created by the nineteenth-century novelist Gustav Freytag:

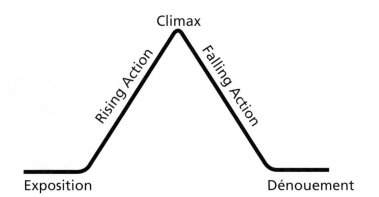

PLOTS

Within the dramatic structure, Shakespeare usually creates several **subplots** involving minor characters. For example in *Twelfth Night*, the subplot involves Sir Toby Belch, Sir Andrew Aguecheek, Fabian, Maria and Feste tricking Malvolio.

❶ Write down the main characters in the Shakespeare play you are studying, then note the plots or the subplots that they are linked to.

❷ The French word **dénouement** means to 'untie' or 'unknot'. In the play you are studying, find examples of a moral being learned or a problem resolved.

APPLYING YOUR SKILLS

❸ Use the structure outlined above to make notes on the main plot of the play you are studying. If you are studying *Henry V*, write down the example notes and add further comments for falling action and dénouement.

Remember:

- The acts do not always fall neatly into each stage for every play (for example, the climax might occur in Act IV), or readers/audiences might disagree on the climax and where it occurs.
- Keep to the main plot and characters, not the subplots.

SHAKESPEARE'S LANGUAGE

Shakespeare was writing over 400 years ago, so the language he uses might seem difficult to understand today. This unit is designed to help you understand and appreciate Shakespeare's language.

READING BLANK VERSE

Shakespeare sometimes uses **prose**, especially for lower-class characters, but large sections of his plays are written in **blank verse** – poetry that is unrhymed ('blank') – and in a **metre** called **iambic pentameter**. In this form, each line has five (*pent*) iams. An iam is a pair of syllables, one unstressed, one stressed.

Read the line below out loud, stressing the underlined syllables:

> O, <u>par</u>don <u>me</u>, thou <u>bleed</u>ing <u>piece</u> of <u>earth</u>

Sometimes Shakespeare varies this:

- To emphasise meaning
- To convey a speaker's emotions
- To make the speech sound more natural

Read these lines from *Macbeth* aloud:

> *Tomorrow, and tomorrow, and tomorrow,*
> *Creeps in this petty pace from day to day*
> *To the last syllable of recorded time.*

None of these lines is quite iambic pentameter. Why? At this point, Macbeth is losing a battle and has just heard of his wife's suicide. The rhythm shows his feeling that life drags on pointlessly. The first line is not iambic at all, and it has an extra syllable. This makes it drag. To make sense of the second line, you have to stress the first word, emphasising the slowness of time. The third line also varies rhythm and has an extra, dragging syllable.

1 Read a verse speech from the play you are studying.
- Read to the ends of sentences, not to the ends of lines.
- Tap out the lines to check their rhythm.
- If a line varies from iambic pentameter, try to work out how the sense is affected.

MAKING THE MOST OF IMAGERY

Shakespeare uses **imagery** to express meaning and reflect the **themes** of the plays. This imagery might be:

- **Metaphor:** *'he sees the Romans are but sheep'* (Cassius, *Julius Caesar*)
- **Simile:** *'As two spent swimmers, that do cling together / And choke their art'* (Sergeant describing warring sides in an indecisive battle, *Macbeth*)
- **Personification:** *'when you depart from me, sorrow abides and happiness takes his leave'* (Leonato addressing Don Pedro in *Much Ado About Nothing*)

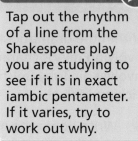

A02

AQA Paper 1, Section A

Edexcel Paper 1, Section A

Eduqas Component 1, Section A

OCR Component 2, Section B

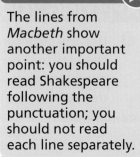

TOP TIP ★

Tap out the rhythm of a line from the Shakespeare play you are studying to see if it is in exact iambic pentameter. If it varies, try to work out why.

GET IT RIGHT! ★

The lines from *Macbeth* show another important point: you should read Shakespeare following the punctuation; you should not read each line separately.

Some plays use a great deal of particular types of imagery. For example, *Macbeth* and *Julius Caesar* have many examples of animal imagery, emphasising the predatory animal aspect of human nature.

❷ Read these lines from *Romeo and Juliet*. Romeo has just seen Juliet for the first time:

It seems she hangs upon the cheek of night
Like a rich jewel in an Ethiope's[1] ear;
Beauty too rich for use, for earth too dear.

Ethiope[1] – Ethiopian (someone who has dark skin)

- How do these lines use all three types of image?
- How do these images suggest what Romeo feels about Juliet?
- How might Romeo's plentiful use of imagery reflect his character?

EXAM FOCUS

Read this extract from a student's essay discussing imagery in *Much Ado About Nothing*. Some of its features have been highlighted:

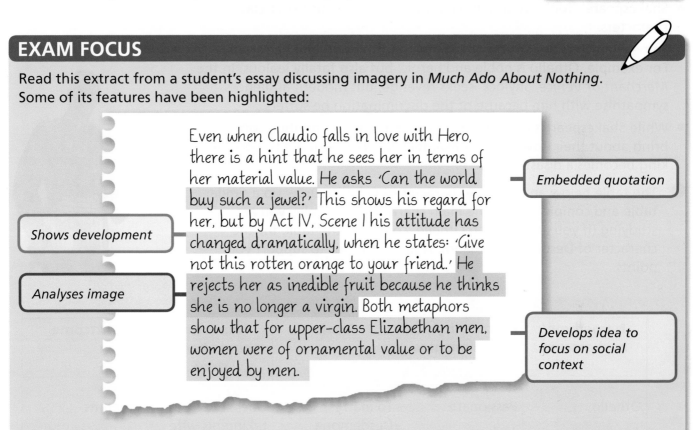

Even when Claudio falls in love with Hero, there is a hint that he sees her in terms of her material value. He asks 'Can the world buy such a jewel?' This shows his regard for her, but by Act IV, Scene I his attitude has changed dramatically, when he states: 'Give not this rotten orange to your friend.' He rejects her as inedible fruit because he thinks she is no longer a virgin. Both metaphors show that for upper-class Elizabethan men, women were of ornamental value or to be enjoyed by men.

Embedded quotation

Shows development

Analyses image

Develops idea to focus on social context

APPLYING YOUR SKILLS

❸ Find a speech in your play that contains imagery. Write a paragraph about it like the one in the Exam Focus response, but include a comment on the rhythm of the language.

Remember:

- Identify the type of image.
- Quote it.
- Analyse its effect.
- Explain how it relates to a character, theme, or both in the play.

PROGRESS LOG [tick the correct box]   Needs more work ■   Getting there ■   Under control ■

SHAKESPEARE'S CHARACTERS

Shakespeare's plays cover a wide cast of characters, and an exam question is likely to focus on character, since key aspects of characters are the central concern of the play. For example:

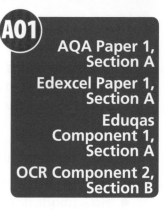

A01

AQA Paper 1, Section A

Edexcel Paper 1, Section A

Eduqas Component 1, Section A

OCR Component 2, Section B

- The **choices** they make and how these affect events
- How they are **affected by events**
- How they **change and develop** through experience

There are many character types in Shakespeare's plays: heroes, villains, soldiers, leaders, lovers, comic characters and many more. Certain types of character often have similar traits:

- Shakespeare's fools are usually clever and mischievous lower-class characters.

- Some characters are antiheroes, showing both good and bad traits. For example, Othello is noble and heroic, but also fatally jealous. In the *Merchant of Venice*, Shylock seeks revenge, but modern audiences sympathise with him because of the discrimination he suffers.

- While Shakespeare's leaders vary in character, their ambitions often bring about their downfall. For example, Macbeth's desire to become king becomes a disastrous force.

1 The table below analyses the character of Othello. Draw up a similar table and complete it for the main character in the play you are studying (if you are studying *Othello*, complete the table for the character of Desdemona or Iago). Add quotations to support your points.

Name/type/ background	Personality and relationships	Goals	Important things he/she does	Outcome
Othello Antihero Impressive general A Moor from a noble line, but an outsider in a white society	Passionate Jealous Loves Desdemona, with whom he elopes Ambitious	To marry Desdemona Seeks equality through his marriage To be the best general	Goes to Cyprus, taking his wife with him, thus allowing himself to be influenced by the villain, Iago Smothers Desdemona	Commits suicide after the murder

EXAM FOCUS

In *Much Ado About Nothing*, Don John is the villain who tries to create problems between the two lovers, Hero and Claudio. Read this extract from one student's successful analysis of the character of Don John. Some of its features have been highlighted:

> Don John admits himself that he is a 'plain-dealing villain', who makes mischief, particularly for Hero and her relationship with Claudio – for example when he tells Claudio the lie that Don Pedro wants to marry Hero in Act II. We do not know why he behaves badly. He is only a minor character and a man of 'not many words', but he has an important impact on the plot. His actions initially separate and eventually (accidentally) bring the lovers together.

Appropriate quote that identifies his main character trait

Reference to action taken as example

Shows the character's main effect

APPLYING YOUR SKILLS

❷ Referring to the table you created for your characters, write a commentary about one of them in no more than 100 words.

Remember:

- Include a quotation that reflects their character.
- Include what others think of them.
- Show how they affect the plot by giving an example.

SHAKESPEARE'S THEMES

A **theme** is a central idea that runs through a work of literature. Shakespeare's themes cover questions about society, politics and morality as well as personal relationships. Even Shakespeare's comedies can include serious themes.

Some common themes in Shakespeare's plays are:

- Parents and children (*Romeo and Juliet*)
- Ambition (*Macbeth)*
- Love, courtship and marriage *(Much Ado About Nothing)*
- Race and the role of women (*The Merchant of Venice*)
- The supernatural (*The Tempest)*
- Disguise (*Twelfth Night*)
- Kingship (*Henry V*)
- Power (*Julius Caesar*)
- Jealousy (*Othello*)

A01

AQA Paper 1, Section A

Edexcel Paper 1, Section A

Eduqas Component 1, Section A

OCR Component 2, Section B

HOW ARE THEMES REVEALED IN THE PLAYS?

Characters' speeches often highlight themes. In *Macbeth*, Lady Macbeth urges her husband to murder King Duncan. When Macbeth falters, she tells him: *'When you durst [dared to] do it, then you were a man.'* She is saying that Macbeth is a coward. However, her words are also linked to the theme of ambition, making us question who is the more ambitious of the two.

Themes can be revealed through characters' words or actions. For example, in *Twelfth Night*, Viola's decision to disguise herself as a man, and her convincing portrayal, highlights the theme of illusion and reality.

❶ Write down the themes listed below that feature in the Shakespeare play you are studying. Choose only the main themes.

> love   patriotism   disguise   betrayal   revenge   power and ambition   friendship   corruption   nature   religion   marriage   magic   kingship   war   jealousy   race   illusion and reality   greed   fate   mercy   parents and children   jealousy   the role of women   friendship   order and chaos.

❷ Consider the plot of your play and make brief notes on where the themes occur. Find quotations to support your points. Note them and keep them for reference.

TOP TIP ★

It is often best to break down general themes into something more specific when commenting on the play. For example, in *Romeo and Juliet*, rather than saying 'love' is a theme, you might mention 'how young people deal with powerful feelings of desire'.

GET IT RIGHT! ★

Remember to use short quotations and embed them in sentences in your exam. You can split quotations, placing a word or words in one part of the sentence and the remaining words in another part, to make your writing more fluent.

EXAM FOCUS

In *Romeo and Juliet*, both young people come into conflict with their parents, but Juliet has less freedom than Romeo. Read this student's extract about Juliet's relationship with her father. Note the detailed comments that break the themes down into smaller parts.

> In Act I, Lord Capulet believes that Juliet is too young to marry. However, by Act III he is less tolerant when she refuses to marry Paris, and determines to 'drag' her to church 'on a hurdle' if she disobeys him. His comments not only reveal his changed attitude to his daughter, but also highlight another theme, the position of women and the pressure on Elizabethan daughters to obey their fathers.

Specific thematic comment linked to context

Shows how the relationship has altered

Identifies a related theme

APPLYING YOUR SKILLS

❸ Choose a theme from a Shakespeare play and write a short commentary on it like the one in the Exam Focus section. Discuss how it is revealed in the play through events or a character's words.

Remember:

- Include a quotation that relates to the theme.
- Note if any other theme is revealed, or focus on a more specific element of the theme.

PROGRESS CHECK FOR CHAPTER 8

GOOD PROGRESS

I can:

- Understand and refer to the context in which the play was written ☐
- Understand and refer to the key events, main plot and subplots in the play ☐
- Explain how Shakespeare uses language to convey relationships and ideas ☐
- Explain the main themes in the play and understand how the characters are presented ☐

EXCELLENT PROGRESS

I can:

- Refer closely to key aspects of the context in which the play was written ☐
- Analyse in detail and refer to literary techniques to show how Shakespeare uses language; refer in depth to key events ☐
- Analyse in detail the way themes are developed and characters presented across the play ☐

CHAPTER 9: The nineteenth-century novel

CONTEXT IN THE NINETEENTH-CENTURY NOVEL

The context of the nineteenth-century novel is the historical time and place in which it was written, who created it and under what conditions. In your exam you will need to link context closely to the novel you are studying.

A03

AQA Paper 1,
Section B

Edexcel Paper 2,
Section A

Eduqas
Component 2,
Section B

OCR Component 1,
Section B

HISTORY AND POLITICS

- With the Industrial Revolution came wealth. Industrialists made fortunes. Rural people moved to the cities to find work, where factory conditions were grim. Various Factory Acts were passed to improve conditions.

- Queen Victoria (1837–1901) ruled over a vast empire, and Britain was a major world power. By the turn of the century, however, the USA and Germany began to dominate economically.

CULTURE AND SOCIETY

- Women had few rights and had not yet won the right to vote (nor had working-class men). They were dependent on their husbands, particularly financially. One of the main concerns of *Pride and* Prejudice is the need for women to find husbands.

- There was a significant gap between rich and poor. There was no National Health Service and infant mortality was high. Charles Dickens draws attention to the plight of the poor in *A Christmas Carol.*

- Progress in the sciences had an important influence on literature, such as *Frankenstein, The Strange Case of Dr Jekyll and Mr Hyde* and *War of the Worlds*, all of which could be seen as early science fiction. Nevertheless, there was also interest in ideas such as spiritualism and psychology.

- Free public libraries were established in 1850 and more people began to read novels.

- Popular entertainment included the music hall, travelling sideshows and sensational stories published in the so-called 'Penny Dreadful'.

RELIGION, BELIEFS AND MORAL CODES

- Christianity was the main religion in Britain. Most people held religious beliefs and many attended church regularly.

- Negative attitudes to those of a different race are disturbing to us today. In the nineteenth century scientific ideas often divided race into classes, and described races as inferior or superior.

- There were strict moral codes about sexual behaviour, although poverty resulted in widespread prostitution, particularly in the cities, which affected all social classes.

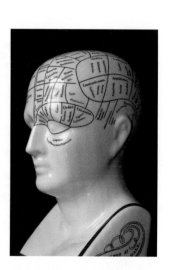

CHARACTER AND CONTEXT

To help you link context closely to the question about the nineteenth-century novel you are studying, ask yourself the following questions:

- What are the circumstances of the main characters in the novel?
- Where and when is the story set?
- What issues is the writer exploring that could be linked to the issues of the period?

How do these aspects of context reveal themselves in the nineteenth-century novel? Here are some examples:

- In *Jane Eyre*, Rochester's wife hidden in the attic raises attitudes to race and mental illness.
- In *Dr Jekyll and Mr Hyde* and *A Christmas Carol*, an interest in the supernatural reflects popular cultural interests.
- In *War of the Worlds*, the clash between reason and religious faith reflects conflicting attitudes at the time.

TOP TIP

Find and keep a note of useful quotations in the novel you are studying that support the context in which the story is set or the author is writing.

APPLYING YOUR SKILLS

❶ Create a 'context' spider diagram for the novel you are studying. An example for *Frankenstein* is shown below.

- In the middle, write the name of the novel you are studying.
- Around this, make notes about the context of the novel.
- Add events and details from the novel that relate to the contexts.
- Finally, add your own explanation or ideas about the links between the context and the novel.

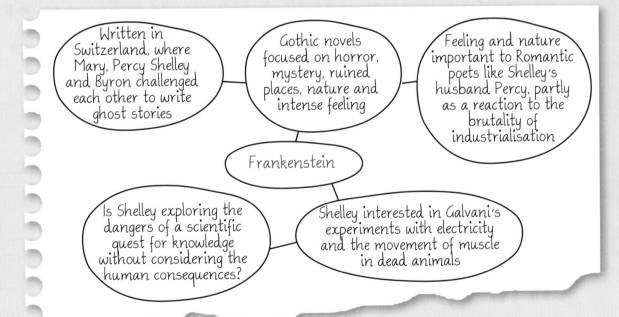

Remember:

- Context can be specific events or wider social beliefs.
- Try to find quotations from the play to add to your diagram to support your points.

STRUCTURE AND VOICE IN THE NINETEENTH-CENTURY NOVEL

Nineteenth-century novelists use a wide range of structures to tell their stories. However, there is usually a strong narrative voice, which you may be asked to discuss in your exam.

A02

AQA Paper 1, Section B

Edexcel Paper 2, Section A

Eduqas Component 2, Section B

OCR Component 1, Section B

STRUCTURE

Nineteenth-century novels may use a range of structural devices and features, which play around with the traditional chronological structure. They might:

- Use **flashbacks**. *A Christmas Carol* also uses **flash-forwards** to reveal a possible future.
- Use **framing** (a story within a story), like *Frankenstein*
- Be in chronological order but use letters to move the plot along, as in *Pride and Prejudice*
- Be told in chronological order with a simple structure, as in *Silas Marner,* which is narrated over a long period in two parts
- Be told chronologically, but present the main character's life from childhood (a **bildungsroman**), as in *Jane Eyre* and *Great Expectations*

It can be useful to work out a general overview of the stages in the novel. The tables below show two examples.

	Stage 1	Stage 2	Stage 3	Stage 4	Stage 5
Jane Eyre	Early childhood at Gateshead Hall with the Reed family	Childhood and adolescence at Lowood School and friendship with Helen Burns	Thornfield Hall as governess	Moor House with the Rivers family	Return to Thornfield Hall and Rochester

	Stage 1	Stage 2	Stage 3
Great Expectations	Childhood in Kent with Joe Gargery	As a reckless young man in London with Herbert Pocket	London and Cairo; learns maturity through Magwitch and Joe's influence

❶ Work out the stages of the novel you are studying. Use a table like the ones above.

POINT OF VIEW

The **narrative viewpoint** of a novel can be written in:

- First person – often in the voice of the **protagonist**, as in *Jane Eyre*, *Great Expectations* and *War of the Worlds*
- Third person, narrated directly by the writer, who has complete knowledge of all the characters (as in *Pride and Prejudice*) but who may at times narrate in a voice that is **ironic**, or judgemental
- Second person (occasionally) when the reader is addressed directly (for example in *Jane Eyre*, where the narrator says: 'Reader I married him ...')

> **TOP TIP**
> Make sure you know who narrates the novel you are studying. If there are multiple narrators (as in *Frankenstein*), make a note of the points at which their narrations occur.

EXAM FOCUS

In *Pride and Prejudice*, Mr Collins is a pompous, narrow-minded clergyman. Read one student's comment about how the narrative voice presents him:

> The narrative voice strikes a sharp tone when we are told that 'Mr Collins was not a sensible man' and the reader feels as if the narrator disapproves of him.

Identifies the mood

Effect on the reader

Compare the response above to the different narrative tone in this student's comment about *The Strange Case of Dr Jekyll and Mr Hyde*:

> The third person narrative voice gives us the lawyer Mr Utterson's authoritative point of view. His 'definite presentiment' that Mr Hyde is 'a fiend' sounds a warning and alarms the reader as well as Utterson himself.

Identifies the type of narrative voice and point of view

Identifies the mood and effect on the reader

❷   Write a paragraph on the narrative viewpoint and voice in a novel you are studying. Include an analysis of their effects, giving examples.

APPLYING YOUR SKILLS

❸   Copy the table below and complete it for the nineteenth-century novel you are studying.
- Choose from the adjectives listed that describe the narrative voice. Add others.
- Find quotations to support the descriptions.

POV(s)	Tone of the narrative voice		Supporting quotations
	humorous	gloomy	Chapter, page
	reliable	ironic	
	commanding	informal	

Remember: There may sometimes be a mixture of narrative voices/points of view.

CHARACTERS AND RELATIONSHIPS IN THE NINETEENTH-CENTURY NOVEL

In the exam, you may be asked to write about a character or their relationship with one or more other people. To do this, you will need to explore:

- Their personality and attitudes
- Their actions
- Their relationships with others
- If and how they change

UNDERSTANDING CHARACTERS THROUGH DIALOGUE

The **dialogue** (what the character says and/or what others say about them) can reveal a great deal about a character. Remember, however that this information may be:

- **Explicit** (stated clearly and openly)
- **Implicit** (suggested or hinted at)

For example:

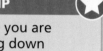

A01

AQA Paper 1, Section B

Edexcel Paper 2, Section A

Eduqas Component 2, Section B

OCR Component 1, Section B

TOP TIP ★

When you are noting down dialogue, remember to indicate who is speaking and about whom or what. Keep a note of the chapter and page for your own reference.

Quotation	What it tells us
Silas Marner Eppie's biological father has come to claim her from Silas. Eppie says: *'And he's took care of me and loved me from the first and I'll cleave to him as long as he lives'*	Silas is loving, caring and responsible, since he has raised Eppie from childhood. Consequently, she views him as her father and will not leave him. (Explicit information)
The Sign of the Four Holmes accuses Watson of romanticising his account of an investigation. He says: *'Detection is, or ought to be an exact science, and should be treated in the same cold and unemotional manner.'*	Although the comment is about detection, it hints that Holmes himself is 'exact' and 'cold' and without feeling. (Implicit information)

❶ Draw up a table like the one above and find some quotations that reveal information about the main character or characters. Try to find both implicit and explicit information.

HOW CHARACTERS AND RELATIONSHIPS ARE PRESENTED

Remember that you can learn about a character by how others react to them as well as by their own words and actions. For example, in *Jane Eyre*, Rochester's willingness to talk openly with Jane suggests a mutual attraction.

Relationships may highlight other aspects of the novel, such as how a **theme** is explored (for example, marriage in *Pride and Prejudice*). Relationships can also affect individual character development. For example, Pip is utterly changed by his relationship with Magwitch in *Great Expectations*, although he comes to value the older man only gradually, over a period of time.

TOP TIP

Sometimes a character will reveal something about themselves by a look or gesture rather than through speech. For example, in *The Strange Case of Dr Jekyll and Mr Hyde*, 'something eminently human beaconed from his [Mr Utterson's] eye' tells us he is probably a compassionate person.

EXAM FOCUS

Read this successful response to a question about the relationship between Pip and Magwitch.

> *Refers to key point in text*

Towards the end of the novel, when Magwitch says that Pip, 'never deserted' him, Pip is troubled, because he knows that he 'had once meant to desert him', despising Magwitch for his low social status. However, through Magwitch's steadfastness and love, Pip learns the value of true friendship and he stands by Magwitch in his time of need.

> *Quotations explain Pip's initial feelings*

> *Shows how the relationship changes Pip and highlights the theme of friendship*

APPLYING YOUR SKILLS

❷ Choose a main character from your novel and pair them with another character from the novel. For example, you could pair the narrator and the curate in *War of the Worlds* or Jane and Rochester (or Jane and St John Rivers) in *Jane Eyre*.

● Write a commentary of no more than 100 words about the relationship between the two characters. Use the Exam Focus paragraph as a model.

● Concentrate on one aspect of the relationship or one point in the text and examine it closely in relation to the two characters (for example, when Elizabeth first meets Darcy in *Pride and Prejudice*).

Remember:

● Include important quotations.

● Mention the effect of the relationship **at that time** on the characters.

PROGRESS LOG [tick the correct box]   Needs more work ▪   Getting there ▪   Under control ▪

THEMES IN THE NINETEENTH-CENTURY NOVEL

Themes in novels and drama can be revealed through almost all aspects of the text, including character, plot, **narrative voice**, **setting** and language. Here are some common themes with examples of how they can be revealed:

A01

AQA Paper 1, Section B

Edexcel Paper 2, Section A

Eduqas Component 2, Section B

OCR Component 1, Section B

- **Theme:** Dual nature
  Example of how revealed: through character. In *The Strange Case of Dr Jekyll and Mr Hyde*, the writer explores the idea that humans are both good and evil.

- **Theme:** Scientific knowledge and its dangers
  Example of how revealed: through plot. In *Frankenstein*, Victor Frankenstein attempts to create life. The terrifying consequences raise several moral issues.

- **Theme:** Marriage
  Example of how revealed: through narrative voice. In *Pride and Prejudice*, the opening sentence introduces the novel's main theme – marriage.

- **Theme:** Lost hope
  Example of how revealed: through setting. In *Jane Eyre*, after the failed wedding to Rochester, Jane's despair is reflected in the change in the weather at Thornfield, when a winter snowstorm descends on the June landscape.

TOP TIP ⭐

A theme may be revealed in more than one way. For example, there may be clues to a theme in events, images and symbols.

RECORDING EVIDENCE

In the exam you may be asked how themes are revealed in your novel. You will need to make references and include short quotations.

The table below shows how **symbolism** in *A Christmas Carol* can reveal a theme.

Theme	How the theme is revealed	Reference and/or quote	Effect
Social injustice	Two poor children called 'Ignorance' and 'Want' appear in the novel as symbols of the way society, as well as Scrooge, fails the poor.	Stave Two: The Ghost of Christmas Present: 'From the foldings of its robe it [the Spirit] brought out two children; wretched, frightful, hideous, miserable …'	The effect on the reader of the image is one of shock and horror – which the author intends.

❶ Look at this list of themes:

| conflict   social class   money   love   friendship   loyalty   crime and punishment   prejudice |
| childhood and growing up   ambition   the position of women   forgiveness   addiction |
| justice   fear   pride   self-knowledge   parenthood   miserliness   poverty |

- Choose a theme from the list that applies to the novel you are studying.
- Draw up a table with the same headings as the table above.
- Find an example of how the theme is revealed through either: character, plot, narrative voice, setting or language (such as symbolism).
- Make a note of where you found it in the text and add a quotation.
- Explain the effect it has on the reader.

EXAM FOCUS

Read how one student presents the notes above to reveal the theme of social injustice in *A Christmas Carol*:

> In Stave Two of 'A Christmas Carol', Dickens uses symbolism to present the theme of social injustice. The Ghost of Christmas Present reveals two 'wretched, frightful, hideous' children called 'Ignorance' and 'Want'. Their names and their poverty are symbols of the way society, as well as Scrooge, fails the poor. The effect on the reader is one of shock and horror, which Dickens intends.

Links theme and symbolism

Embedded quotation

Identifies the mood and effect on the reader

APPLYING YOUR SKILLS

❷ Write a commentary (about 100 words) about a theme you identified from the notes you made in the table in Question 1.

Remember:

- Make a reference and/or include a quotation.
- Describe the effect on the reader.

PROGRESS CHECK FOR CHAPTER 9

GOOD PROGRESS

I can:

- Understand and refer to the context in which the novel I am studying was written ☐
- Understand the plot and refer to key events ☐
- Explain how the narrator's voice is presented and recognise multiple narrations ☐
- Explain the main themes and understand how the characters are presented ☐

EXCELLENT PROGRESS

I can:

- Understand the context in which the novel was written and refer closely to key aspects of context ☐
- Refer in depth to the plots and show how they relate to the characters ☐
- Analyse how the narrator's voice is presented and recognise multiple narrations ☐
- Analyse in detail the way themes are developed in the novel ☐

CHAPTER 10: Modern prose and drama

CONTEXT IN MODERN PROSE AND DRAMA

In Literature, the word 'modern' covers quite a long period of time. The text you are studying could have been written more than eighty years ago (*Journey's End,* 1928) or in the twenty-first century (*Pigeon English,* 2011). For your exam, make sure you can link the text you are studying with the time in which it was written and set.

A03

AQA Paper 2, Section A

Edexcel Paper 1, Section B

Eduqas Component 2, Section A

OCR Component 1, Section A

HISTORY AND POLITICS

- The first half of the twentieth century was dominated by war – the First World War (1914–18) and the Second World War (1939–45). *An Inspector Calls* is set in 1912 but was written in 1945. *Journey's End* is set during First World War.
- The Russian Revolution of 1917 resulted in the overthrow of the monarchy and the rise of Communism. These events influenced *Animal Farm.*
- In 1928, women over the age of 21 gained the right to vote.
- The world was gripped by economic recession (the Great Depression) throughout the 1930s, which allowed Hitler and his Nazi Party to come to power in Germany.
- After the Second World War, there was a 'Cold War' between Eastern and Western Europe and the USSR (now Russia), which lasted until 1989.
- Several British colonies achieved independence in the post-war period, including India, Pakistan and Nigeria.
- The Northern Ireland conflict ('The Troubles') began in 1968.

TOP TIP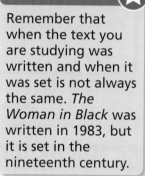

Remember that when the text you are studying was written and when it was set is not always the same. *The Woman in Black* was written in 1983, but it is set in the nineteenth century.

CULTURE AND SOCIETY

- Women were employed to do men's work in both world wars, which meant they had greater freedom than ever before.
- In the post-war period, housing in Britain was poor and food was rationed until 1954. *A Taste of Honey* is set in the late 1950s.
- Britain grew more culturally diverse. *Anita and Me* and *Pigeon English* explore cultural diversity and race.
- The position of women, a **theme** in *The History Boys* and *Oranges Are Not The Only Fruit,* changed and issues such feminism and female sexuality began to be explored.

❶ Note down when the story you are studying was written and the historical period in which it is set. Do some research to find out more about what was happening in both these periods.

THEMES

You can sometimes identify themes by examining the **setting**. For example, the play *A Taste of Honey* was written in the 1950s:

- The story is about a **girl** who gets **pregnant.**
- The story is also about a **girl** whose **mother neglects** her.
- The story is also about a **lonely girl.**
- Its setting is in a **rented attic room in a deprived part of Salford.**

From this information, the themes of the play could be growing up in poverty, mothers, neglect, responsibility, loneliness.

② Complete these statements for the modern text you are studying, then to identify the themes.

- *The story is about …*   - *Its setting is …*

(If you are studying *A Taste of Honey,* think about what else happens in the story and add more statements to the bullet list above.)

APPLYING YOUR SKILLS

❶ Create a 'context' spider diagram for the novel you are studying. An example for *An Inspector Calls* is shown below.

- In the middle, write the name of the text you are studying.
- Around this, make notes about the context of the text.
- Add events and details from the text that relate to the contexts.
- Add your own explanation or ideas about how the contexts and the text are linked.

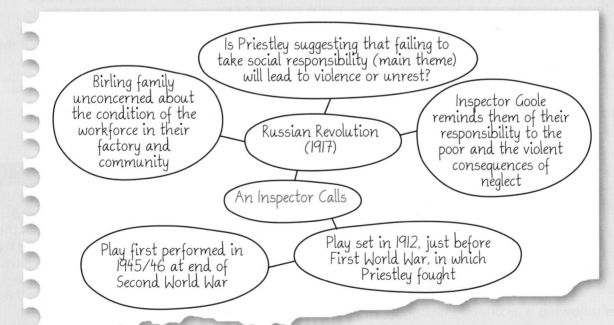

Remember:

- Context can be specific events or wider social beliefs.
- Try to find quotations from the play to add to your diagram to support your points.

STRUCTURE IN MODERN PROSE AND DRAMA

The structure of a play or novel is the way that it is organised and how the events unfold.

BASIC STRUCTURE

In most novels and plays, the narrative is told chronologically. A novel is usually divided into chapters and a play into acts and/or scenes. For example:

- *Lord of the Flies* has twelve chapters, each with a title that gives us a clue to the focus of the chapter (for example, 'Chapter 1 The Sound of the Shell')
- *An Inspector Calls* follows the traditional three-act play, with a series of important events in each act.
- *A Taste of Honey* is a play with two acts, each containing two scenes.

Tension often builds throughout a chapter or an act to a crisis point or revelation, until eventually the **climax** is reached.

❶   Look at the chapter headings or the progress through the scenes in the novel or play you are studying. Make notes on how the plot develops in each chapter or scene.

VARIETIES OF STRUCTURE

Within this broad organisation, a novel or play might include other structural features. For example:

- *The Women in Black* uses **framing**. The first chapter is set in the present time and prepares us for the main ghost story that the narrator recounts from his past.
- **Flashbacks** and **flash-forwards** occur in *Never Let Me Go*. The story is told by the main character, who jumps around chronologically.
- In the musical *Blood Brothers*, the narrator speaks directly to the audience (this is called 'breaking the **fourth wall**') and asks them to consider what they witness. The narrator helps to move the plot along, as do the songs.
- *The Curious Incident of the Dog in the Night-time* was originally a novel. It was adapted into a drama that has a play within a play. The main character, a child, Christopher, has written a play, which the audience is watching and which will be performed in his school.
- **Foreshadowing** is a common technique in which the writer hints at events to come. There are several examples of foreshadowing in *Lord of the Flies*.

A02

AQA Paper 2, Section A

Edexcel Paper 1, Section B

Eduqas Component 2, Section A

OCR Component 1, Section A

★ GET IT RIGHT!

Do not confuse form and structure. 'Form' is the particular type of text the writer chooses to tell their story – for example, short play, **novella**, fable (such as *Animal Farm*). Structure is the organisation and development of the plot within that form.

★ TOP TIP

In the exam, you should be able to quickly recall all the main events and the sequence in which they occur. Make sure you revise the structures of the novel or play you are studying.

EXAM FOCUS

Read how one student describes foreshadowing in *Lord of the Flies.* Some features have been highlighted:

Accurate literary term

Golding uses foreshadowing when Roger bullies the younger Henry. He throws stones towards him, but he leaves 'a space round' him so the stones miss, because despite his bullying, he still obeys some rules of civilised behaviour. This foreshadows the incident in Chapter 11. Roger rolls a boulder downhill and kills Piggy. Golding shows us at this point that all rules have now gone.

Example of foreshadowing

Notes what is foreshadowed in the structure of the text

Effect on reader

APPLYING YOUR SKILLS

❸   Write 100 words on one aspect of the structure of a text you are studying.

Remember:

- Open with information about the basic structure of chapters or acts.
- Identify a structural feature, with an example.
- Explain its effects.

PROGRESS LOG [tick the correct box]   Needs more work ■   Getting there ■   Under control ■

CHARACTERS IN MODERN PROSE AND DRAMA

In modern texts, characters are usually presented realistically and are easily recognisable to a modern audience. However, writers reveal information about characters in many different ways.

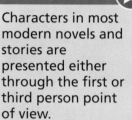

A01

AQA Paper 2, Section A

Edexcel Paper 1, Section B

Eduqas Component 2, Section A

OCR Component 1, Section A

NARRATIVE VOICE

The **narrative voice** is who tells the story. To find out more about them, try to identify the narrator's **tone**. Think about the language they use – is it chatty and informal or formal and unemotional? Is the narrator a child or an adult? Do you trust them? For example:

- In *Anita and Me*, we trust the narrator Meena because although she lies, she tells us that she does.

- In *Pigeon English*, Harrison speaks in **dialect** and we have a strong sense of his presence. The pigeon also speaks, giving us another perspective on aspects of Harrison's life.

FIRST PERSON POINT OF VIEW

If a character tells us a story in the first person, we only see their point of view – about themselves and about other characters. We may learn what other characters think, but this is often through the perspective of the first person narrator.

- In *The Woman in Black*, the narrator is Arthur Kipps, a man haunted by the past. This is a ghost story, and Arthur's personality changes because of his experiences, so can we be sure that what he says is reliable?

- *Anita and Me* and *Never Let Me Go* are written in the first person and, like Arthur Kipps, the narrators are adults looking back on their lives.

- The first person character/narrator, Harrison, in *Pigeon English* is a child, relating events as they happen.

TOP TIP ★

Characters in most modern novels and stories are presented either through the first or third person point of view.

THIRD PERSON POINT OF VIEW

The third person point of view gives the reader access to the thoughts and actions of a wider range of characters.

- *Lord of the Flies* is not told from the perspective of any one character. However, Ralph's perspective is **foregrounded** and he emerges as the main character.

- In *Animal Farm,* a **fable**, the animal characters are used to **satirise** what happened in Russia after the 1917 revolution. The animals represent different types of people. The third person narrator is detached and without opinions, so the animals seem to speak for themselves.

TOP TIP ★

Use the term 'register' when referring to the particular language and vocabulary used by a character related to their class, age or status.

STAGE DIRECTIONS IN DRAMATIC TEXTS

Stage directions can give an impression of a character. In *An Inspector Calls*, the playwright describes Sheila as 'a pretty girl in her early twenties'. Stage directions may even give us an insight into character. Eric, Sheila's brother, is described as 'not quite at ease'.

In drama, characters are revealed through their actions as well as their words. Their actions reflect their **motivation**. For example, in *Blood Brothers*, Mickey agrees to help his brother Sammy take part in a robbery. Mickey has no job and has low self-esteem. He is easily undermined by Sammy, who humiliates him by suggesting he has achieved nothing in life.

❶ Make notes on the important actions the main characters take in a play or novel you are studying. What do these actions tell you about the character?

DIALOGUE

Characters are also revealed through **dialogue** in prose and drama. For example:

Key points and dialogue: *An Inspector Calls*	What it tells us about the characters	
	Mr Birling	**Inspector Goole**
Mr Birling has been mayor and is still a magistrate. He says angrily: *'I'm a public man.'* (Act II) Inspector Goole, who has come to question him, replies: *'Public men have responsibilities as well as privileges.'*	Priestley presents him as self-important – a man who believes he has standing in the community.	He is not in awe of Mr Birling, but is ready to tell him what he thinks. The emphasis the Inspector gives to 'responsibilities' echoes one of Priestley's major themes.

APPLYING YOUR SKILLS

❷ Draw a table like the one above. Choose a short dialogue between two characters in the modern text you are studying and make notes on what it tells you about them.

Remember:

- Note any effects created by the writer.

- Consider what the character's words say about them but also what they say about each other.

PROGRESS CHECK FOR CHAPTER 10

GOOD PROGRESS

I can:

- Understand and refer to the context in which the text was written ☐
- Understand the plot in the text I am studying and refer to key events ☐
- Identify the themes in the texts ☐
- Understand how the characters are presented ☐

EXCELLENT PROGRESS

I can:

- Analyse in depth the context in which the text was written, plots and key events ☐
- Analyse several themes and how characters behave and develop ☐

CHAPTER 11: Poetry

POETRY AND CONTEXT

In the exam, you will be expected to link one or more anthology poems to their contexts. This means exploring links between the time and place in which it was written, and the ideas and language of the text. The sections below outline some key contextual ideas for the different styles of poetry you may have studied.

A03

AQA Paper 2, Section B

Edexcel Paper 2, Section B, Part 1

Eduqas Component 1, Section B

OCR Component 2, Section A

THE ROMANTICS

Poets such as Blake, Wordsworth, Keats, Byron and Shelley are referred to as the Romantics. Romanticism began in the late-eighteenth century and reached its height in the early- to mid-nineteenth century. The literary movement arose partly as a reaction to existing attitudes that favoured logic and reason over feeling. It was also a reaction to the Industrial Revolution, which had resulted in huge economic and social changes. In 'London', for example, William Blake draws attention to the dire conditions and poverty in the city.

GOTHIC POETRY

The Gothic movement grew out of Romanticism in the late-eighteenth century. It was also concerned with feeling, but of a more extreme kind, often referred to as Gothic horror.

The **settings** in Gothic poetry are typically wild landscapes, and the poems often reference crime, insanity or the supernatural. Characters follow their deepest desires. For example, Browning's 'Porphyria's Lover' has links to the Victorian Gothic in its concern with murder, insanity and isolation.

THE NATURAL WORLD

Nature is portrayed in a wide variety of ways, and reflects a range of attitudes and perspectives. For example, its glory is evoked in Byron's 'She Walks in Beauty' and its necessity for human well-being in the poem 'Leisure' by W. H. Davies. However, in Ted Hughes' 'Hawk Roosting', the hawk has no sense of right or wrong – it is a bird perfected by nature that practises 'perfect kills'. Seamus Heaney's 'Death of a Naturalist' charts a child's fascination with frogspawn, but also his fear of 'the great slime kings' that emerge.

WAR

A number of real wars provide the backdrop for poems. Some, such as Wilfred Owen's 'Dulce et Decorum Est' and 'Anthem for Doomed Youth' explore issues of suffering and blame as a result of the First World War. 'Vergissmeinnicht' ('Forget-Me-Not'), by Keith Douglas, is an intensely personal poem commenting on the Second World War.

Even poems whose main focus is not war may draw on more general ideas about war. In Vernon Scannell's 'Nettles', many images of the nettles ('*a regiment of spite*', '*a fierce parade*') suggest the poet's deep connection to the Second World War.

DIVERSE CULTURES AND GENDER

Many of the poems you will study are about individual experiences, but some may have clear links to a cultural or political context.

- Daljit Nagra's 'Singh Song!' uses the **dialect** of English speakers whose first language is Punjabi.
- 'Kamikaze' by Beatrice Garland is about a Japanese pilot who does not carry out his suicide mission.
- John Agard's 'Checking Out Me History' is a political poem, commenting on the lack of black history taught to students.
- The picture painted of the speaker in Elizabeth Barrett Browning's 'Sonnet 29 – I think of thee!' is submissive, but it subscribed to the Victorian view that a woman's place was under the protection of a man.
- In the nineteenth-century poem 'The Farmer's Bride' by Charlotte Mew, a modern reader would be struck by the control exercised by the farmer over his young wife, when he 'turns the key upon her' and locks her up.

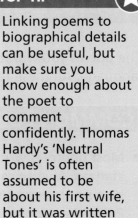

TOP TIP

Linking poems to biographical details can be useful, but make sure you know enough about the poet to comment confidently. Thomas Hardy's 'Neutral Tones' is often assumed to be about his first wife, but it was written long before he met her.

EXAM FOCUS

Read this part of a successful response to a question about language in 'Before You Were Mine' by Carol Ann Duffy. Some of its features have been highlighted:

The references to Edinburgh and Glasgow and the Scottish names, 'McGeeney' and 'Duff' set the poem in Scotland. Colloquialisms, such as 'pals' and 'hiding' (meaning 'a beating'), also have an effect. They reinforce the image of Scottish urban life as the young women joke, 'shrieking' with laughter on 'the pavement'.

Specific references to place

Notes how everyday language can also affect the reader's perception of context

APPLYING YOUR SKILLS

❶ Look closely at the poems in your anthology and try to find words and images that:
- Suggest a specific place or time
- Suggest a particular historical period or cultural context

❷ Choose a poem and write fifty words about its context.

Remember:

- Look for references to place.
- Link language to context if you can.

POETIC LANGUAGE, FORM AND STRUCTURE

The poems you will study have a wide range of forms, structure and language. All these features are used to create a variety of effects.

COMMON POETIC FEATURES

- Most poetry is written in lines and some are arranged in verses or **stanzas**. A verse can refer to lines of any number and a whole poem can be a single verse. A stanza has a specific pattern of lines. For example, a Petrarchan **sonnet** such as Elizabeth Barrett Browning's 'Sonnet 43' has an octave and a sestet (two stanzas). A **ballad** has four lines in a stanza called a quatrain.

- A **caesura** is a pause in a line of poetry. In Keats's celebratory poem 'To Autumn' a caesura is used in the line 'With a sweet kernal, to set budding more,'. This halt comes after a series of fast-paced images that appeal to the sense of taste and touch and helps to emphasise nature's lush harvest.

- An **enjambment** continues the words from one line to another, carrying the thought with it. In Simon Armitage's 'Mother Any Distance', a tape measure is the central metaphor. The effect of the frequent enjambment is to suggest that the tape measure is unreeling behind the speaker.

- Poems often contain words or images that can be grouped together. In Owen Sheers's 'Winter Swans', there are several images of the swans, from their feathers like icebergs, to the boat-like quality of their bodies and fragile whiteness. In Percy Shelley's 'Ozymandias', the hard 'k' sound often occurs as **alliteration** or at the end or middle of words and seems to reflect the destruction of Ozymandias, his statue and empire.

A02

AQA Paper 2, Section B

Edexcel Paper 2, Section B, Part 1

Eduqas Component 1, Section B

OCR Component 2, Section A

TOP TIP ★

When examining the structure of a poem, try to trace the pattern and find a turning point when it starts moving towards a resolution. Remember that sometimes a poem seems to have no obvious resolution and returns to the beginning (for example, Byron's 'When We Two Parted').

RHYME, RHYTHM AND CADENCE

Rhythm always forms the movement of the poem, as does **cadence** and **metre**. The rhythm can be strong (as in Tennyson's 'Charge of the Light Brigade' with its rushing beat that mirrors the soldiers' charge):

> *Half a league, half a league,*
> *Half a league onward,*

Or it can be gentle or even monotonous as in Hardy's 'Neutral Tones', in which the speaker's despair cannot be lifted, for example:

> *The smile on your mouth was the deadest thing*
> *Alive enough to have strength to die*

Rhyme usually works with rhythm, so a regular rhyme scheme with full rhymes – such as 'tears' and 'hears' – often stresses the rhythm. Half-rhyme, (such as 'fold' and 'yield') is usually found with a less accented rhythm. This can make the language sound more natural, or create slight uncertainty, as if grasping for meaning.

FORM AND STRUCTURE

The form and structure of a poem are similar, but there are some subtle differences.

FORM

What is form?	How the poem is presented, or set out on the page (as a shape poem is). Some poems (such as sonnets) follow specific conventions. Others have no regular rhythm or obvious design (free verse).
Example	The form of Robert Browning's 'My Last Duchess' is a dramatic **monologue**, a first-person narrative poem in which the poet chooses a persona (in this case the duke) as the speaker to tell the tale.
Effect	To create a convincing and dramatic portrait of a character/speaker who holds centre stage as he addresses both another character and the reader. As the tale unfolds, the form helps to give maximum impact to the duke's sinister deeds.

STRUCTURE

What is structure?	The structure refers to the underlying patterns in a poem and how these develop.
Example	In Cecil Day Lewis's 'Walking Away', the speaker begins by recalling parting from his small son when he began school. He describes the scene, but cannot quite express the feeling of loss. As he reflects and the poem develops, he finds the words he needs.
Effect	The poem's development reveals how the difficulty is resolved in the speaker's mind: having weighed his feelings against the need for children to leave home to achieve independence, his parental love is revealed in the final words – 'the letting go'.

APPLYING YOUR SKILLS

❶ Choose a poem from your anthology and describe its form in approximately fifty words.

Remember:

- Name the form (if the poem has a specific one).
- Show the effect of the form – what it helps the poet to do in the poem.

UNSEEN POETRY

You will be given poems you have not studied before (unseen poems) printed on the exam papers. The questions will focus on how the poet presents certain feelings or ideas. The stages below explain how to approach these questions.

A01 A02

AQA Paper 2, Section C

Edexcel Paper 2, Section B, Part 2

Eduqas Component 1, Section C

OCR Component 2, Section A

STAGE 1: READ THE POEM AND THE QUESTION

- First read the poem through and try to understand what it is broadly about (such as conflict, relationships or a poem related to time and place).
- Read the poem again, keeping the exam question in mind.
- Reread any part of the poem (for example, a particular phrase, line or verse) if you are uncertain about its meaning. Try to understand it in relation to what the poem is broadly about.

STAGE 2: MAKE NOTES AND ANNOTATIONS ON THE PAGE

- Underline key words, phrases or lines in the poem, particularly in relation to the focus of the task.
- Identify the main **theme** or themes.
- Underline any images or techniques that might help you answer the question.
- Note any special features (layout or repeating patterns, such as recurring words or sounds) that enhance the meaning in relation to the question.
- Note what form (type of poem) it is where possible (such as **sonnet**, free verse) and whether this aids understanding (is there a change in **tone** or perspective after the first eight lines, as in a sonnet?)
- Note down some short questions or notes to help you. For example: *'alliteration stresses the stormy sea?'* or *'Image of a lost love, means honesty is important.'*

STAGE 3: WRITE YOUR RESPONSE

Organise your answer into six or seven paragraphs, referring to the main points from your annotations.

- Discuss (briefly) what happens in the poem; the 'story' and the context (setting, location, etc.) (Introduction).
- Explain what the speaker's feelings are in relation to the focus/theme of the question.
- Discuss images in the poem that relate to the focus or theme of the question.
- Describe the techniques the poet uses to enhance or elaborate on the key ideas, theme or focus of the question.
- Discuss the form and structure of the poem, and the effect each of these has on the reader.

- Sum up (concisely) what ideas the poet presents to the reader. (Conclusion)

For example, you might be asked:

> *How does the poet present the speaker's feelings about love and marriage in the poem?*

This suggests you should be looking for:

- What **sort of 'story'** the poet tells about love and marriage
- The **viewpoint** or **emotions** that suggest an attitude to love and marriage
- Positive or negative language or descriptions
- The effect of the poet's choices

> **GET IT RIGHT!**
>
> Remember that the poet is not necessarily speaking about their own feelings or situation in a poem, so it is safer to refer to 'the speaker'.

Study the poem 'Postponement' below, and the annotations written in response to the question above:

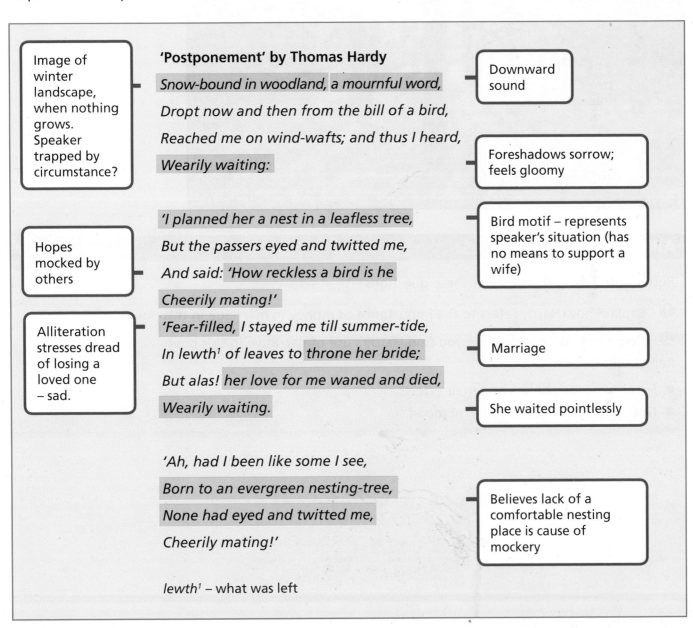

Image of winter landscape, when nothing grows. Speaker trapped by circumstance?	Downward sound
	Foreshadows sorrow; feels gloomy
Hopes mocked by others	Bird motif – represents speaker's situation (has no means to support a wife)
Alliteration stresses dread of losing a loved one – sad.	Marriage
	She waited pointlessly
	Believes lack of a comfortable nesting place is cause of mockery

'Postponement' by Thomas Hardy

Snow-bound in woodland, a mournful word,

Dropt now and then from the bill of a bird,

Reached me on wind-wafts; and thus I heard,

Wearily waiting:

'I planned her a nest in a leafless tree,

But the passers eyed and twitted me,

And said: 'How reckless a bird is he

Cheerily mating!'

'Fear-filled, I stayed me till summer-tide,

In lewth[1] of leaves to throne her bride;

But alas! her love for me waned and died,

Wearily waiting.

'Ah, had I been like some I see,

Born to an evergreen nesting-tree,

None had eyed and twitted me,

Cheerily mating!'

lewth[1] – what was left

Story: The speaker is trapped in a wood at winter and waits for help to come. He hears a bird singing and imagines his own situation is like the bird's.

Overall picture:

- The speaker's situation is represented by the bird **motif**.
- The speaker has no financial means to keep a wife. Born into a low social class, as represented by the bare tree.

APPLYING YOUR SKILLS

Reread the poem, then answer these questions.

❶   Explain how Hardy refers to the importance of money in marriage in this poem.

❷   Comment on how effective you find Hardy's use of narrative in this poem.

Remember:

- Focus on word choices and their effects.
- Notice the effects of rhythm on mood.

COMPARING UNSEEN POEMS

HOW CAN YOU COMPARE TWO POEMS?

You will be asked to compare two poems (one or both 'unseen'). The questions will focus on the similarities and differences between the poems, how the poets present their ideas and the effects of the language they use.

For example, you might be asked a question similar to this:

> *Read the two poems below and answer the question.*
>
> *Compare how the poets present ideas about the natural world in 'The Eagle' and 'I think I could turn and live with animals'.*
>
> *You should compare:*
>
> - *What the poems are about and the ideas in the poems*
> - *The words and images and their effects*
> - *The **tone** or mood*
> - *The poems' form and structure*
> - *Your feelings about the poems*
>
> *Use evidence from the poems to support what you say.*

AQA Paper 2, Section C

Edexcel Paper 2, Section B, Part 2

Eduqas Component 1, Section C

OCR Component 2, Section A

WHAT SHOULD YOU DO IN THE EXAM?

- First, underline the key words in the question.
- Read the second poem through once, without making notes but with the focus of the task in the back of your mind.
- Read it again, making notes, annotations and highlights around it, focusing on the similarities and differences between the two poems.
- Write your response.

Look at these two poems and the notes on each of them.

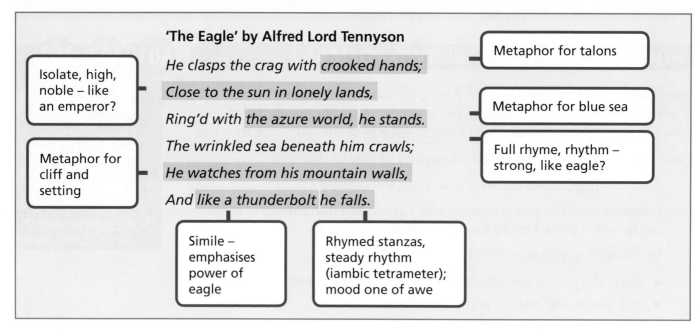

'The Eagle' by Alfred Lord Tennyson

He clasps the crag with crooked hands; — Metaphor for talons

Close to the sun in lonely lands,

Ring'd with the azure world, he stands. — Metaphor for blue sea

Isolate, high, noble – like an emperor?

Metaphor for cliff and setting

The wrinkled sea beneath him crawls; — Full rhyme, rhythm – strong, like eagle?

He watches from his mountain walls,

And like a thunderbolt he falls.

Simile – emphasises power of eagle

Rhymed stanzas, steady rhythm (iambic tetrameter); mood one of awe

Story: Speaker watches an eagle on a mountain swoop down to the sea.

Point of view: In awe for the eagle's power.

Form: Two tercets.

Structure: As though we are observing the eagle. We look up at it on its crag then our eye follows its swooping down to the see, like a camera following the eagle.

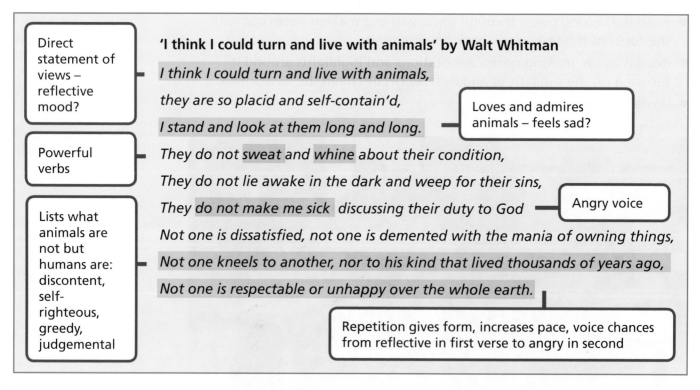

'I think I could turn and live with animals' by Walt Whitman

I think I could turn and live with animals,

they are so placid and self-contain'd,

I stand and look at them long and long. — Loves and admires animals – feels sad?

Direct statement of views – reflective mood?

Powerful verbs

They do not sweat and whine about their condition,

They do not lie awake in the dark and weep for their sins,

They do not make me sick discussing their duty to God — Angry voice

Lists what animals are not but humans are: discontent, self-righteous, greedy, judgemental

Not one is dissatisfied, not one is demented with the mania of owning things,

Not one kneels to another, nor to his kind that lived thousands of years ago,

Not one is respectable or unhappy over the whole earth.

Repetition gives form, increases pace, voice chances from reflective in first verse to angry in second

Story: Speaker watches animals and thinks how different they are from humans.

Point of view: Seems to envy the animals' contentment and prefer them to humans.

Form: Free verse. **Monologue?**

Structure: As though the speaker is talking to himself and we are listening in.

The main similarities are that both poems are about creatures in the natural world. The creatures are 'complete' in themselves. Both speakers admire them. The main differences you might note in a comparison include:

- **First poem:** Eagle majestic and proud, isolated. Speaker feels awe. Vivid imagery. Strong regular rhythm, full rhyme. Traditional form.
- **Second poem:** 'Animals' peaceful, have simplicity. Speaker feels unhappy with life. Animals offer comfort. Simple images, direct language, powerful verbs used to express unhappiness and discontent. Free verse poem.

APPLYING YOUR SKILLS

1 Use the annotated poems and guidance to write a full comparison between these two poems.

Remember:

- Focus on their similarities **and** differences.
- Consider features such as story, form, structure and point of view.

PROGRESS CHECK FOR CHAPTER 11

GOOD PROGRESS

I can:

- Explain the methods poets use and understand the context of the poem. ☐
- Comment on an 'unseen' poem clearly, referring to a range of techniques ☐
- Explain the similarities and differences between two poems ☐

EXCELLENT PROGRESS

I can:

- Analyse the methods poets use and the context of a poem ☐
- Interpret an 'unseen' poem, selecting apt and precise evidence and referring to a wide range of techniques ☐
- Make a convincing comparison and well-judged analysis between two poems ☐

CHAPTER 12: GSCE English Literature practice papers

SHAKESPEARE QUESTIONS

The exact wording may differ, but answering the question for your Shakespeare set text will help you prepare for this part of the exam.

AQA Paper 1, Section A

Edexcel Paper 1, Section A

Eduqas Component 1, Section A

OCR Component 2, Section B

MACBETH

Read *Macbeth* Act III Scene 4, from 'Avaunt! and quit my sight!' to 'I am a man again. Pray you, sit still', then answer the question that follows.

At this point in the play Macbeth and his wife are holding a banquet. Macbeth is speaking to the ghost of Banquo.

Starting with this section, explore how Shakespeare presents Macbeth's strengths and weaknesses.

Write about:

- How Shakespeare presents Macbeth in this speech
- How Shakespeare presents Macbeth in the play as a whole

ROMEO AND JULIET

Read *Romeo and Juliet* Act IV Scene 3, from 'Alack, alack, is it not like ...' to the end of the scene, and then answer the question that follows.

At this point in the play Juliet is alone in the Capulet vault.

Starting with this section, explore how Shakespeare engages our sympathies with Juliet.

Write about:

- How Shakespeare presents Juliet in this speech
- How Shakespeare presents Juliet in the play as a whole

THE TEMPEST

Read *The Tempest* Act I Scene 2, from Prospero's words 'Thou most lying slave ...' to 'Who hadst deserved more than a prison', and then answer the question that follows.

At this point in the play Prospero and Miranda are outside Caliban's cave. Prospero is addressing Caliban.

Starting with this conversation, explain how far you think Shakespeare presents Prospero as using his power for the good.

Write about:

- How Shakespeare presents Prospero at this point in the play
- How Shakespeare presents Prospero in the play as a whole

SHAKESPEARE QUESTIONS

THE MERCHANT OF VENICE

> Read *The Merchant of Venice* Act III Scene 1, from Salarino's words 'Why, I am sure, if he forfeit ...' to Shylock 'I will better the instruction', and then answer the question that follows.

At this point in the play Shylock is discussing his contract with Antonio.

Starting with this conversation, explore how Shakespeare presents the theme of revenge.

Write about:

- How Shakespeare presents the theme of revenge at this point in the play
- How Shakespeare presents the theme in the play as a whole

AQA Paper 1,
Section A

Edexcel Paper 1,
Section A

Eduqas
Component 1,
Section A

OCR Component 2,
Section B

MUCH ADO ABOUT NOTHING

> Read *Much Ado About Nothing* Act I Scene 1, from Beatrice's words 'I wonder that you will still be talking' to 'You always end with a jade's trick: I know you of old', and then answer the question that follows.

At this point in the play Beatrice and Benedick have just met up again after some time.

Starting with this conversation, explain how far you think Shakespeare presents Beatrice and Benedick as suitable marriage partners for each other.

Write about:

- How Shakespeare presents the two characters at this point in the play
- How Shakespeare presents them in the play as a whole

JULIUS CAESAR

> Read *Julius Caesar* Act I Scene 2, from Cassius's words 'Why, man, he doth bestride ...' to 'But it was famed with more than with one man?', and then answer the question that follows.

At this point in the play Cassius is speaking to Brutus against Caesar's growing power.

Starting with this speech, explore how Shakespeare presents the theme of fate and free will.

Write about:

- How Shakespeare presents the them of fate in this conversation
- How Shakespeare presents the theme in the play as a whole

SHAKESPEARE QUESTIONS

HENRY V

> Read *Henry V* Act IV Scene 1, from the King's words 'I, or more then we should seek after; for we know enough,' to 'he let him outlive that day, to see his Greatness, and to teach others how they should prepare', then answer the questions below.

AQA Paper 1, Section A

Edexcel Paper 1, Section A

Eduqas Component 1, Section A

OCR Component 2, Section B

a) Look at how the characters speak and behave here. How do you think an audience might respond to this part of the play? Refer closely to details from the extract to support your answer.

b) Write about times in the play when the audience may feel Henry is a man as well as a king. Give reasons for what you say.

OTHELLO

> Read Act IV Scene 3, from Desdemona's words 'Pr'ythee unpin me, – have grace and favour in them' to '*Emilia*: It is the wind', then answer the questions below.

a) How does Shakespeare create mood and atmosphere for an audience here? Refer closely to details from the extract to support your answer.

b) How does Shakespeare present relationships between men and women in the play?

TWELFTH NIGHT

> Read Act I Scene 1, from 'If music be the food of love, play on' to 'That it alone is high-fantastical', then answer the questions below.

a) Explore how Shakespeare presents Orsino's feelings in this extract. Refer closely to the extract in your answer.

b) In this extract, Orsino speaks about the kind of love he feels. Explain the importance of love elsewhere in the play.

In your answer you must consider:

- The different kinds of love presented and by whom
- The reason Orsino's love changes in the play

You should refer to the context of the play in your answer.

NINETEENTH-CENTURY NOVEL QUESTIONS

The exact wording of your exam question may differ, but answering the question for your nineteenth-century novel below will help you prepare for this part of the exam.

> AQA Paper 1,
> Section B
>
> Edexcel Paper 2,
> Section A
>
> Eduqas
> Component 2,
> Section B
>
> OCR Component 1,
> Section B

ROBERT LOUIS STEVENSON: *THE STRANGE CASE OF DR JEKYLL AND MR HYDE*

> Read Chapter 3, from 'The large handsome face of Dr Jekyll ...' to the end of the paragraph beginning 'Well, but since we have touched upon this business ...', and then answer the question that follows.

In this extract, Mr Utterson has just raised the subject of Jekyll's will, and offered to help him.

Starting with this extract, how far does Stevenson encourage readers to sympathise with Dr Jekyll?

Write about:

- How Stevenson presents Dr Jekyll in this extract
- How far Stevenson presents Dr Jekyll as someone we might sympathise with in the novella as a whole

CHARLES DICKENS: *A CHRISTMAS CAROL*

> Read Chapter 4, from 'Still the Ghost pointed downward ...' to the end of the chapter, and then answer the question that follows.

In this extract, Scrooge is with the Ghost of Christmas Yet To Come.

Starting with this extract, explore how Dickens presents the process of Scrooge's transformation as a character.

Write about:

- How Dickens presents Scrooge changing in this extract
- How Dickens presents Scrooge changing in the novella as a whole

CHARLES DICKENS: *GREAT EXPECTATIONS*

> Read Chapter 54, from 'You have a returned Transport there,' to the end of the paragraph beginning 'It was but for an instant ...', and then answer the question that follows.

In this extract, Pip is in a rowing boat on the Thames, trying to get Magwitch on to a steamer.

Starting with this extract, explore how Dickens creates suspense and drama.

Write about:

- How Dickens creates suspense and drama in this extract
- How Dickens creates suspense and drama in the novel as a whole

NINETEENTH-CENTURY NOVEL QUESTIONS

CHARLOTTE BRONTË: *JANE EYRE*

> Read Chapter 4, from 'Psalms are not interesting,' to the end of the paragraph beginning 'Deceit is, indeed, a sad fault in a child', and then answer the question that follows.

AQA Paper 1, Section B

Edexcel Paper 2, Section A

Eduqas Component 2, Section B

OCR Component 1, Section B

In this extract, Jane is being questioned by Mr Brocklehurst at Lowood School.

Starting with this extract, explore how Brontë presents the difficulties and challenges that Jane faces.

Write about:

- How Brontë presents Jane's difficulties in this extract
- How Brontë presents the difficulties and challenges that Jane faces in the novel as a whole

MARY SHELLEY: *FRANKENSTEIN*

> Read Chapter 15, from 'I continued to wind among the paths of the wood' to the end of the paragraph beginning 'This was then the reward of my benevolence!', and then answer the question that follows.

In this extract, the Creature is telling Victor Frankenstein about the life he has lived so far.

Starting with this extract, explore how far Shelley presents the Creature as a victim.

Write about:

- How Shelley presents the Creature as a victim in this extract
- How Shelley presents the Creature in the novel as a whole

JANE AUSTEN: *PRIDE AND PREJUDICE*

> Read Chapter 22, from 'Why should you be surprised, my dear Eliza?' to the end of the chapter, and then answer the question that follows.

In this extract, Charlotte Lucas has just told Elizabeth that she is engaged to Mr Collins.

Starting with this extract, explore how Austen presents attitudes towards love and marriage.

Write about:

- How Austen presents attitudes towards love and marriage in this extract
- How Austen presents attitudes towards love and marriage in the novel as a whole

NINETEENTH-CENTURY NOVEL QUESTIONS

SIR ARTHUR CONAN DOYLE: *THE SIGN OF THE FOUR*

> AQA Paper 1, Section B
> Edexcel Paper 2, Section A
> Eduqas Component 2, Section B
> OCR Component 1, Section B

> Read from the start of Chapter 4 ('We followed the Indian down ...') to 'This is Mr Sherlock Holmes, and this is Dr Watson', and then answer the question that follows.

Starting with this extract, explore how Conan Doyle presents Thaddeus Sholto as an unusual and exotic character:

Write about:

- How Conan Doyle presents Thaddeus Sholto in this extract
- How Conan Doyle presents Thaddeus Sholto in the novel as a whole

H. G. WELLS: *WAR OF THE WORLDS*

> Read Chapter 2 from Book 2, from 'The fifth cylinder must have fallen ...' to '... scarcely realise that living quality'.

Write about the theme of chaos and order in the novel. In your response you should:

- Refer to the extract and the novel as a whole
- Show your understanding of characters and events in the novel
- Refer to the contexts of the novel

GEORGE ELIOT: *SILAS MARNER*

> Read Chapter III, from 'Godfrey bit his lips and clenched his fist' to 'I'll bid you good-bye, though I'm sorry to part.'

Write about the character of Godfrey Cass in the novel and how he changes. In your response you should:

- Refer to the extract and the novel as a whole
- Show your understanding of characters and events in the novel
- Refer to the contexts of the novel

MODERN PROSE AND DRAMA QUESTIONS

The exact wording of your exam question may differ, but answering the question for your modern prose and drama set text below will help you prepare for this part of the exam.

AQA Paper 2, Section A

Edexcel Paper 1, Section B

Eduqas Component 2, Section A

OCR Component 1, Section A

J. B. PRIESTLEY: *AN INSPECTOR CALLS*

What is the role of the Inspector in *An Inspector Calls*?

Write about:

- How the Inspector behaves towards the other characters
- How Priestley presents the Inspector by the ways he writes

WILLY RUSSELL: *BLOOD BROTHERS*

How and why does Russell contrast the lives and characters of Mickey and Edward?

Write about:

- How Russell presents Mickey and Edward
- What ideas Russell explores by comparing these characters

ALAN BENNETT: *THE HISTORY BOYS*

How does Bennett use the characters Hector and Irwin to explore ideas about education?

Write about:

- How Bennett presents the characters of Hector and Irwin
- How Bennett uses Hector and Irwin to explore ideas about education

DENNIS KELLY: *DNA*

How does Kelly explore the theme of bullying?

Write about:

- How Kelly presents characters who are bullied, or who bully others
- How Kelly uses these characters to explore ideas about bullying

SIMON STEPHENS: *THE CURIOUS INCIDENT OF THE DOG IN THE NIGHT-TIME*

How does Stephens present the ways Christopher relates to other people?

Write about:

- How Christopher relates to other people
- How Stephens presents Christopher's relationships

MODERN PROSE AND DRAMA QUESTIONS

SHELAGH DELANEY: *A TASTE OF HONEY*

How does Delaney explore the theme of love and marriage?

Write about:

- Attitudes towards love and marriage in the play
- How Delaney presents love and marriage by the way she writes

> AQA Paper 2, Section A
>
> Edexcel Paper 1, Section B
>
> Eduqas Component 2, Section A
>
> OCR Component 1, Section A

WILLIAM GOLDING: *LORD OF THE FLIES*

Compare the leadership styles of Ralph and Jack.

Write about:

- How Golding presents the characters of Ralph and Jack
- How Golding explores ideas about leadership in the way he writes about Ralph and Jack

AQA ANTHOLOGY: *TELLING TALES*

How do writers present relationships between adults and children in 'Odour of Chrysanthemums' and one other story from the collection?

Write about:

- Some of the ideas about adult–child relationships presented in the stories
- How the writers present these ideas by the way they write

GEORGE ORWELL: *ANIMAL FARM*

How does Orwell use characters to explore ideas about the abuse of power?

Write about:

- How some characters abuse power
- How Orwell presents the abuse of power by the way he writes

KAZUO ISHIGURO: *NEVER LET ME GO*

How does Ishiguro present attitudes towards duty and obedience?

Write about:

- How Ishiguro uses different characters to present ideas about duty and obedience
- How Ishiguro presents these ideas by the ways he writes

MODERN PROSE AND DRAMA QUESTIONS

MEERA SYAL: *ANITA AND ME*

How does Syal present the ways in which Meena changes during the course of the novel?

Write about:

- How Syal presents Meena's development as a character
- How Meena's development is influenced by other characters, and by events

> AQA Paper 2, Section A
> Edexcel Paper 1, Section B
> Eduqas Component 2, Section A
> OCR Component 1, Section A

STEPHEN KELMAN: *PIGEON ENGLISH*

How does Kelman present ideas about immigration and culture?

Write about:

- What we learn about how Harrison adapts to life in London
- How Kelman presents Harrison's experience of immigration by the ways he writes

HAROLD BRIGHOUSE: *HOBSON'S CHOICE*

Maggie: 'If you're dealing husbands around, don't I get one?'

Explore Maggie's attitude to marriage in *Hobson's Choice.* You must refer to the context of the play in your answer.

R. C. SHERRIFF: *JOURNEY'S END*

Raleigh: 'the finest officer in the battalion, and the men simply love him'.

Explore the theme of heroism in *Journey's End.* You must refer to the context of the play in your answer.

CHARLOTTE KEATLEY: MY MOTHER SAID I NEVER SHOULD

Read Act 3 Scene 5 from Jackie's words 'Rosie...? *Silence* Hold this for as long as possible ...' and 'If you were really my Mum ...' to 'Rosie: ... Have them all. Have them all.'

Explore how Rosie responds to Jackie in this scene and why.

Choose one other moment in *My Mother Said I Never Should* that reveals how Rosie struggles in her relationships with Jackie and Margaret.

MODERN PROSE AND DRAMA QUESTIONS

SUSAN HILL: *THE WOMAN IN BLACK*

Read the chapter 'Across the Causeway', from 'In the greyness of the fading light,' to 'I would drop dead on that wretched patch of ground'.

Write about how the writer creates a mood of anxiety and fear in the novel. In your response you should:

- Refer to the extract and the novel as a whole
- Show your understanding of characters and events in the novel

> AQA Paper 2, Section A
> Edexcel Paper 1, Section B
> Eduqas Component 2, Section A
> OCR Component 1, Section A

JEANETTE WINTERSON: *ORANGES ARE NOT THE ONLY FRUIT*

Read the chapter Genesis, from 'My mother out walking that night dreamed a dream …' to 'You can change the world'.

Write about Jeanette's journey from her religious beginnings and how this changes in the novel. In your response you should:

- Refer to the extract and the novel as a whole
- Show your understanding of characters and events in the novel

POETRY QUESTIONS

The exact wording of your exam question may differ, but answering the question for your poetry anthology below will help you prepare for this part of the exam.

AQA Paper 2, Section B

Edexcel Paper 2, Section B, Part 1

Eduqas Component 1, Section B

OCR Component 2, Section A

AQA ANTHOLOGY

Either

Compare how poets present relationships between children and their parents in 'Mother Any Distance' and one other poem from the 'Love and relationships' cluster.

Or

Compare how poets present ideas about conflict in 'Bayonet Charge' and one other poem from the 'Power and conflict' cluster.

EDEXCEL ANTHOLOGY

Either

Read 'Valentine' by Carol Ann Duffy. Choose one other poem from the 'Relationships' anthology. Compare how attitudes to love are presented in the two poems.

Or

Read 'The Charge of the light Brigade' by Alfred Lord Tennyson. Choose one other poem from the 'Conflict' anthology. Compare how tension is presented in the two poems.

Or

Read 'Nothing's Changed' by Tatamkhulu Afrika. Choose one other poem from the 'Time and place' anthology. Compare how the passing of time is presented in the two poems.

EDUQAS ANTHOLOGY

Read 'Dulce et Decorum Est' by Wilfred Owen, then answer both parts of the question:

a) Write about the ways in which Owen presents war in this poem.

b) Choose one other poem from the anthology in which the poet also writes about war. Compare the presentation of war in your chosen poem to the presentation of war in 'Dulce et Decorum Est'.

In your answer to part b) you should compare:

● The content and structure of the poems – what they are about and how they are organised

● How the writers create effects, using appropriate terminology where relevant

● The contexts of the poems, and how these may have influenced the ideas in them

POETRY QUESTIONS

OCR ANTHOLOGY

AQA Paper 2, Section B

Edexcel Paper 2, Section B, Part 1

Eduqas Component 1, Section B

OCR Component 2, Section A

Either

Love and Relationships

Read 'Love and Friendship' by Emily Brontë and 'Friendship after Love' by Ella Wheeler Wilcox. Then answer both parts of the question.

a) Compare how the speakers in these poems express feelings about different kinds of love.

b) Explore in detail one other poem from your anthology, which expresses feelings about love of some kind.

Or

Conflict

Read 'The Man he Killed' by Thomas Hardy and 'The Volunteer' by Herbert Asquith. Then answer both parts of the question:

a) Compare how the speakers in these poems express feelings about war.

b) Explore in detail one other poem from your anthology that expresses feelings about war.

Or

Youth and Age

Read 'Cold Knap Lake' by Gillian Clarke and 'On my First Son' by Ben Jonson. Then answer both parts of the question.

a) Compare how the speakers in these poems explore feelings about children and childhood.

b) Explore in detail one other poem from your anthology that expresses feelings about children and childhood.

CHAPTER 1

GRAMMATICAL TERMS [p. 6]

1 *We were all sitting on the harbour wall, watching the boats sail by, when suddenly a cry went up. 'Man overboard!', someone called. There was a terrific crack and I saw a huge wooden mast fall from a yacht. It crashed into the sea near where a man in a yellow lifejacket was floundering around. I called out in disbelief, 'That's my dad!'*

2

Nouns		Pronouns	Verbs		Adjectives
common	proper		auxiliary	main	
hat	London	I	have	see	big
book	**Saturday**	who	**will**	**book**	**happy**
table	**Italy**	**his**	**may**	**go**	**responsible**
actor	**April**	**himself**		**make**	**tall**
		you		**run**	
		me			

Adverbs	Determiners	Prepositions	Conjunctions	
			coordinating	subordinating
quickly	the	of	or	because
together	**his**	**to**	**and**	**while**
sharply	**my/your**	**on**	**but**	**although**
soon	**a/an**	**in**		**if**

3 For example: 'university teacher', 'cream tea'.

4 *Uncle Ray's rabbit in the hutch* **is snoring.**

The small boy *was* ***a lost and bewildered newcomer.***

5 *She's annoyed* **because of the holiday cancellation.** (adverbial – shows the relationship between 'annoyed' and 'cancellation').

It seems the robin **on the windowsill** *visits daily.* (adjectival – shows the relationship between the robin and the windowsill).

SENTENCE CONSTRUCTION AND CLAUSES [p. 8]

1 Simple sentence; minor sentence; compound sentence

2 'because they need money'; 'in order to cultivate the coca plant'; 'While tribespeople use rainforest resources'

3 Examples:

Jake always ate well **because** *he was a great chef,* **who** *cooked at home.*

Although *Sian had a strong voice, she didn't practise enough* **because** *she had too much to do.*

Having *finished work, Kai,* **who** *loved sky-diving, had training* **and** *practised his skills.*

SENTENCE TYPES AND TENSES [p. 10]

1 Suggested starters: 'The geese are …'; 'The book of rules is …'; 'Kate or Jack is …'; 'Either of the acrobats is …'; 'Neither of the clowns are …'

2 *A series of hits was performed by the rapper.*

Her intentions were declared. ('by her' not needed.)

The result was anticipated by Danny and Marlon.

3 *I* **was** *the first to get home on Wednesday, so I* **made** *myself a cup of cappuccino with our new coffee maker. It* **does** *you good to relax sometimes. It* **wasn't** *for long though, because five minutes later there* **was** *a loud banging on the door. When I* **opened** *it I* **saw** *my little brother* **standing** *there, sinking under the weight of his schoolbag, with tears streaming down his face.*

PUNCTUATION [p. 12]

1 Answers will vary.

2 *Mr Bennet told his family that about a month ago he received a letter and answered it about a fortnight later, since he thought it was a matter of some delicacy that needed early attention. It was from his cousin, Mr Collins, who, when Mr Bennet was dead, could turn the whole family out of the house as soon as he pleased.*

PARAGRAPH ORGANISATION [p. 15]

1 *Exceptionally heavy rain … (as given)*

In addition, rail and property …

Finally, heavy rain is expected …

SPELLING [p. 16]

1 Corrected spellings: 'heroes', 'countries', 'valleys', 'libraries', 'roofs', 'dreadful', 'irrigation', 'advantageous'.

Exceptions: 'motifs'.

Literary terms: 'parodies', 'motifs', 'ironies', 'paradoxes', 'ambiguities'.

2 Answers will vary.

3 Corrected spellings: 'losing', 'pieces', 'fibrous', 'tied', 'knot', 'seen', 'until', 'break', 'threw', 'higher'.

homophones spelled incorrectly: 'tied', 'knot', 'seen', 'break', 'threw', 'higher'.

Homophones spelled correctly: 'time', 'two', 'not', 'to', 'one', 'missed'.

CHAPTER 2

FINDING EXPLICIT INFORMATION [p. 20]

1 It is a hot afternoon. There are two small girls, a small boy, their aunt and a man they do not know in the carriage. The children and their aunt talk to each other and the children ask lots of questions.

2 The 'next stop' is at Templecombe, but there is no mention of the children and aunt getting off.

3 The child does not want to move to the window. They pass fields of sheep and cattle. The aunt attempts to answer the child's question. The bachelor is beginning to scowl.

FINDING IMPLICIT INFORMATION [p. 22]

1 The girl may be bored and want to distract the aunt. The girl is determined. The girl likes the poem but not enough to learn it all.

2 The bachelor sees the likelihood of the girl continuing in terms of a 'bet', a 'wager'. This suggests that he is familiar with betting, and that he has the time, money and inclination to make bets like this himself.

3 The children do not want to hear the aunt's story. The aunt does not want to irritate the bachelor further by telling the story. The aunt is a poor storyteller. The bachelor listens to the story and is critical of it.

QUOTING OR PARAPHRASING EFFECTIVELY [p. 24]

1 Strong, decisive character: 'imperious mien', 'definite black eyebrows', 'parted exactly', 'calm and set'.

Reason to be unhappy: 'disillusionment'.

2 For example: *The fact that the mother speaks 'distinctly' shows that she knows her son can hear her and expects him to answer her; Her looking 'piercingly' suggests that she is a strict and vigilant mother whose children cannot easily get away with misbehaviour.*

3 For example: *The boy is five years old, small but well built. He likes playing by the brook and is 'defiantly' reluctant to come home, even to please his mother.*

ANALYSING LANGUAGE FEATURES AND EFFECTS [p. 26]

1 'bounding', 'running', 'great roar', 'vast deafening snarl'.

2 'Bounding' and 'running' suggest urgency; 'great roar' and 'vast deafening snarl' suggest a noise like a savage, dangerous animal.

3 The repetition of 'too lazy' emphasises Yvette's idleness, almost as if she cannot be bothered to think of another phrase. 'Strayed' and 'dreamy' suggest purposeless wandering.

4 Simile ('like a wet, shuddering cat'); personification ('the water raved').

5 The simile makes her sound like an animal, as if she is reduced to the level of animal survival, while 'shuddering' emphasises her physical response to fear and trauma. The personification presents the water as a 'raving' mad person, who cannot be reasoned with.

6 For example: *The simple verb 'gone' suggests the shock of finding the bridge simply swept away. The simile personifying the house as leaning as if making a bow makes it sound like a person acknowledging the power of the water. The nouns 'wreckage' and 'debris' suggest the high level of destruction, while the personification of 'gaping mouths' for the now empty rooms suggests mouths gaping in horror, or even death.*

ANALYSING THE EFFECTS OF DIFFERENT TYPES OF SENTENCES [p. 30]

1 Compound ('The pack ice seemed to have closed and the ship ...'); minor ('Nothing for it').

2 The compound sentence links the fact and its consequence as if they are inseparable. The minor sentence expresses the Captain's grim resignation to the loss.

3 A simple sentence makes a dramatic opening. Grammatical inversion (instead of saying, 'It happened just before nightfall') delays the event, creating drama. The complex sentences 'Although ...' and 'Grabbing ...' also delay the information, building suspense by suggesting danger first. Two short simple sentences create a sense of urgency. A longer one suggests the size of the bear. Finally, a dramatic simple sentence reveals the nature of the danger.

ANALYSING THE STRUCTURE OF A TEXT [p. 32]

1 A The men are fixated on the fast-moving, rough sea, probably because they are worried about their situation. The grey sea, reflecting the sky, suggests bad weather.

B It is winter and the weather is bad. The narrator and others are 'wandering', suggesting purposeless exercise on a cold wintry day.

C Suggests that marriage and money will be key themes. The statement could be ironic, as not all unmarried and wealthy men are looking for a wife.

2 A How did the men get into this situation? Will they survive?

B Why are the children wandering about in the cold? Who is Mrs Reed? What will the narrator and the other wanderers do now?

C Does the author really believe that this is a 'universal truth'. Is she about to introduce a wealthy male character and some possible wives?

3 For example: *This reveals more of the narrator's character: she is a child, is not an 'outdoor type', and feels physically weak. She seems unhappy – told off by Bessie, and excluded from the group of children. She refers to 'their mama', implying that Mrs Reed is mother to three children, but not the narrator – perhaps why she is excluded, which begins to win our sympathy. The mother seems content, pampered and perhaps lazy.*

4 For example: *The waggoner leaves; What is on the wagon; What the girl does.*

5 For example: *Hardy creates atmosphere with the 'stillness' – apart from the canary. He makes the package seem significant by describing it without*

saying what it is. He implies that the girl is tempted to do something that she does not want the waggoner to see. Her smiling at herself implies that she is secretly vain.

6 For example: *Brontë uses parallel sentences to emphasise the contrast between the pair: 'He wanted all to ... I wanted all to ...'; 'I said his ... He said mine ...'. The sentences become shorter, indicating a rise in tension as Cathy and Linton come close to falling out.*

FORMING AN INTERPRETATION: EVALUATING A TEXT [p. 36]

1 For example: *The writer also reveals that the narrator is contradictory in another way: he dislikes work but appreciates that it is character-building.*

2 Exam Focus, page 39.

3 What characters do: Errol looks at his watch and drums his fingers (shows his anxiety).

Descriptive language: 'haunted face creasing' (shows anxiety, strain).

Detail: 'stuffed owl' is unsettling.

Ideas: Errol's sense of being 'trapped' makes the reader wonder who or what is trapping him.

4 Errol's repeated glances at his watch and his drumming on the table [Evidence] are effective ways to show that he is tensely waiting for something, [Analysis and evaluation] revealing his anxious nature. [Point]

5 For example: *A persuasive sense of menace is created by the adjectives 'trapped, vulnerable', and the strong verb 'glaring', which all imply threat, showing that the character feels in danger.*

6 For example: *The author makes us imagine the narrator's experience in several ways. He uses repetition of 'trees' and a list of adjectives to convey the overpowering nature of the forest. The description of the steamboat 'hugging the bank', makes it, and the man, sound insecure, as if threatened, and 'little begrimed' emphasises how small human beings are compared with this environment. The simile of the boat being like a 'small ... grimy beetle' in a big hallway adds to this sense of overwhelming size. At the same time, the boat 'crawled on', so we see the man is not completely overwhelmed.*

7 For example: *The mood of the extract is one of combined horror and mystery. The narrator is 'chilled and horrified' but can only strain 'to listen through the mist'. The mist creates a sense of mystery and prevents him from seeing what is happening, and so he relies on the frightening evidence of sounds, which are vividly described: 'draining, sucking, churning'. In a way, the effect is intensified by it* *being reduced to one sense. The author creates a strong sense of the narrator feeling 'absolutely helpless' and feeling intense 'frustration'. The fact that a child seems to be dying makes the experience traumatic.*

CHAPTER 3

EFFECTIVE DESCRIPTIVE WRITING [p. 42]

1 Rain trickling from caps and hoods; streets and boulevards; umbrellas; cars.

2 Rain 'assaulted meagre streets'; umbrellas 'collapsed from exhaustion'.

3 Powerful verbs – 'drenched', 'streamed', 'squelched'; vivid adjectives – 'waterlogged', 'miserable'; repetition – 'water streamed ... Water ran ... waterlogged'; other vocabulary choices – 'Rivulets'.

4 Answers will vary.

5 Answers will vary.

CREATING ATMOSPHERE AND MOOD [p. 44]

1 Alarm, horror, fear.

2 Questions: 'And this Thing I saw? How can I describe it?'; semicolon, commas: 'career; a walking engine' and several commas; short sentences followed by a long one: opening two short sentences followed by a long one.

3 Rhetorical questions: viewpoint; contemplate the unanswerable; emphasis.

4 Exclamation mark and full stops after minor sentences.

5 Answers will vary.

GENERATING IDEAS AND STRUCTURING A DESCRIPTION [p. 46]

1 Answers will vary.

2 For example: *The speeding express train was crammed full of tired commuters when it happened.*

3 For example:

- *The glowing fairground lights, which drew her like a moth, twinkled and dazzled in the dark.*
- *They walked in mournful silence along the windswept beach for the last time.*
- *The brand new laptop, with which he had been so delighted, had been completely dismantled.*

4 Answers will vary.

CREATING CONVINCING CHARACTERS AND VOICES [p. 48]

1 For example: *She seems a strong, possibly stubborn character, resistant to persuasion.*

2 For example: *Maggie has a sense of morality and is aware that she can prevent others suffering by her choices.*

3 For example: *She seems to be very sure of herself, and determined to resist the new road. She regards the officer as a minor difficulty. She seems blunt – taking him literally and simply refusing to move.*

4 For example: *She stood in the kitchen, dark eyes glaring at her father, arms tightly folded, bright red nails digging into her upper arm.*

'I don't see why you need to know where I'm going. I don't even know myself. I'm meeting Kylie – that's all. Anyway, why do you care all of a sudden?'

5 Joe seems heroic in the third-person version, but rather vain in the first-person.

6 Answers will vary.

GENERATING IDEAS AND STRUCTURING A NARRATIVE [p. 50]

1–3 Answers will vary.

4 For example: *Dad hauled the faded, velvet armchair through the rickety gate and swung the gate shut with his right boot. It shuddered on its hinges. He grinned. That stain on the armrest was where Cherry had spilt her coffee the evening he'd proposed to her. She'd been shocked into silence for ten seconds, then flung herself at him. They'd been married in spring, in the church on the edge of the moors. She'd looked as pretty as the crocuses that lined the path. That little rip in the cushion was ... His reverie was interrupted by a creak on the stairs behind him. He turned – to face a man in a balaclava. He held a gun.*

CHAPTER 4

IDENTIFYING FACTUAL INFORMATION [p. 56]

1 Any of these: Stephen King, Bram Stoker, James Herbert.

2 'the intense pressures and stresses of exams'.

3

- True.
- False (Her mother disapproved of her reading horror stories.)

4 Kittens.

5 'Children who are disobedient will be subject to such terrible tribulations.'

6

- False. (Even though he disapproves of the content, he says the illustrations were 'beautifully executed'.)
- True.

SELECTING AND SYNTHESISING INFORMATION FROM TWO TEXTS [p. 58]

1 Points that could be included about Text A: Morgan thinks there is a value in reading horror stories because they help us control the fears that preoccupy modern humans and help us to deal with them in a useful way; these are fears of 'human cruelty', 'being insignificant'. Imprisonment – both in a place and in our own bodies. Abandonment. Helplessness. Pain, loss and grief. In addition, horror stories allow us to explore these fears only as far as we want to: 'we can lift up the lid and look at the darkness … and close it again when we've had enough'.

Points that could be included about Text B: Osborne says the purpose of horror stories is to send a moral message: as the kittens in the book were disobedient and punished, so disobedient children will be punished too; 'children who are disobedient will be subject to such terrible tribulations' as those experienced by the kittens.

UNDERSTANDING PERSUASIVE LANGUAGE [p. 60]

1 'dreams and screams': rhyming is apt in a text about children, but also emphasises how wrong it is to scare them, because 'dreams' should be innocent and positive; 'all kinds of intestinal torture': alliteration adds impact, helping to create grimly humorous exaggeration, as if doctors are torturing children in various ways; 'intoxicating literature': compares stories with alcohol, even poison.

2 Possible points: Opens with rhetorical question effectively comparing 'food' for body and brain, suggesting that we should see them in the same way. Use of 'we' draws in the reader. Uses metaphor effectively in 'rubbing off the natural angles' and 'wrapping up'. 'Dumb animals and their young' sums up his view of what appeals to children in a way that will faintly amuse adult readers. 'I never fear …' makes a point that is persuasive because it makes obvious sense. The final sentence uses a semicolon to make two linked, balanced points. The second appeals to adults because they will identify with the idea that in adulthood we have to accept 'sorrow'.

COMPARING WRITERS' VIEWPOINTS AND TECHNIQUES [p. 62]

1 Text A techniques and effects:

- Light-hearted phrase 'my corner of Twitter' (Twitter is not a place) flags up the 'unscientific' nature of the 'survey'. Listing modern fears (e.g. 'Pain, loss and grief') emphasises their extent. Repetition of 'These' in two sentences is powerful, as is turning 'sabre-tooth tigers' into a metaphor.

- Makes readers picture themselves 'faced with a sabre-tooth tiger'.
- Asks two questions about coping with fear, and then answers 'Simple' (effective minor sentence).
- Onomatopoeia and metaphor describe fear in 'so much of it sloshing around in our heads that we drown in it'.
- Metaphor of 'pocket' or 'box' in a story that we can fill with our fears.
- Lists modern sources of anxiety: 'technology, zombies, dystopia and psychological terrors'.
- Effective return to personal anecdote in final paragraph, with 'fear of not being able to trust your own mind' earning our respect.

Comparison:

- Both use personal anecdote (Morgan's teenage book-buying; Osborne's picking up a children's book). Morgan more humorous ('sabre-tooth tigers', etc.).
- Both use lists: Morgan lists horror authors and modern fears; Osborne lists frightening features illustrated in the children's book.
- Morgan asks questions, then answers them herself; Osborne uses a rhetorical question in the final paragraph to emphasise that it is time we took more care with children's literature.
- Morgan uses colloquial but effective metaphor ('sloshing around …'); Osborne uses metaphor less obviously ('rubbing off … wrapping up').
- Morgan uses the deliberately clichéd image of the 'sabre-tooth tiger' to sum up primitive dangers and fears; Osborne is more visual and original in listing frightening features of the children's book: 'awful owls with eyes of fire'.

2 Headings might be: 'The terrifying children's book'; 'How frightening books make children ill and nature cures them'; 'Children's book should be joyful, not frightening'.

3 A high-level response should be in fluent prose, using connectives where appropriate and should combine:

- Comparison of attitudes (see 'Selecting and synthesising information from two texts' in Chapter 4)
- Comparison of style and techniques (see answer to Question 1 above)
- Comparison of structure (see Question 2 above)

CHAPTER 5

WHAT IS WRITING TO EXPRESS A VIEWPOINT? [p. 66]

1 Zoos: purpose = explain views; audience = educated readers interested in topical issues; form = weekend magazine article (audience will have leisure to read it in detail, but may want to be entertained as well as informed).

Television: purpose = influence, persuade; audience = informed media professionals; form = speech (so might make more use of rhetoric than an article).

2 The second is more formal. Vocabulary: 'colleagues', 'appreciate', 'provide ... adequate facilities', 'maximise our efficiency', etc.

The second is more persuasive, despite being too formal. For example, it could say 'have to come out on strike'.

3 Purpose = explain views, persuade; audience = internet users interested in social media; form = blog.

Example sentences: *Endangered elephants, dolphins, the blue whale – you name it, I've done my bit to save it. Am I a dedicated environmental activist, prepared to put in time and effort to protect the planet and my fellow creatures? Er ... sort of – that is, I will happily fill in the first letter of my email address so that the rest pops up for me to sign an online petition.*

KEY FEATURES OF NON-FICTION TEXTS EXPRESSING A VIEWPOINT [p. 68]

1 For example: *Who wants to look like someone washed up on the shores of an island called 'Out of Touch'? Not me. I've got the right trainers, the right jeans, the right sweatshirt. You, of course, might say that I have the wrong views, the wrong priorities, the wrong attitude, but face it, you'd be in a miserable minority.*

2 For example: *I took my little sister Mandy to the park the other day. She was proudly wearing her new jeans. While there, we saw a teenage girl also wearing brand new jeans. The difference was that hers had slashes carefully cut into them. 'Look at her,' said Mandy. 'I bet she wishes she had nice jeans like mine.' And to me, five-year-old Mandy has the right idea.*

3 For example: *Hoodies, heels or horrendous haircuts: everyone seems to feel a need to make their personal style statement. But are they declaring their individuality or announcing their stupidity? A few stars, like Gaga or Rita Ora, may make a statement, but everyone else looks around like lost sheep for someone to follow, and then plays safe.*

USING LANGUAGE TO ARGUE OR PERSUADE [p. 70]

1 Figurative language techniques:
- Simile. Sounds as if the economy is not under control and cannot easily be brought under control, which could be disastrous.
- Simile. Makes it clear that such a law is useless because a chocolate teapot would melt.
- Metaphor. Implies that some effort is needed to succeed through education.
- Personification. Makes war sound merciless and destructive.

2 For example:
- *School pupils all in their identical uniforms, like a shoal of sardines.* (simile)
- *She took to the job as easily as a duck to water.* (simile)
- *The window of opportunity opened and I climbed through it.* (metaphor)
- *The steady march of progress has transformed this community.* (personification)

3 For example:
- *This senseless new road will desecrate a part of our rural heritage.*
- *Many talented but unqualified school-leavers find themselves the victims of unemployment.*

4 For example: *Introducing a tax on sugary foods: According to the nursery rhyme, 'Sugar and spice and all things nice' are what little girls are made of, but for both girls and boys in today's society sugar is no innocent matter. More and more young children are visiting dentists with rotting and painful teeth caused by this supposedly simple pleasure. Sugar has become the curse of the young – hidden in supposedly healthy juice drinks and even savoury items like ketchup. It's time to highlight the damage done by this silent stalker by making it more expensive!*

USING DIFFERENT TYPES OF SENTENCES [p. 72]

1 Main: 'Owain plays for England'; subordinate: 'although he lives in Wales'.

Main: 'They are completely bilingual'; subordinate: 'Having been brought up in the UK'

Main: 'Switzerland gave women the vote only in 1990'; subordinate: 'which is advanced in many ways'.

2 For example: *We used to be limited to face-to-face communication – before social media apps became the new social glue, enabling us to talk to each other in so many ways. With Facebook – so easy to use that even my granddad uses it – we can invite all our friends to a party in seconds. Some people talk about the threat of social media, pointing to cyber-bullying and terrorism. But any form of communication can be used for good or bad. The internet is a way to join our intelligences, turning us into one huge* *interconnected human mind – which could be the way forward for humanity.*

USING PUNCTUATION TO PERSUADE [p. 74]

1 Punctuation:

- *Although many apps are free, downloading them uses up your data.*
- *It is free, simple to use, and readily available, and, what's more, it works.*

2 Comma after 'However' avoids confusion. Round brackets show that the reference to Ozzie is an optional extra. The question mark indicates a question.

3 Answers will vary.

USING STRUCTURES CREATIVELY [p. 76]

1 For example: *We will all need to speak to people, in and out of work, for the rest of our lives, but relatively few people will need to do a lot of writing. Therefore schools should focus on verbal communication, not written. It is often said that writing is a mark of civilisation. However, being able to express yourself verbally is far more useful. Moreover, verbal skills fulfil emotional needs: few of us make real friends just by writing to them. In short, schools are currently preparing us for exams, but not for life.*

2 Example plan:

- *We live in a democracy, and we need to be informed to take part in it.*
- *Being politically aware involves knowing about history.*
- *We need history to avoid the mistakes of the past and to plan a better future.*
- *We also need history to give us a sense of context – where we come from.*
- *Conclusion: we need more history in school, not less.*

3 Example opening paragraph: *Dear Governors, I feel that the move towards phasing out history in school is potentially disastrous. We live in a democracy, and for it to work properly, without it being hijacked by wealthy elites, we need to understand the trends and mistakes of history. Dictators like Hitler thrive on ignorance, which is why we need to study history in school.*

Example conclusion: *We live in ever more complicated times, when political questions often seem to be beyond the reach of the ordinary person. But whether we are contemplating leaving the EU or abandoning nuclear missiles, we cannot avoid our personal responsibility. This is why we need history – to help us choose politicians and policies that will promote peace, wealth and justice.*

CHAPTER 6

PAPER 1 SECTION A: READING [p. 79]

1

- He is not a scientist.
- He does not seem to be someone who lives a healthy outdoor physical life.
- He is interested in the cholera bacillus.
- He is impressed by the destructive power of the bacillus.

2

- Emphasis on his paleness, 'deep grey eyes' suggesting a 'deep' character – an intellectual type, not e.g. a sportsman.
- Adjectives 'haggard', 'nervous' and 'fitful' suggest a mentally unwell person, perhaps unbalanced or obsessive, working too hard.
- His 'gleam of satisfaction' when he thinks of destruction is menacing, and his 'morbid' interest implies an unhealthy interest in death.
- 'devouring' – strong verb implying unhealthy interest in the bacillus, as if he cannot get enough of it.

3

- At the beginning the writer focuses on the bacillus itself – looks unimpressive, yet has huge destructive potential. Writer introduces the two men – scientist and visitor. Scientist is helpful and knowledgeable; visitor is mysterious, but seems to have an unhealthy interest in disease and death.
- Focus gradually shifts to the scientist's perception of the visitor, who is so unlike the down-to-earth fellow scientists he is used to. Physical description of visitor (a little vampire-like!) makes reader suspect him.
- Scientist taking 'the most effective aspect' implies that he is going to respond somehow to the visitor being so 'impressionable'.
- Scientist then does respond, dramatising the lethal potential of the bacillus, personifying it as if it is a villain that can be instructed to destroy human life. He tells a story of this 'criminal' bacillus destroying thousands of lives.

4

- The writer describes the scientist holding the tube 'thoughtfully', suggesting detached scientific interest. The scientist describes bacillus impartially as 'minute particles of life', treating it as a fact of life rather than simply an evil.
- Writer dramatises bacillus through the words of the bacteriologist. Use of 'pestilence' creates strong negative impression, emphasised by alliteration in the 'p' sound of 'imprisoned'.
- Use of 'Imprisoned' also subtly introduces personification of bacillus as a criminal who may be set loose to destroy.

- Scientist contrasts tiny size of bacillus with awful effects.
- 'Go forth and multiply' is a biblical phrase, so this suggests someone – perhaps the scientist – playing God, ordering the bacillus to destroy.
- Writer, through the scientist, creates a highly imaginative account of what would happen if the bacillus was released. Several adjectives emphasise the awful and unavoidable death that would result: 'mysterious, untraceable death, death swift and terrible'.
- Writer personalises the effects in 'husband from the wife', etc.
- Repetition of 'He would' creates powerful and personified sense of possible destruction.
- 'decimated the metropolis': strong verb-noun combination on which to end.

PAPER 1 SECTION B: WRITING [p. 83]

5 Write a description suggested by the picture.

Extract from a mid-level response

All around the laboratory there are men and women in crisp white coats looking at test tubes. They hold them up to the light, heat them over Bunsen burners, or compare them in little racks. The morning light comes in through the high windows, but these scientists seem unaware of that. Their investigations take up all their attention. Some are frowning, as if there is some mystery that they just cannot understand.

In the centre of the room is a huge bubbling vat with a guard rail all around it and gleaming silver pipes coming out and going off in all directions, like a motorway junction. The steam gives off a horrible smell, like old socks, but everyone here seems to have got used to it. One man with lank black hair stands next to a collection of dials and gauges, now and again he writes down figures from the dials in small handwriting in a big book. He smiles faintly sometimes, with a look of someone who is determined to do an experiment and thinks it is beginning to go well.

But the most interesting thing in the laboratory is what hangs overhead – an enormous tank full of a liquid that ripples like a rainbow. It catches the light and seems to shine brilliantly. If you stand close, you can hear it humming, like bees.

Comment

An organised response, with competent use of sentence structures and punctuation. There is some evidence of thoughtful word choice ('crisp', 'gleaming') and some fairly effective figurative language ('like a rainbow'). There is some appeal to the senses. Paragraphs are used appropriately for shifts in focus.

A 'good' level response needs:

- More interesting and effective word choices to replace phrases such as 'horrible smell'
- More development of focus (e.g. could have focused in more on the man with lank hair)
- More detail (e.g. the faces of the scientists looking at test tubes)

Extract from a high-level response

The eager young researchers in their starched white coats stand in a huddle, concentrating hard on what they see through the elongated lens of the high-powered microscope. Tiny filaments of pink and blood red swirl and separate. Could this be the beginnings of new life – or the end of all life as we know it?

Zooming out from the focused group reveals a strange scene – one that resembles a cross between a zoo and a Victorian carnival freak show. In the corner, a cage of headless chickens strut around as if having no head was as normal as pecking corn – though of course they cannot do that. Nearby, a grotesque monstrosity of a baboon jabbers to itself – literally, because its two heads seem to be in conversation. Its fur is long, and unnaturally silky, like human hair. In the centre of the room an oblong tank is filled with dogfish – but not the ordinary kind: these are the horrific product of more scientific meddling, mixing the genes of a goldfish and a Labrador. A bored technician drops in weighted sticks, and the dogfish swims to fetch them.

But pride of place in this freak show goes to the cage at the centre of the room, where the huge figure of a human-like creature paces up and down like a caged lion, grunting in a way that cannot be understood. The stitches around his scalp and wrists show where his white-coated creators have recently assembled his parts to make something like themselves.

Comment

A well-crafted description, moving in a structured way from the scientists to their creations, climaxing in the attempt to create a human being. Effective use of descriptive language, with varied sentence types, and figurative language (e.g. 'a cross between ...'), and the rhetorical question at the end of the first paragraph.

A 'very high' level response needs:

- More connection between the scientists in paragraph 1 and the rest of the description
- Slightly more originality (e.g. 'like a caged lion' is a cliché and is too obvious)

- Some more effective word choices (e.g. 'in a way that cannot be understood' could be replaced by 'incoherently')

Write a story about a scientific experiment that goes wrong.

Extract from a mid-level response

Professor Jones – Tracy to her friends – was excited. This could be the making of her career. A degree in biochemistry, higher qualifications specialising in skin nutrition, and a special study in human ageing. Now she was the world expert in research into anti-ageing. She looked at herself in the mirror of the ladies' toilet. She was a thirty-year-old woman, brown-eyed, pretty but with very strong eyebrows. 'Could this be the face behind world-famous cosmetics?' she asked herself.

For four long years she had led research funded by Laboratory Dernier into what they called the 'holy grail' of cosmetics – a skin cream that would halt the ageing process. But she was an ambitious woman, so that wasn't enough. She wanted to reverse back the ageing process.

At last the time had come to begin the trials. Four women had volunteered and were going to be paid a shedload of money. There was a bit of a risk involved after all. All were over 60, wrinkled and saggy, way past their prime. But all hoped to be transformed – and not just financially.

On day one the women applied 'Factor X', the top-secret new preparation. They did it for a week. After a week they all looked a lot younger – perhaps by about ten years. After another week of treatment, the results were astonishing.

'I've been given a new lease of life,' one woman said. 'My husband hardly recognises me!'

After a further week of treatment, the women had teenage skin – smooth and tight, but without any spots. But that's when things started to go horribly wrong ...

Comment

An engaging response that sets up an imaginative and effective scenario with narrative potential. The candidate uses details and descriptive language to establish a believable character. There is some variety of sentence structure, and competent use of paragraphs. The device of having the character see herself in the mirror and speak to herself is effective.

A 'good' level response needs:

- A consistent register and tone (e.g. 'shedload' and 'bit of a risk' are too informal)

- More interesting and effective descriptive language
- Avoidance of accidental repetition (e.g. 'for a week. After a week ...').

Extract from a high-level response

Damian Scrupleforth was a remarkable baby. Smiling amiably at the world within a few days, crawling in a matter of weeks, and speaking his first words, quite distinctly, at two months: 'More formula milk, please.'

The 'please' was the cause of particular delight, because Damian had been designed to be polite and considerate at all times. At the government Alpha Project playgroup, where he played intelligent and character-building games with his fellow toddlers, Damian was politely assertive: 'I think you'll find that I was already playing with those Lego bricks, Robert.' This was when he had reached the age of two.

By the time Damian entered the choppy waters of the teenage years, he was doing quadratic equations, contributing to New Scientist *magazine, and, of course, helping the elderly across the road. His physique was strong, and his health as sound as a bell. This was no surprise. He was, after all, a product of the latest twenty-first-century genetic engineering.*

The first signs of it began when Damian turned fifteen. There was a girl who lived near the government compound that he called 'home'. She was just a 'normal', but somehow whenever he glimpsed her his heart fluttered like a caged canary, and his mouth went dry. One day she smiled at him in passing – a smile like the sun emerging from the clouds, and a symphony of sensations seemed to go through him. ...

Comment

The response shows a varied and inventive use of structural devices, including withholding information (e.g. who is delighted at his politeness). Sentences are varied and effective (e.g. opening with a short simple sentence, followed by a long minor one). Language devices are used well (e.g. groups of three such as 'solving quadratic equations ... road').

A 'very high' level response needs:

- More consistently interesting and effective word choices (e.g. 'go through him' could be 'flood through him')
- More descriptive detail (e.g. what he looks like)
- Avoidance of accidental repetition (e.g. 'polite ... politely' – could use 'courteous')

PAPER 2 SECTION A: READING [p. 84]

1 A, D, E, G

2

- Writer A, Alice Fisher, regards fashion as entertaining, though sometimes silly; calls celebrity styles 'vivid and fun'. Enjoys individuality of fashionable display.
- Writer B, George Bernard Shaw, has no objection to fashion being regulated, as by Covent Garden Opera. He sees this regulation as functional, but thinks it should apply to women as well as men.
- Fisher compares catwalk fashion with celebrity styles, saying the latter have become more 'outrageous', which she seems to enjoy.
- Shaw objects to the vulgarity of showy female fashion, and especially to the distasteful fashion of having dead birds or parts of them on hats. Thinks the public should be protected from shocking or offensive fashion.

3

- Presents himself as a reasonable man who accepts Covent Garden's rules for male clothing. Lists arguments supporting them.
- Uses this to launch a criticism of female fashion, using popular expression that reinforces view of himself as reasonable and normal – 'sauce for the goose ...'
- Uses anecdote – the woman in front of him.
- Uses ironic humour – 'I wish she had come later ...'
- 'pitiable corpse' emphasises reality of what it is – a dead bird, not just an accessory.
- Uses rhetorical question, followed by humour in exaggerated description of how he might appear – 'dead snake round my neck', etc.

4

- Fisher regards fashion as fun and interesting, even if not of 'vast cultural significance'.
- Shaw sees no virtue in fashion, focusing on the offence it can cause.
- Both writers use language that is partly playful (e.g. Fisher beginning 'Spring is a fertile time', and the humorously exaggerated tone-setting 'orgy of style', and Shaw's suggestion that the bird was 'nailed ... to the lady's temple').
- Fisher covers a range of incidents and celebrity moments (e.g. Björk's egg-laying); Shaw focuses on one incident at the opera, and backs it up with a memory of the theatre.
- Fisher uses visual detail for entertainment value; Shaw uses it more critically, and sharply, in an emotive way, to emphasise the offensiveness of dead birds as fashion accessories.

PAPER 2 SECTION B: WRITING [p. 87]

Mid-level response:

At school we have to wear uniform and dress in a conventional way, day in, day out – the same old navy blue jumpers and grey skirts or trousers. It's dull but practical, and avoids making difficult decisions every morning. However, you might think that on 'mufti days' students would jump at the chance to be individual and show off their style. Instead of that, what they mostly wear is just a different kind of uniform: jeans, designer t-shirts, etc. The fact is, no one wants to stand out and look like a freak. Perhaps there is the occasional Goth, but they are just wearing a different uniform, playing safe, not expressing themselves.

Fashion is actually ridiculous a great deal of the time. Yet people more or less stick to it because they want to be part of a particular set. Teenage girls wear heels so high it looks like they'll fall off them, boys wear their jeans so low that they're always about to fall down. Hoodies are supposed to be cool, but really they are just a disguise – either a real one so that the wearer can commit a crime without being identified, or a mental one because they want to hide who they are, not display it.

The worst thing about clothes is the way people get mocked for what they wear. Girls get called all sorts for having their skirts too short, boys get teased for wearing the wrong make of jeans. It is all just another way for humans to show themselves off as better than others, like peacocks spreading out their feathers in a display.

I think it was King Charles who first wore high heels – because he was short, but now we have tall women tottering about on them because of him. It is simply stupid. Even jeans, the commonest clothing in the western world, started off as hard-wearing practical work clothes, not fashion wear. People wore them to identify with the poor.

In my view, clothes should be practical: hard-wearing and comfortable. I don't want to wear a mini-skirt and skimpy top on a December night, just because it looks good. On the other hand, if I'm going up a mountain I want a proper waterproof, not a leather jacket. Fashion is for those who are frightened of being left out of the in-crowd. It certainly has nothing to do with individual expression.

Comment

This response makes a clear, coherent case, with some use of figurative language and some language devices (e.g. parallelism in 'so high ... so low') and lists of three. The structure is effective, moving from the personal example of school uniform, to a logical conclusion.

A 'good' level response needs:

- Some more interesting language choices
- More use of effective techniques, such as imagery and emotive language
- A more vivid use of details – such as what people wear

High-level response

Fashionable self-expression is not just for showing off – it's the first instinct of human life. From the earliest caveman who had the idea of leaving the paws on his leopard skin, to the first cavalier who had his tailor cut slits in his velvet doublet to reveal his silk shirt underneath, humans have always wanted to show their individual style. Of course, it's partly about showing off in other ways. The caveman wanted to say, 'I'm rough and tough enough to hunt leopards'. The cavalier wanted to impress his foot soldiers, and his fellow officers, to show that he could buy all that fancy outfitting. And just as in those times, the dedicated follower of fashion nowadays wants to impress as well as express.

But it's not that simple. Clothes are about two opposing human needs: individuality, on the one hand, and the urge to merge, on the other. If I wear jeans and a t-shirt, I'm merging into the crowd, becoming one with the great mass of humanity – which we all want. However, if I slash my jeans, wear a rhinestone-studded belt, and paint 'Eat the rich' across my t-shirt, I'm suddenly an individual. Like Wally of the 'Where's Wally?' books, I'm one of the crowd, but if you look closely, you can see how I stand out from it.

So, it may be fashionable – ironically – to mock the excesses of fashion, and even more of celebs like Lady Gaga, with her meat dress, but these all express a normal human need. Moreover, it is actually quite a useful need. Just as medieval soldiers knew who to hack to pieces by what coat of arms they had on their tunic, we modern, civilised types know who we might have things in common with by what they are wearing. Cut-off leather jerkin with half-inch studs and oily jeans? Mmm ... perhaps not quite my sort. Tweed jacket and leather elbows – well, not quite me either.

So, clothes are so much more than just for covering up and keeping warm: they identify us, gain us membership to the right club, and give us a chance to shout out our individuality all at once. What a brilliant invention. Chimpanzees don't know what they're missing!

Comment

A well argued, well structured response that uses anecdote, entertaining examples and some effective visual details, as well as language devices such as rhetorical question, and connectives that help the flow of the text.

A 'very high' level response needs:

- Some slightly more interesting word choices (e.g. 'exhibit' for 'show')
- More effective language devices (e.g. find a better way to begin the final paragraph and avoid repeating 'So')
- Some further use of descriptive adjectives (e.g. '<u>bright</u> idea', '<u>showy</u> silk shirt', '<u>dangerous</u> leopards').

CHAPTER 7

HOW TO COMMENT ON TEXTS AND USE QUOTATIONS [p. 88]

1 For example: *Meena describes how the Tollington women 'snarl and send death rays to each other', showing their mutual dislike.*

2 For example:

- *The author <u>reveals</u> that the main character ...*
- *In this scene Shakespeare <u>demonstrates</u> ...*
- *As events unfold, the audience <u>perceives</u> ...*
- *The sense of fear is <u>conveyed</u> by ...*

3 Answers will vary.

WRITING ABOUT AN EXTRACT [p. 90]

1 *With close <u>reference</u> to the <u>extract</u> show <u>how</u> a character is <u>presented</u>.*

Write about the way <u>suspense</u> is treated in the <u>novel</u>.

- *Refer to the <u>extract</u> and the <u>novel as a whole</u>*
- *Show your <u>understanding</u> of <u>characters</u> and <u>events</u> in the novel*

Refer to the <u>context</u> of the <u>novel</u>.

2 Answers will vary.

COMMENTING ON KEY LITERARY TECHNIQUES [p. 92]

1 Joe is very strong and perhaps even heroic.

2 The adverb and verb create a shocking image using sound as well as sight.

3 For example: *The use of 'Sir' and 'my master' implies that the speaker is a servant and respects the person he is addressing, yet his rhetorical questions suggest that he is challenging the listener's opinion. The simple simile 'like a rat' is appropriate for a servant and conveys his revulsion for the man he is describing. His passing 'a hand over his face' suggests that that he finds this situation stressful.*

CHAPTERS 8–11 [pp. 96-129]

Answers will vary.

CHAPTER 12

SHAKESPEARE QUESTIONS [p. 130]

MACBETH

- Only Macbeth can see Banquo's ghost: he is either psychic or suffering from guilt-stricken delusions.
- He challenges the ghost, rather than fleeing from it – suggesting bravery.
- He insists that he is as brave as any man, and could face a rhino or fierce tiger: he just cannot face the ghost – or his own ghost. He is very concerned about his masculinity.
- He has proven himself a brave warrior and, at one time, a loyal follower of Duncan.
- He is ambitious and also susceptible to Lady Macbeth's taunts about his masculinity. Therefore he allows himself to be led by her and by the Witches.
- He earns the title 'tragic hero' in the end by taking responsibility for his deeds.

ROMEO AND JULIET

- Juliet has bravely followed the Friar's plan to avoid having to marry Paris, and to be with her husband, Romeo, by taking a sleeping draught.
- Much of the speech is made up of questions – showing uncertainty and insecurity.
- Her speech is fragmented. She interrupts herself with 'O, if I wake', suggesting her great agitation – hardly surprising in the vault, and about to take a mystery potion.
- Shakespeare shows her as a brave girl, prepared to go against the wishes of her parents, and against the longstanding Capulet-Montague feud, for the love of Romeo.
- She is loving and passionate, and hates the fact that Romeo has to leave her, as shown by her insistence that the 'lark' they hear at dawn is a 'nightingale' (bird of night).
- Her suicide is tragic – undertaken because Romeo is dead and she will not remarry.

THE TEMPEST

- Prospero seems full of hatred towards Caliban, calling him 'lying slave' and 'Filth', and saying only whipping will do him any good.
- His control of Caliban could be seen as justified – Caliban tried to rape Miranda, but a modern audience might also compare Prospero with a colonial power.
- Prospero is harsh towards Caliban, but also quite harsh to Ariel, whom he has enslaved.
- Prospero causes the shipwreck, but ensures that no one is hurt.
- He severely tests Ferdinand. This could be for Miranda's good, or because he is a jealous parent who does not want to lose her.
- In the end he forgives those who have wronged him, and renounces magical power to return to his worldly responsibilities.

THE MERCHANT OF VENICE

- Salarino cannot believe that Shylock will insist on his agreement with Antonio and take his 'pound of flesh'.
- Speech shows that Shylock, despite being a merchant, is strongly motivated by revenge. He wants Antonio's flesh even if it is only good for fish bait.
- Shylock's list of grievances against Antonio argues that he is justified; it goes on to become a persuasive attack on anti-Semitism and racial prejudice.
- Shylock loses our sympathy when he insists on his 'pound of flesh', and on taking it in such a way as to kill Antonio.
- Portia, posing as a judge, puts forward a strong case for mercy in her 'quality of mercy' speech; Shakespeare opposes this ideal to revenge.
- It could be argued that in the end Portia, Antonio and the Duke take revenge on Shylock.

MUCH ADO ABOUT NOTHING

- Beatrice and Benedick enter into competitive, mutually insulting banter as soon as they see each other again after Benedick's return. Beatrice says no one listens to Benedick. He calls her 'Lady Disdain' and pretends to be only mildly interested when he finds she is still alive.
- Benedick claims that all ladies love him, but he loves 'none'; Beatrice matches this by saying 'I am of your humour for that': she is equally opposed to marrying.
- Their humour is well-matched, and shows similar temperaments: neither seems to be conventionally romantic – despite which they are tricked into falling in love. This reflects Shakespearean comedy being largely about marriage as a social harmoniser.
- They both lose a certain amount of dignity when they fall in love, being mocked by other characters, but they never complain.
- Benedick shows himself more seriously suited when he agrees to challenge Claudio because of his humiliation of Hero, Beatrice's cousin, which, in Elizabethan terms, reflects on Beatrice.
- Both are loyal friends who want to see justice: they deserve each other.

JULIUS CAESAR

- Cassius resents Caesar's growing power, and speaks ironically of him as a Colossus, and he and Brutus as 'petty men' who 'peep about' like frightened children.
- Shakespeare addresses a popular debate of the time: are we ruled by fate, represented here by astrology ('our stars'), or by ourselves?
- Cassius insists that they only have themselves to blame if they remain 'underlings'.
- Storms and odd behaviour in the animal kingdom (mentioned in Plutarch, Shakespeare's historical source) seem to be omens pointing to disturbing political events.
- The soothsayer warns Caesar ('Beware the Ides of March'), and Calpurnia wants him to stay at home. Caesar seems to accept fate when he asks, 'What can be avoided / Whose end is purposed by the mighty gods?'
- Shakespeare seems to leave the question open.

HENRY V

a)

- Henry goes in disguise amongst the common soldiers, so the audience sees him as an ordinary man.
- He speaks in prose (informally) to the soldiers, rather than in blank verse (formally).
- The soldiers argue that they are only fighting because they are Henry's subjects and are not responsible for the cause being right or wrong. The king is responsible if they die in a sinful state (without a priest).
- Henry listens as though the men are his equals, arguing that the soldiers are responsible for their own consciences since 'every subject's soul is his own' and before battle should prepare themselves for the afterlife, as they might on their deathbed. Shakespeare is exploring the nature of kingship here, through prose.

b)

- Henry speaks in prose to Katherine, as a man rather than a king, while her lady-in-waiting translates, since Katherine speaks little English.
- She knows the words for body parts, so the audience would witness a comic and daring interlude between herself and Henry.

OTHELLO

a)

- The mood of the extract is one of deep sadness. Desdemona's melancholy suggests depression and bewilderment at Othello's questioning in the previous scene.

- The audience fears for Desdemona's safety through her comment to Emilia: 'If I do die before thee … shroud me in one of those same sheets.' This foreshadows her murder in Act V.
- The willow song mirrors Desdemona's fear that Othello will desert her. The willow is the symbol of deserted love: 'I called my love, false love.'

b)

- Relationships between men and women are often marked by suspicion, jealousy, violence and/or death.
- Desdemona's genuine love is destroyed by Othello's jealousy and Iago's plotting.
- Iago seems to despise Emilia (as he does everyone) and in Act V, he murders her.
- Cassio exploits his mistress Bianca and is cruel when he dismisses her (Act III Scene 4).

TWELFTH NIGHT

a)

- The speech opens the play and introduces one of its most important themes: love.
- For Orsino, music is 'the food of love' because it inspires melancholy and romantic love, and also the idea of being in love.
- The focus of his love is Olivia and his mood is contrary. He believes that if he can have a 'surfeit' of music he will become sick of love, suggesting that his love is fickle.
- The 'spirit' of this love is like 'the sea' (and music) rises and 'falls into abatement' (decline). Again, the effect is to suggest that such love is egotistical, unrealistic and changeable.

b)

- There are different kinds of love in the play, for example: Olivia's idealised love for her dead brother and impulsive love for Cesario; Viola's true love for Orsino; Malvolio's love founded on vanity; Antonio's platonic love for Sebastian.
- Orsino's romantic love changes to mature love when he realises that his respect for Cesario (Viola) are genuine feelings of love for Viola when she reveals herself as a woman.
- Since Twelfth Night is a romantic comedy, the nature of love as one of its main themes is appropriate and is frequently explored in Shakespeare (such as in Romeo and Juliet).

NINETEENTH-CENTURY NOVEL QUESTIONS [p. 133]

ROBERT LOUIS STEVENSON: THE STRANGE CASE OF DR JEKYLL AND MR HYDE

- Jekyll is presented as troubled ('grew pale to the very lips'); he is 'painfully situated'.
- That he can only refuse Utterson's help, and cannot benefit by confiding in him, argues that his case is very serious and deserves sympathy.

- Jekyll's gratitude to Utterson, just for wanting to help, shows how much he needs sympathy, and makes him more deserving.
- Jekyll is respectable and has many friends. The fact that Utterson is Jekyll's friend and wants to help him is itself a recommendation.
- Jekyll is a risk-taker and sees Lanyon as 'hidebound' – making him both appealing, especially to modern readers, yet guilty of hubris (ambitious pride).
- Jekyll is a truth-seeker, and believes in the dual nature of man ('not truly one, but truly two'). Could argue that his real crime is honesty about his own darker side. We sympathise because in the end he suffers and is condemned to lose his better self to Hyde – almost as if damned.

CHARLES DICKENS: *A CHRISTMAS CAROL*

- Scrooge is terrified by the ghost. We see his desire to change, and be saved from the fate of dying with no one caring, with his appeal, 'Say it is thus ...' that 'the ends will change'.
- Words 'crept' and 'trembling' show that Scrooge has become afraid, a prelude to change, rather than 'Hard and sharp as flint'.
- Insists 'I am not the man I was' and reasons that there must be hope for the ghost to show him the vision of his grave.
- Over the course of the novella he changes from being mean, scorning the spirit of Christmas (e.g. in his rudeness to Fred in Chapter 1), to being joyful and generous.
- The Ghost of Christmas Past shows how Scrooge has become what he is. Christmas Present shows him poor families, especially Cratchits, and Want and Ignorance (reflecting Dickens's social views). But Scrooge only completes his change when made aware of his own mortality.
- Finally Dickens shows a humorous but sympathetic view of Scrooge, so happy he is 'giddy as a drunken man', ending the story with a strong moral conclusion.

CHARLES DICKENS: *GREAT EXPECTATIONS*

- Pip and friends are close to getting Magwitch onto the steamer so he can escape to the country and avoid arrest. Dickens creates suspense by leaving it until they have almost managed to do this for an officer to challenge them.
- Action happens swiftly, 'before we knew what they were doing'. Sentence beginning 'This caused ...' emphasises rapid events, like the steamer paddles turning, accentuated by a list with 'and' repeated: 'and I heard them ... and heard the order ... and heard them stop ...'.
- Phrases such as 'In the same moment', 'quite frantically', 'white with terror', 'felt the boat sink' create suspense and drama.

- Novel begins with drama – when Pip meets convict in the graveyard. Develops with Pip being made to steal a file and food, and then with the convicts being hunted.
- Mrs Havisham presents a different kind of Gothic drama.
- Often there is the threat of violence, either veiled, as with Jaggers, or openly physical, e.g. vengeful Orlick lures Pip to the sluice-house.

CHARLOTTE BRONTË: *JANE EYRE*

- Jane makes a mistake in honestly saying 'Psalms are not interesting'. Her honesty in not humouring Brocklehurst contradicts Mrs Reed's claims.
- Brocklehurst's reply shows his ignorant lack of sympathy with children and his extreme religious views (not unusual at the time), as does his reference to fire and brimstone.
- Mrs Reed's accusation of 'deceit' and Brocklehurst's unquestioning belief in it are unjust. Jane has to battle prejudice. Mrs Reed is 'already obliterating hope' for her.
- Jane's first problem is in being (apparently) poor – which is why she is sent to Lowood. She is also unloved. As an adult she believes herself too plain for a man to love her.
- Rochester seems to change her fortunes, but her discovery that he is married to Grace Poole dashes Jane's hopes. Her challenge is to behave morally and leave him.
- She manages to avoid marriage to the emotionally cold, repressed St John Rivers. Eventually 'rewarded' by marriage to Rochester.

MARY SHELLEY: *FRANKENSTEIN*

- The Creature appreciates nature. Notices trees 'budding with fresh spring'.
- He saves girl 'with extreme labour', risking own life, and succeeds – only to be shot and wounded by 'rustic'.
- 'Writhed', 'miserable pain', 'shattered' and 'agony' emphasise his suffering. Clearly blames incident for his conversion to 'eternal hatred and vengeance'.
- The Monster is created huge and ugly – likely to cause revulsion; doomed to loneliness unless Frankenstein will make him a partner. Pleads for this and almost gets it – then Frankenstein destroys his work.
- Monster appreciates poetry – e.g. Milton, and seems to identify with Milton's Satan. Intelligent and speaks eloquently.
- Shelley ambiguous. Monster is badly mistreated by Frankenstein and humanity, but he does do some evil things – e.g. framing Justine.

JANE AUSTEN: *PRIDE AND PREJUDICE*

- Elizabeth shows vanity and insensitivity in her negative reaction to Charlotte's engagement. Elizabeth is more attractive than Charlotte, so has more chance of marriage.
- Austen presents Charlotte as marrying for financial support and to avoid spinsterhood, rather than for love – arguably the best a woman in her position could do in Austen's time. Collins simply wants to marry – not concerned about love. It does seem ridiculous for him to propose to two women in three days.
- Novel opens with a line ironically assuming that a single man with a fortune must be looking for a wife – signalling link between marriage and money.
- Austen presents the Bennets as an example of an unhappy marriage. Mr Bennet married an unintelligent woman for her youthful charms.
- Some see purpose of marriage to cement family connections and keep wealth within family – e.g. Lady Catherine. Wickham shows another side of marriage – the opportunist.
- Elizabeth and Darcy make the perfect marriage because they are suited in character and intelligence, despite unequal rank – Austen was making a radical point at the time.

SIR ARTHUR CONAN DOYLE: *THE SIGN OF THE FOUR*

- Sholto is exotic in having an Indian servant, and in living in a 'little sanctum' at odds with the 'sordid and common passage' leading to it.
- First appearance dramatic, framed in 'yellow light', odd looks: 'small man with a very high head, a bristle of red hair all round the fringe of it, and a bald, shining scalp'. Strange simile comparing his head to a 'mountain peak'. Bad teeth.
- Nervous, never still, 'in a perpetual jerk'. Prematurely bald. Strange voice and affected style of speech: 'oasis of art'.
- Exotic, tasteful decor, 'a diamond of the first water'; tiger-skins, rugs, hookah.
- Worries about own health, asking Watson to check his heart. Sensitive about himself but not others – e.g. Miss Morstan's feelings on way to Pondicherry Lodge.
- Elsewhere in novel self-preoccupied. Announces Captain Morstan's death insensitively.

H. G. WELLS: *WAR OF THE WORLDS*

Extract, examples of chaos:

- The extract opens with a detailed description of destruction, using lengthy sentences and powerful verbs, in which a suburban house is 'completely smashed, pulverised and dispersed'.

- The earth lies 'in heaped piles' and hides the other houses as though they have been subjected to 'a violent blow of a hammer'.
- The house the narrator is in is severely damaged, leaving only kitchen and scullery.

Extract, examples of order:

- The Martians' success must involve good organisation and efficiency. Their fighting-machines are 'swift, complex and perfect'.
- The Martians' machines are so well constructed and effective that the narrator does not see them as machines but having a 'living quality'.

Novel, examples of chaos:

- The Martian invasion has created disorder and chaos.
- The destruction of the church on which the curate comments 'Gone – swept out of existence' in Chapter 3 symbolises religious belief being swept away.
- The curate's mental instability is reflected in his erratic behaviour.
- In despair, the Artilleryman gives way to chaotic drinking and aimlessness.
- The exodus from London 'lashing in a foaming tumult' (Chapter 16) symbolises society breaking down.

Novel, examples of order:

- The Martians are ruthlessly efficient in their attacks.
- The narrator's plans and calm determination to survive suggests, for the most part, a logical, well-ordered mind.
- The narrator's brother also has a logical mind.

Context:

- The Martians represent imperialism, in which H. G. Wells was interested – i.e. how dominant countries conquer other countries to build empires.
- The Martians' dependence on machines echoes the Industrial Revolution (the development of manufacturing using machines) of the nineteenth century, through which Wells lived.
- The descriptions of the Martian machines resemble robots, which suggests that H. G. Wells's ideas about technology were prophetic.

GEORGE ELIOT: *SILAS MARNER*

In the extract:

- Godfrey Cass is presented as a desperate young man as he 'bit his lips and clenched his fists' at his brother's remarks. He is in difficulties, with a potentially damaging secret: he is married to Molly Farren, an opium addict, and we can assume pregnant with Eppie at this time. He therefore appears weak and foolish.

- His relationship with his brother, Dunsey Cass, is quarrelsome and destructive.
- Godfrey's lack of courage is evident in his inability to deal with his brother. The adverb 'quivering' is used to describe Godfrey when he fears Dunsey will reveal his secret to Squire Cass.
- However, we could also say that Godfrey possesses some decency for marrying Molly.

In the novel as a whole:

- We see how Godfrey values money and the status it gives him. He tries to pay off Molly to ensure her silence.
- Although Godfrey is married to Molly, he is in love with Nancy Lammeter and had hoped to marry her. Nor does he acknowledge Eppie as his daughter, so he is also capable of deceit.
- Later, he matures when he finally marries Nancy. She has a calming influence and Godfrey genuinely loves her.
- Godfrey also learns that money cannot buy love when Eppie rejects him as her father and refuses to live with him and Nancy.
- He is generous to Eppie and contributes to her wedding, though he does not attend, because we can assume it is too painful for him, which suggests he feels regret.
- **Context:** As the Squire's son, Godfrey is from a high social class and money and position. He assumes superiority over those of a lower class, evident in his dealings with Molly and Eppie.

MODERN PROSE AND DRAMA QUESTIONS [p. 136]

J. B. PRIESTLEY: *AN INSPECTOR CALLS*

- Appears at first to be ordinary police inspector, but is more sympathetic to Eva Smith, and makes more moral judgements than a real inspector would.
- His dramatic role is to make each character in turn see their guilt: withholds information and asks questions to make them incriminate themselves.
- This fits with his pursuing 'one line of enquiry at a time', so focus is on one character at a time.
- We learn about Eva Smith from him – background and how she died.
- Mouthpiece for Priestley's moral message of social responsibility: 'fire and blood and anguish' will come 'if men will not learn that lesson'.
- Mystery of who he is, or was – a ghost (ghoul – Goole), voice of conscience. Twist of phone call announcing that an inspector is coming.

WILLY RUSSELL: *BLOOD BROTHERS*

- Identical twins – so should be similar in character and abilities.
- Sensitive scene when they meet as boys. Contrast in speech (Edward 'posh', Mickey working-class Liverpool) and attitudes: Edward offers Mickey sweet. Both equally innocent in discussing 'plate' in Sammy's head.
- Remain friends, despite Mrs Lyons' efforts – threesome with Linda. Edward more confident and sophisticated – encourages Mickey to make Linda his girlfriend.
- Incident with police officer – his attitude towards Mickey and Edward very different.
- Edward going to university is beginning of end for friendship. Edward cannot understand Mickey's situation. Mickey says Edward has never had to grow up.
- Mickey's unemployment, prison, depression, addiction, while Edward becomes a councillor. Russell's message is that 'fate' is really the result of social situation.

ALAN BENNETT: *THE HISTORY BOYS*

- Hector opposes education for exam system. Wants to expand boys' thinking. Special focus on literature and the arts.
- Irwin, a supply teacher, is given job of preparing boys for Oxbridge entrance exams. Encourages boys to be controversial just to impress – to 'pretend' rather than say what they really think. Thinks Hector encourages dull interpretations of history.
- Hector thinks education is for life – opposite of head's view which is that it is just to achieve status (especially for the school).
- Head hires Irwin to bring grammar-school boys up to independent-school level – highlighting social inequalities in education, preserving elitism.
- Hector eccentric. Boys practise subjunctive tense in French by role-play set in a Paris brothel. Also gets them to learn and recite poetry.
- Hector relatively open with the boys – they learn from his personality; Irwin more guarded. Hector treats history, especially the First World War, as a literary context. He believes in power of literature. Irwin glib and cynical: history is 'a performance'. His methods get Posner into Cambridge but fail him in life.

DENNIS KELLY: *DNA*

- Main victim is Adam – tortured and thought killed when he fell through a grille, then found alive, and finally (we assume) actually killed to protect gang.

- Importance of loyalty to gang versus individual morality and compassion; Leah on chimps and bonobos.
- Leaders replaced when they can no longer hold on to position and protect group: John Tate (finds God), Phil (becomes silent), Cathy (even more extreme – cuts off a first year's finger).
- Phil bullies Brian into incriminating postal worker in Adam's death. Bullying connected to refusal to take responsibility. Leah denies group responsible, then says should share blame ('we haven't done anything ... but if we have ...')
- Effects of bullying (e.g. Brian goes mad and eats earth) and question of whether bullied are in any way to blame. Mark and Jan say Adam was 'laughing' and was a 'nutter'.
- Kelly asks, are we chimps or bonobos? Is bullying inevitable in groups – in our DNA?

SIMON STEPHENS: *THE CURIOUS INCIDENT OF THE DOG IN THE NIGHT-TIME*

- Christopher autistic (not made explicit). Brilliant at maths and science but has difficulty 'reading' and relating to people. Cannot empathise and understand what they need to know – e.g. when policeman asks what he is doing in garden.
- Cannot bear to be touched – father (fingertips only), mother, policeman.
- His determination can irritate others – his refusal to drop investigation into who killed Wellington. Sticks to goals.
- Tries not to get involved with other people, like elderly neighbour Mrs Alexander. Interacts to some extent, despite instructions and own reservations.
- Use of Siobahn reading from Christopher's account to narrate. Gives us insight, e.g. 'I find people confusing.'
- Christopher's honesty (but lies to father about investigation); shocked and angered by dishonesty of others – especially Ed saying Judy dead. Heroic effort when he goes to find her – must really care for her.

SHELAGH DELANEY: *A TASTE OF HONEY*

- Main love relationship is mother (Helen) and daughter (Jo). Like a marriage in that they are more equal than in a typical parent–child relationship. Helen neglects Jo, but loves her in her way. Jo criticises Helen but loves her. They bicker like a couple.
- Helen a poor example. Married once before. Conceived Jo in an affair (she 'had nothing better to do'). Peter is a selfish, unfaithful man. Helen seems to want his money, and security. Helen wishes Jo could 'learn from my mistakes'.
- With no father and a neglectful mother, not

surprising that Jo is won over by Boy's affection and promises. Boy seems to care for Jo, but does either of them believe he will return to her?
- Ironically, homosexual Geof supports Jo more than anyone else. Even offers to marry her. Says he doesn't mind that she is having another man's baby. Committed to her: 'I'd sooner be dead than away from you.'
- Sad that Helen drives Geof away when he is devoted to Jo, but at least Helen makes an effort for Jo at the end.
- Perhaps Delaney is saying that all relationships are flawed and disappointing, and that all we can expect is temporary sweetness – a 'taste of honey'.

WILLIAM GOLDING: *LORD OF THE FLIES*

- Ralph associated with symbol of conch – standing for democracy, Jack with spear.
- Ralph supports rule of law, protection of younger, weaker boys, and importance of keeping fire alight to be seen and rescued. Jack more interested in hunting.
- Ralph has charisma to become leader, but his rationalism cannot manage boys' deep fears and savage impulses. Reluctant to believe in the beast; Jack exploits fear of it; says he and 'his' hunters will kill it.
- Ralph wants to preserve adult civilisation, and comes to respect Piggy's intelligence. Jack sees island as opportunity to shed civilised restraints and become a tribal leader ('my tribe'), breaking from Ralph and his few remaining supporters.
- Ralph is kind-hearted; Jack has a powerful streak of cruelty and ruthlessness, rules by fear and intimidation (has Wilfred beaten, perhaps an idea from school). He offers meat; Ralph offers rules. Jack prepared to hunt Ralph to the death.
- When officers arrive, Ralph accepts responsibility – says he is leader; Jack shrinks away. They represent two types of political leader in adult world: democrat and dictator.

AQA ANTHOLOGY: *TELLING TALES*

- In 'Odour of Chrysanthemums', mother speaks firmly to 'sulky', 'resentful, taciturn' boy, then more 'gently'. Sees her husband's self-centredness in him.
- Daughter more sympathetic. Tries to manage mother when she is bitter about husband's drinking. Daughter dreamy about fire and has 'a little rapture' over flower in mother's apron; mother practical, dismissive – perhaps was like daughter once.
- Mother loves children – partly angry with father on their behalf. Tries to protect them (pointlessly) from knowing he is dead ('nothing to make a fuss about').

- In 'The Darkness Out There', teenagers slightly patronising about the old people, but want to help them.
- Mrs Rutter assertive, not slow to give Sandra and Kerry tasks. They are shocked by her account of letting the German airman die, as if in revenge for her husband.
- Children in both stories represent hope: all that is left of the failed marriage in 'Odour of Chrysanthemums', and a more forgiving compassionate view in 'The Darkness Out There'.

GEORGE ORWELL: *ANIMAL FARM*

- Novel is allegory of Russian Revolution and its aftermath. Jones represents tsar and old regime. Napoleon can be seen as Stalin and Snowball as Trotsky.
- Jones exploited animals; after takeover, Napoleon exploits them instead.
- Pigs (intelligent animals) can be seen as Communist Party elite. Use propaganda and speeches to manipulate animals, and gradually take benefits for themselves – milk and apples, claiming it is for social good.
- Pigs' power and privilege depends on the unquestioning hard work of animals like Boxer, representing Russian peasantry, and obedient savagery of dogs – representing roles of security forces in repressive USSR.
- In the end, pigs become indistinguishable from the men with whom they now do business. They are the new ruling class.
- Orwell's style is simple (he called it a 'fable'), with restrained irony, allowing readers to draw their own conclusions – more effective than being heavy-handed or showing pigs' manipulation and animals' suffering in vivid detail.

KAZUO ISHIGURO: *NEVER LET ME GO*

- Dystopian novel. Clone children brought up at Hailsham to believe they have a special role, and must look after themselves, but not told what. They accept this. Actually society is prejudiced against them – even disgusted.
- Told they must produce art. Accept that this is somehow important. Learn later that this is meant to help argue the case that they are individuals.
- Roy challenges the token system for art going into the gallery: actually a pathetic rebellion in the context of the much larger injustice of cloning for body parts.
- Kathy prides herself on being a good 'carer', minimising the suffering of her 'donors'. She is dutiful in her work, is grateful for small perks, and accepts her fate.

- Ishiguro uses Kathy as first-person narrator: calm voice, sometimes wistful, never rebellious.
- To many readers it would seem strange that even the clones never rebel against being exploited. They accept the euphemism of 'completion' for their early deaths. Ishiguro never describes the network behind the exploitation – making a point about society?

MEERA SYAL: *ANITA AND ME*

- Meena is a first-person narrator, so we find out about her directly through her comments on herself and others. Narrative filters the child's voice through often ironic adult perspective.
- At start, Meena is a liar (or fantasist), who lies to get out of trouble, and to make life more interesting. Also loves drama, e.g. story of hot dog, and her wanting to hear the 'rickshaw story' repeatedly.
- She is naive – believes that Anita's father was a sailor, and easily impressed by charismatic Anita, whose rebelliousness challenges Meena's desire to please her parents.
- Reaches a moral low-point when she steals collection tin from Mr Ormerod and blames Baby.
- Gradually becomes aware of growing racism in village, represented by Sam, and approved of by Anita. Meena very opposed – start of rift with Anita.
- Through knowing Nanima, breaking leg, loss of Anita's friendship, and moment when she chooses to tell the truth to the police, Meena learns to become more secure in her identity, and rejects the idea that she has to choose between two cultures.

STEPHEN KELMAN: *PIGEON ENGLISH*

- He misses father and baby sister Agnes in Ghana – can only keep in touch by Skype; often recalls life in Ghana – presented as innocent and relaxed, though poor.
- Family in debt to thuggish Julius, with his baseball bat, 'the Persuader'. Auntie Sonia has to burn off her fingerprints.
- Is called 'Ghana' by the Dell Farm Crew, but does not seem to experience racism in multicultural society; no mention of any character's ethnicity.
- In some ways has an African attitude to luck and superstition – e.g. his alligator's tooth.
- Pakistani butcher, Nish, and wife deported; mixed response – women mostly concerned about where they will get their meat now. Harrison worries about own family's visa.
- Adapts well to life in UK: mostly happy, but caught up in youth violence.

HAROLD BRIGHOUSE: *HOBSON'S CHOICE*

Maggie's attitude to marriage:

- Maggie views marriage largely as a business proposition. 'I'm value to you, so's my man' she says to her father. This ties in with her ambitious nature and her view of herself as a woman who can mange her own affairs.
- She chooses her husband, Willy Mossop (and proposes to him) because she recognises his skills as a bootmaker and sees his potential.
- Although there is a marked difference in social status between herself and her husband, this does not worry her and she regards them both as equal partners.
- Maggie's age (thirty), when most women of the period were married, may also propel her towards marriage, particularly because her father belittles her about her single status.
- While Maggie is domineering (and remains dominant), mutual respect develops between her and Willy. Her father's traditional attitude to marriage, in which authority lies with the husband, is a view Maggie firmly resists.
- Maggie wishes to mould her husband to her idea of what he should be, but she also wants him to recognise his own potential. This seems to suit Willy, who initially lacks faith in himself, but becomes confident enough to assert himself and even challenge Maggie.
- Maggie's attitude to marriage does not involve romance, but love develops between Maggie and Willy and they form a successful, equal partnership.

Context: The play was set in 1880, at a time when wives were still largely under the control of their husbands. However society's attitudes were beginning to shift, and Maggie represents the generation of women who challenged this convention through ambition and independence.

R. C. SHERRIFF: *JOURNEY'S END*

Heroism is explored in various ways:

- The comment by Raleigh is about Stanhope. It is revealed in a letter that Raleigh has written to be sent home and Stanhope opens it.
- The most obvious example of heroism is Stanhope. Though young, he has received the Military Cross for his bravery. We learn that he fought at Vimy Ridge, a horrific battle, which further emphasises his heroism.
- However, Stanhope has become an alcoholic as a result of his experiences, which reveals the consequences of such heroism. His real fear is that his family will find out and his reputation will be tarnished. Consequently, he does not go home on leave. He opens the letter out of fear that Raleigh has mentioned his drinking.
- Since whisky is easy to obtain, and drinking is a social activity, we get the impression that Sherriff is suggesting that many soldiers drink to calm their nerves or as a form of escape.
- Trotter, who is from a lower social class than Stanhope, is also brave. He is an unconventional hero, down-to-earth with a sense of humour, commenting: 'you'll feel you've been 'ere a year in about an hour's time'. We assume that humour is his way of controlling his fear and coping with the confusion of war.
- Raleigh is new to the war, and the audience would see him as naïve, since he still believes in the war-hero as a glorious figure. He hero-worships Stanhope.
- The men also gain courage in unusual ways. (For example reading *Alice in Wonderland* as a simple pleasure, and a metaphor for innocent childhood, as well as emphasising the absurdity of war.)

Context: The First World War. Sherriff wrote the play ten years after the end of the war, in which he fought and was badly injured. In the aftermath of the war, society questioned the morality of modern warfare that could inflict so much damage. Society had also changed a great deal and many values and beliefs were called into question. The audience of the time would have been aware of the effects of the 'Great War'.

CHARLOTTE KEATLEY: *MY MOTHER SAID I NEVER SHOULD*

Rosie directs all her anger at Jackie in response to:

- The discovery that Jackie is her mother and not her older sister
- The death of Margaret, who raised her and whom Rosie thought was her mother

Dramatic effect serves to heighten Rosie's detached manner (in contrast to her anger later in the scene). Effects are achieved by:

- Rosie's cold, sarcastic attitude to Jackie, when she insists on implying that Jackie is more concerned about her work as a painter than she is about Rosie or was about her mother Margaret: 'Did you sell all your paintings?'
- Rosie's determination to refer to Margaret as 'Mum'
- When Rosie systematically throws down the family photographs one by one
- The use of stage directions, in which moments of silence underline the failing relationship between Rosie and Jackie, particularly when Rosie reveals she has her birth certificate

Act I, Scene 10, 1979: Rosie's eighth birthday reveals her erratic behaviour with Margaret and Jackie:

- Rosie compares Margaret unfavourably with Jackie (whom at this point she assumes is her older sister), impressed by Jackie's seemingly sophisticated life, while also daunted by her artistic skill ('Rosie: I can't paint like you can!').
- Simultaneously Rosie is protective towards Margaret, whom she needs more than Jackie. ('She (Rosie) doesn't need me, does she?')
- The baby doll Suky that Rosie buries in the garden and Jackie resurrects, is a symbol of the connection, sometimes frayed, between Margaret, Jackie and Rosie, who all played with the doll. It can also be seen as a symbol of both childhood and motherhood.

SUSAN HILL: *THE WOMAN IN BLACK*

Extract: The following induce a mood of anxiety and fear:

- Emotive adjectives ('ravaged', 'desperate') and nouns ('malevolence') emphasise the threatening presence of the woman in black.
- Dramatic images ('its extreme pallor', 'my heart gave a lurch') and similes ('pounding in my chest like a hammer on an anvil') suggest violent emotion.
- The increase in pace (achieved through lengthy sentences) mirrors the increase of Kipps's heart rate and fear. These are followed by a short, abrupt sentence ('It was though I had become paralysed') presenting him in shock.
- There is a dramatic change in Kipps's mood, from an inquisitive rational one to one of terror 'never knowing [himself] gripped and held fast by such dread'.

Novel as a whole:

- Prior to the extract, Kipps has been impressed by the beauty of the quiet marshes and contrasts with his fearful mood in the extract. However there is also an intimation that this peaceful mood will change when he sees the 'satanic-looking' bird on entering the churchyard.
- At the start of the novel, we see Kipps in the present, as a family man, but haunted by the past. When the story goes back in time, the young Kipps's rational character becomes a fearful one as events develop.
- The ghost story form, with its focus on the supernatural, helps the writer create a mood of anxiety and fear.
- The isolated setting of Eel House, in a ghostly landscape, enhances the mood of anxiety.
- Kipps's early sighting of the woman in black (and the children) at the funeral are mysterious. We realise they are ghosts. A mood of increasing anxiety and fear builds throughout the novel, until the dénouement and shock ending.

JEANETTE WINTERSON: *ORANGES ARE NOT THE ONLY FRUIT*

In the extract:

- Jeanette's journey is defined by her mother, who dreams of adopting a child and raising her to become an evangelical missionary who will change the world.
- Like the Christmas story, a star guides the way to the 'crib', in which the child is found. The dream is told as a myth or parable, in an archaic, biblical style through expressions such as 'And so it was …'.
- 'For seven days and seven nights' is a reference to Christian creation story.
- In the dream there is an emphasis on sexual temptation and demonic visitations.

In the novel as a whole:

- Mythic tales or fairy stories are frequently used to symbolise Jeanette's journey and the problems she faces.
- Jeanette's world is the fundamentalist church. Her interaction in society is limited, so she also sees herself becoming a preacher.
- The chapters of the book take their names from the books of the Old Testament and reflect the changing nature of Jeanette's journey.
- When she reaches adolescence, her sexuality becomes a barrier and her church's punishments are cruel and alienating. The direction of her journey shifts away from the church.
- She finds that she has an artistic temperament and ability, which is increasingly at odds with the restricted view of the church. Her destiny is to become a writer.
- Ultimately, her self-belief allows her to leave the church, although her experiences do not equip her to deal easily with the wider society.

POETRY QUESTIONS [p. 140]

AQA ANTHOLOGY

'Mother Any Distance' and 'Before You Were Mine'

- Focus in 'Mother Any Distance' is on poet's feelings about his mother. All we learn about her, perhaps, is that she is reluctant to let go of him, just as he is of her. She still pinches the end of the tape, even outstretched. In 'Before You Were Mine' we learn much more about Duffy's mother. Could even call it a tribute to her. Duffy names her mother's friends, pictures them on the corner, the mother in 'a polka dot dress'.-

- Both poems address the mother, but in mood there is more sense of anxiety and the drama of suspense in Armitage. Duffy is affectionately admiring. Her poem is more comfortable.
- Armitage pictures his mother helping him measure his new home. Duffy imagines her mother's life before she became a mother – her dancing, her dreams – 'fizzy, movie tomorrows', her 'high-heeled red shoes'. The picture is glamorous (especially the reference to Monroe) and fictional, perhaps based on a photo.
- Armitage's imagery focuses on the tension between his wanting freedom and opportunity and his fear of it; 'acres' and 'prairies' are ironic, as if he has too much space. The tape measure is an umbilical symbol. Most vivid contrast is 'Anchor. Kite': security versus freedom. The tension reaches a peak at the end in the pun of 'hatch' (opening on to roof), and 'hatch' as in baby bird that will 'fall or fly'.
- Duffy uses hardly any figurative language – only 'clear as scent', but the poem is full of images in the broader sense – very visual, painting a picture of the mother in her youth.

'Bayonet Charge' and 'Exposure'

- 'Bayonet Charge' is a snapshot – a moment of extreme violence, fear and tension. A third person, past tense narrative describing the immediate experience of the soldier: uncomfortable uniform, sweat, the rifle's weight, his panicky feelings.
- 'Exposure', unusually, is first person plural (we), present tense, not a narrative but describing the on-going, almost unchanging experience of all the men in the trenches. 'Bayonet Charge' focuses on the survival of one man, 'Exposure' on the ordeal of thousands.
- 'Bayonet Charge' implies reasons for the man signing up: the 'patriotic tear' now seems transformed by fear of death; his reasons for signing up – 'King, honour, human dignity, etcetera' are now made to seem meaningless by being listed like this. 'Exposure' gives reasons for the men being there – 'not otherwise can kind fired burn', but the overall experience still seems futile. They suffer the ordeal of weather ('iced east winds', intensified by alliteration) and waiting (numbing repetition of 'But nothing happens').
- In Owen's poem there is context in the men thinking of home – the home fires made precious by the image of 'dark-red jewels'; in Hughes the context is in the man momentarily wondering about the 'cold clockwork of the stars and the nations', puzzling over the apparent callousness of fate and politics.

- In both poems the men seem neglected and abandoned to their fate.

EDEXCEL ANTHOLOGY

'Valentine' by Carol Ann Duffy. Suggested comparison: 'i wanna be yours' by John Cooper Clarke

- Both poems present unusual attitudes to love through humorous metaphors. Instead of a 'satin heart' the speaker in 'Valentine' offers to the lover an onion, a surprising extended metaphor that runs through the poem and challenges the sentimental, conventional view of love, as does Cooper Clarke's poem. It consists of a long list of everyday objects that represent the lover and are both mundane and comic.
- Duffy's images of the onion can also be associated with 'tears', bringing the thornier aspects of love into focus, and the poem seems to be asking for honesty or 'light' in a relationship, which the onion 'promises'.
- Cooper Clarke's poem is addressed to the desired woman. The images are less serious, but they suggest determination. The speaker's attempts at persuasion end with a jibe – he doesn't want to be with another woman, only her.
- Duffy's poem is free verse with several full stops at the end of lines and lines set apart that encourage the reader to pause and reflect. The single line 'Here' has the effect of engaging the reader, as though they too are receiving the onion and being asked to reflect on its meaning.
- By contrast 'i wanna be yours' has a strong rhythm, regular rhyme scheme and is highly musical. The poem has no punctuation, uses slang and is written in lower case as if dashed off on a keyboard (or even an old typewriter), which suits the fast beat and impatient attitude to love.
- **Context:** Carol Ann Duffy often presents poetry from an unconventional perspective, and 'Valentine' can be seen in this light. Her poetry usually has a feminist dimension. The metaphor of the onion also challenges the idea that the 'cute' sentimental 'card' is what necessarily appeals to women.
- John Cooper Clark is a performance poet and worked as an MC in a nightclub. 'i wanna be yours' can also be regarded as a song. It has been set to music and recorded by the band the Arctic Monkeys.

'The Charge of the Light Brigade' by Alfred Lord Tennyson. Suggested comparison: 'Poppies' by Jane Weir

- Although both poems are about loss and death in war, Tennyson's poem is about a national event. It details the battle charge and the pounding of the cavalry horses. Tension is achieved through the fast rhythm, heavy repetition ('Theirs', 'Cannon', 'Flashed') strong rhyme ('reply', 'why', 'die') and vivid images ('jaws of Death'). Each verse slows towards the end to emphasise the loss of life. The final sestet is a tribute to the battalion, while also presenting a glorified image of war through the 'Noble six hundred!' – the Light Brigade.

- 'Poppies', a contemporary poem, is about personal grief, the loss of a son in war. The metaphor of the poppy evokes blood and the soldier's death throes.
- Like Tennyson's poem, Weir's has a clear form (though different in style and pace), with a sestet at the beginning and end.
- It uses caesura to slow the poem while also using enjambment so that thoughts run on. The effect is to create a halting tension that mirrors the grief and pain expressed. This tension is supported by the way the poem shifts back and forth between past and present, with images of the son's childhood and the son as a man in which the speaker, the mother, pins a poppy to his lapel.
- The images of birds flying signal the son's departure into the world and the dove is a common symbol of peace and life against death. In the final sestet, the speaker is at the war memorial, but caught between the present and past, yearning to recall her son's voice.
- **Context:** 'The Charge of the Light Brigade' retells the events of a disastrous battle (1854) of the same name that took place during the Crimean War in which 'someone' of senior rank 'blundered'. The poem became very popular with the Victorian public.
- 'Poppies' refers to Armistice Day, which began after the First World War (1918) to remember those that died, so is pertinent to the loss explored in the poem.

'Nothing's Changed' by Tatamkhulu Afrika. Suggested comparison: 'Absence' by Elizabeth Jennings

- In 'Nothing's Changed', the speaker returns to where he once lived – 'District Six', a South African township that was broken up under the apartheid regime (segregation between black people and white).
- He sees that superficial changes have occurred, none of which has had an effect on racism and inequality. The 'haute cuisine' restaurant has a 'guard at the gatepost' and though 'No board says it is', he knows it is a 'whites only inn'. It is compared to the 'working man's café' where cheap food is sold.

- The speaker's mood is 'a hot white inwards turning anger' that feeds into memories of injustice and he imagines hurling a stone or bomb.
- The poem is free verse, written mainly in short, sharp lines that suit the angry mood, along with forceful words such as 'flaring', 'crushed', burn', and alliteration that uses the hard 'c/k' sound, particularly in the early verses.
- 'Absence' is also concerned with the passing of time, but focuses on a past relationship as well as an associated place, some public gardens that the speaker returns to.
- In contrast to Afrika's poem, most of the images are of the natural world – gentle and ordered. However, the speaker also feels that 'Nothing has changed' (using almost the same words as Afrika's poem). Both poems also deal with memories becoming more acute because of this lack of change.
- In 'Absence', the speaker's feelings are initially constrained, but violent ones described in a powerful metaphor ('an earthquake tremor') erupt when the speaker recalls the person's name, shaking the ordered world around her. Here these feelings are associated with loss not anger, as in Afrika's poem.
- Unlike Afrika's poem, 'Absence' is a lyric poem and has a very regular form of three quintains, with a simple *ababa* rhyme scheme, and is written in iambic pentameter, so it is tightly controlled. It suits the speaker's restrained voice, and even when the feelings held in check emerge, the final stanza remains true to the form.
- **Context:** District Six was broken up in the 1960s to discourage racial interaction. Tatamkhulu Afrika was imprisoned for eleven years with Nelson Mandela. The poem was probably written about 1990 and the poet regards it as autobiographical.
- **Context:** Much of Elizabeth Jennings's poetry appears simple, but is hard to create. She tried to achieve what she described as 'true clarity' in her poems. She lived in Oxford for most of her life and was a devout Catholic.

EDUQAS ANTHOLOGY

'Dulce et Decorum Est'

Content: The speaker sees a soldier dying from poison gas and is haunted by the image.

Structure: Written in iambic pentameter, with regular rhyme scheme ('sacks', 'backs').

Effects:

- The sombre tone has a trudging beat, like a dirge (sad chant).
- The regular rhythm and rhyme, like soldiers marching, imposes order on the confusion and horror the speaker feels.

- Caesura and enjambment threaten to break the ordered movement, though they emphasise the speaker's voice and his struggle to cope with the horrors.
- Uses graphic images such as similes ('men like old beggars', 'like a man in fire or lime') to show the destructive nature of war.

Context:

- The poem's title means 'it is sweet and appropriate to die for your country' and is ironic, because the speaker points to the difference between the brutal reality of war and what the public assume is the glory of war.
- Owen, a soldier, experienced the horrors of the First World War, in which he died.

Suggested comparison: 'The Soldier' by Rupert Brooke

- Both are war poems, but there are few other similarities.
- In contrast to 'Dulce et Decorum Est', 'The Soldier' is a patriotic poem of self-sacrifice. The speaker believes that if he dies in war, wherever he is buried becomes a part of England.
- While both poems have a regular rhyme scheme, 'The Soldier' follows a traditional pattern as a Petrarchan sonnet (an octave and a sestet).
- Again, in contrast to 'Dulce et Decorum Est', the images in 'The Soldier' are lush, depicting England as a rural haven, and the soldier's body will be 'blest by suns of home' despite being buried in a foreign land. England is personified as a woman with 'her sights and sounds; dreams happy as her day'.
- Both poems are influenced by the First World War (1914–18). 'The Soldier' was written in 1914, when patriotism was high, and Brooke is often seen as a poet writing before the full effects of the war were understood. 'Dulce et Decorum Est' was written in 1917 and depicts the reality of war.

OCR ANTHOLOGY

Love and Relationships

'Love and Friendship' by Emily Brontë and 'Friendship after Love' by Ella Wheeler Wilcox

- Brontë uses nature imagery to compare friendship and love. The 'holly-tree' that blooms 'constantly through the year' is a metaphor for friendship and suggests that friendship is also constant. The metaphor for love, 'the wild-rose briar', blooms only in spring and summer, implying that love is only 'sweet' for a while.

- The speaker urges the reader to choose friendship over love, which will last when 'December blights thy brow', which we can read as an unhappy relationship, or that love is unsatisfactory in some way.
- The structure of the poem is a regular simple pattern of three quatrains, with full rhyme in most stanzas that suits the simple images. The poem is deceptively light in mood and suggests an underlying sadness in the last stanza in the reference to winter.
- Like Brontë's poem, 'Friendship after Love,' has nature imagery. Here, love (fierce midsummer') is compared to friendship ('mellow') autumn, and both seasons are personified as 'he'. Love 'tires' of passion, but does not die. It turns into friendship. However, for the speaker friendship is cold by comparison. Although the 'pain' of love is not missed, friendship alone does not feel complete, as it does for the speaker in Brontë's poem.
- The poem is a Shakespearean sonnet and appropriate for a poem about love. The turn comes before the couplet at the end, when the mood shifts to one of yearning.

Context: As a Victorian woman, Emily Brontë would not have had the same freedom as a man. Most women were expected to marry. Both men and women were encouraged to make good marriages, often for financial reasons, so choosing a suitable partner could be dofficult. The poem could be read in this light.

Context: Ella Wheeler Wilcox (1850–1919) was a popular American poet, who often wrote in rhyme.

Suggested poem from anthology: 'An Arundel Tomb' by Philip Larkin.

Conflict

'The Man he Killed' by Thomas Hardy and 'The Volunteer' by Herbert Asquith

- The speaker, an ordinary soldier, describes how, having shot an enemy soldier, he believes they would have been friends in different circumstances. He imagines that the two of them may even have enlisted for the same reasons, such as being 'out of work'.
- The poem's theme is the absurdity of war, and implies that the ordinary soldier is often caught up in war because of circumstance rather than patriotism.
- In the third stanza, the speaker tries to justify his actions with difficulty: '… my foe … he was; / That's clear enough although' and doubts if the man can be thought of as an enemy.

- Hardy uses the working-class vernacular of the time, such as 'nipperkin' (meaning a drink, probably of whisky) to convey the soldier's origins. It helps to create the jaunty story-telling voice, similar to a tale being told in a pub or bar, along with the bouncing rhythm, rhyme scheme and frequent repetition.
- Asquith's poem also has an ordinary soldier as its focus, a 'clerk' (office worker) who is the volunteer of the title and who has died in battle. Beyond that, there are few similarities between the poems.
- The speaker imagines why the soldier enlisted, suggesting that his work 'Toiling at ledgers' was unsatisfying, and that the battlefield provided the excitement and idealism he needed for 'life's tournament' (life's game).
- The depiction of the soldier is heroic, for although his 'lance has broken' (a metaphor for death), he has experienced his 'high hour' on the battlefield and 'lies content' in his grave. This depiction, and the references to the clerk's imaginings of historical warfare, whether to Roman 'legions' or the 'oriflamme' (sacred French banner) of the Middle Ages signals a romantic view. The poem's theme is the glory of war.
- The poem is written in a traditional form, two octaves in iambic pentameter, with a regular rhyme scheme that suits the traditional theme.

Context: 'The Man he Killed' was written in response to the Boer War (1899–1902), which Hardy was against.

Context: 'The Volunteer' was written in 1912 before the First World War and at a time when public opinion viewed war as heroic. Herbert Asquith fought in the First World War and was greatly affected by it. He was the son of the Liberal prime minister, also Herbert Asquith.

Suggested poem from anthology: 'What Were they Like?' by Denise Levertov

Youth and Age

'Cold Knap Lake' by Gillian Clarke and 'On my First Son' by Ben Jonson

- In 'Cold Knap Lake', a free verse poem, the speaker recalls an incident she witnessed as a child, during the war years, in which a girl is pulled from Cold Knap Lake, 'blue lipped'. The speaker's mother ('a heroine') revives the child by mouth-to-mouth resuscitation.

- Part of the tension is created because we do not know if the child will live. The crowd watches 'drawn by the dread of it', until the child recovers and is taken home to a poor house, where, shockingly, she is 'thrashed' for 'almost drowning'.
- In the fourth verse, the poem shifts. The speaker explores what memory is. She considers whether or not the incident is a real childhood memory or a story she has been told. Expressed in nature imagery, the language is lyrical, but disturbing. The lake and its depths are a metaphor for memory, 'where satin mud blooms in cloudiness'.
- The final lines, a rhyming couplet, bring strong closure and have the feel of an allegory, suggesting that some (or even all) memories are 'lost things', unclear, shifting and buried, like the story of 'the poor man's daughter'.
- 'On my First Son' describes the depths of the speaker's sorrow at the death of his seven-year-old son. Its sentiments contrast strongly with those of the parents in 'Cold Knap Lake', who show no love for their small daughter. Here the speaker feels that God is punishing him for too much devotion (and by implication, not loving God enough).
- The poem is an elegy, written in six rhyming couplets of iambic pentameter. It also has three linked sections. In the first four lines the speaker says farewell to his son and explores the meaning of his death. In the second four lines, he rejects fatherhood (and possibly God as the father) but takes comfort that the child is spared the misery of life and old age. In the final lines he lays his son to 'rest in soft peace'. The final couplet provides strong closure (as in 'Cold Knap Lake') and a sad resolution. The speaker vows never to love too much again.

Context: The tourist attraction Cold Knap Lake is part of a beach near Barry, South Wales. Gillian Clarke states that the poem is based on an incident that took place in her childhood.

Context: We can assume the speaker of 'On my First Son' is the poet. Ben Jonson (1572–1637) was a playwright, poet, actor and critic, and a contemporary of Shakespeare. He had a huge impact on English literature.

Suggested poem from anthology: 'You're' by Sylvia Plath

abstract noun a noun that refers to feelings, concepts, states that do not exist physically (e.g. hope, love)

adjective a word used to describe something or somebody (e.g. 'the **red** hat')

adverb a word used to modify a verb, adjective or another adverb, usually formed by adding 'ly' to an adjective

adverbial a word or phrase that is used in the same way as an adverb, to modify a verb or clause

adverbial clause a clause that functions like an adverb

agent the 'doer' – who or what performs the action, introduced by the word 'by'

alliteration where the same sound is repeated in a stretch of language, usually at the beginning of words

anecdote a short, usually entertaining story about a personal experience, used to make a point

auxiliary verb verbs used with other verbs such as 'be', 'do', 'have'; also modal verbs, which express possibility or necessity: 'must', 'shall', 'will', 'could', 'should', 'would', 'can', 'may' and 'might'

ballad a simple song usually made up of several short stanzas

bildungsroman a novel about the development of the main character from childhood to adulthood

blank verse poetry that is unrhymed; Shakespeare's plays are mostly written in blank verse

broadsheet a newspaper in a large format, usually considered more serious than 'tabloid' newspapers

cadence the recurring rise and fall of the rhythms of speech; it can also refer to a rhythm that comes at the close of a line or a poem

caesura a pause in a line of poetry, intended for effect

characterisation the creation of characters in a dramatic work and how they are presented through description, speech and action

clause a special phrase whose head is a verb; a clause can be a complete sentence

cliché an image that is overused and so becomes boring

cliffhanger a dramatic ending to an episode, leaving the audience or reader in suspense

climax the high point of a play, act or story

colloquialism everyday speech used by people in ordinary situations

colon (:) a punctuation mark that precedes a list, or when a character speaks in a play script or an expansion in a sentence

comma splice an error of punctuation in which a comma is used to link two independent clauses

complex sentence a sentence usually made up of a main clause and one or more subordinate clauses

compound adjective a single adjective made of more than one word (e.g. 'four-legged')

compound sentence a sentence made up of two independent clauses joined by a coordinating conjunction

conjunction a word that links two words or phrases together; there are two types: coordinating conjunctions and subordinating conjunctions

connective a word such as 'however' or 'moreover', used to link paragraphs or sentences and show the relationship between them

coordinating conjunction a conjunction that links two words or phrases together as an equal pair

courtly love An idealised way of expressing love that involved praising the perfection of the desired person, often through poetry or song

dash (–) a punctuation mark used to set off a word or phrase after an independent clause

dénouement the final part of a story, play or film

determiner a word that specifies a noun as known or unknown (e.g. 'the', 'a', 'this', 'my', 'some')

dialect accent and vocabulary, varying by region and social background

dialogue speech and conversation between characters

direct speech words that are actually spoken by a character in a novel or story

discourse marker a word or phrase that helps organise speech into sections (e.g. 'well', 'so', 'anyway')

dramatic irony when the reader or audience is aware of something that a character in a novel or play is not

ellipses (...) a series of dots to show where words have been deliberately left out of a sentence ('ellipsis' is the singular)

emotive language language chosen especially to create an emotional response in the reader

enjambment when a thought runs from one line to the next in a poem

explicit refers to information that is stated openly in a piece of writing

fable a story, usually with animal characters, that conveys a lesson or moral

figurative language words or phrases that are used to express a meaning that is different from their literal meaning

finite clause a clause that makes sense on its own as a complete sentence

flashback a scene or part of a play, novel or film that goes back in time to reveal past events

flash-forwards a scene or part of a play, novel or film that goes forward in time, beyond the main story

foregrounded a literary term used to point to a feature of the text that is emphasised

foreshadowing a hint of what is to come in a work of poetry, fiction or drama

fourth wall when the narrator or character in a novel or play addresses the audience directly (originally, an imaginary wall on stage that faces the audience who are outside the action, which is broken)

framing a story within a story

genre a type of story, based on its style (e.g. horror, science fiction, romance)

homophones words that sound the same but that have different spellings and meanings

iambic pentameter a line of poetry consisting of five iambic feet (iambic means each foot has a weak syllable followed by a strong one)

imagery descriptive language that uses images to make actions, objects and characters more vivid in the reader's mind

implicit refers to information that is hinted at or suggested in a piece of writing, rather than being stated openly

in media res when a story starts in the middle of events

indirect object a noun phrase referring to a person or object that is affected by the action of the verb but is not the main object

irony deliberately saying one thing when you mean another, usually in a humorous, sarcastic or sometimes thoughtful way

main clause a sentence contains at least one main clause, which makes sense on its own

metaphor when one thing is used to describe another to create a striking or unusual image

metre the pattern of stressed and unstressed syllables in a line of verse

minor sentence a sentence that is grammatically incomplete, perhaps not containing a subject or verb

mnemonic a memory aid that can help with remembering spelling, for example

modifier a word or phrase that alters the meaning of another

monologue a long speech by a character in a play, used to move the plot along or explain things that the audience might not otherwise realise

mood the tone or atmosphere created by an artistic work

motif a recurring image in a story or poem

motivation the reason that a character in a novel or play acts the way they do

narrative viewpoint the point of view from which a story is told; this might be first person ('I') or third person ('he', 'she', 'they')

non-finite clause a clause that cannot stand on its own as a complete sentence but which relies on the main clause to make sense

noun phrase a phrase with a noun as its head

novella narrative prose longer than a short story, but shorter than a novel

onomatopoeia a word that suggests its meaning through its sound (for example 'meow', 'squelch')

parallelism achieving contrast by repeating a grammatical formation

participle English verbs have two participles: present (e.g. 'talking') and past (e.g. 'talked')

personification describing an object or idea as though it was human, with human feelings and attributes

phrase a group of words that are grammatically connected

prefix a letter or a group of letters added to the start of a word, which alters its grammatical form and sometimes its meaning ('**aero**plane', '**il**legal')

preposition a word that tell the reader the relationship between things or people, such as 'near', 'by', 'under', 'towards', etc.

prepositional phrase a phrase with a preposition as its head, followed by a noun, pronoun or noun phrase

pronoun words that are used instead of nouns (e.g. personal pronouns: 'it', 'they', 'this', 'she', 'him')

prose the natural flow of speech used in novels and other works, unlike poetry which has a more emphasised rhythmic structure

protagonist the main or a major character

refrain repeated lines or groups of words that convey the same meaning

register the style of language based on choice of vocabulary and grammar

relative pronoun a word used to link a clause to a noun or pronoun (e.g. 'which', 'that', 'who')

reported speech an account of what has been said, without using the exact words spoken

resolution the end of a conflict, when issues are worked out

rhetorical question a question asked for effect, rather than to elicit an answer

rhyming couplet a couplet (two paired lines) that rhymes

round brackets () used to include extra information or an afterthought

satirise to ridicule something using humour or irony

semicolon (;) a type of punctuation that links two idea, events or pieces of information

setting where and when the action of a story takes place

sibilance strongly stressed consonants that make a hissing sound when spoken aloud

simile when one thing is compared directly with another using 'like' or 'as'

simple sentence a sentence with one main clause, usually containing a subject, verb and object

soliloquy a dramatic techniques that allows a character to speak as if thinking aloud, revealing their inner thoughts and intentions to the audience

sonnet a fourteen-line verse with a rhyming couplet at the end

square brackets ([ ]) a form of punctuation mainly used to enclose words not said by the original speaker or writer to clarify (e.g. 'He [the red fox] slipped away, unseen.')

stage directions advice printed from time to time in the text of a play, giving instructions or information to the actors, or on setting and special effects

Standard English the form of English most widely accepted as the conventional form

stanza a group or pattern of lines forming a verse

subordinate clause a clause that is secondary to another part of the sentence

subordinating conjunction a conjunction that introduces a subordinate clause

subplot a secondary storyline that supports the main one, often by reinforcing the theme

suffix a letter or a group of letters added to the end of a word, which alters its grammatical form ('sweet**ness**', 'advent**ure**')

symbol something that represents something else, usually with meanings that are widely known (e.g. a dove as a symbol of peace)

tautology saying the same thing twice over in different words, usually as an error of style (e.g. 'They spoke together simultaneously.')

theme an idea running through a work of literature or art

tone see mood

topic sentence a sentence that expresses the main idea of a paragraph, sometimes the first of the paragraph

triad list of three

tricolon using three words or phrases in a row for effect